Elements *of* Discipline

11/13

STEPHEN GREENSPAN

ELEMENTS *of*
DISCIPLINE

Nine Principles
for
Teachers and Parents

Foreword by Arnold J. Sameroff

TEMPLE UNIVERSITY PRESS
Philadelphia

TEMPLE UNIVERSITY PRESS
Philadelphia, Pennsylvania 19122
www.temple.edu/tempress

Library of Congress Cataloging-in-Publication Data

Greenspan, Stephen.
    Elements of discipline : nine principles for teachers and parents /
Stephen Greenspan ; with a foreword by Arnold J. Sameroff.
        p.   cm.
    Includes bibliographical references and index.
    ISBN 978-1-4399-0896-9 (cloth : alk. paper)
    ISBN 978-1-4399-0897-6 (pbk. : alk. paper)   28.95
    ISBN 978-1-4399-0898-3 (e-book)
    1. School discipline.   2. Problem children—Behavior modification.
I. Title.
    LB3012.G76 2012
    371.5—dc23   2012008294

Printed in the United States of America

2 4 6 8 9 7 5 3 1

This book is dedicated
to my wife, Helen Apthorp,
and to my sons, Alex and Eli Greenspan.

They helped me discover
that being a parent can be
a painless and joyful experience.

Contents

Foreword

Raising a child involves many years of work with the hope that the outcome will reward parental efforts in the home and teacher efforts in the classroom—the hope that children will end up as happy and competent adults who will go on to successfully raise their own children. But parents and teachers also hope to experience rewards along the way so the process of child-rearing will provide enjoyment in addition to the satisfaction derived from a successful outcome. However, the pleasures of caregiving are tempered by the need to move children in a specific direction, and this movement requires some degree of control. Parents and teachers must have a way of indicating when their charges are on track (i.e., engaging in constructive or positive behaviors) and when they are off track (i.e., engaging in nonproductive or negative behaviors).

This book by Stephen Greenspan focuses on the issue of discipline—more specifically, on successful discipline. This is an important distinction, because where discipline itself is directed at achieving control or obedience, successful discipline includes the idea that the child will move in a more positive direction. This direction is in tune with the short- and long-term goals of parents and teachers. One of the most important contributions of child-development research to helping parents raise their children is the information that, in many cases, what parents intuitively believe about child-rearing may be wrong. In the case of discipline, for centuries parents and teachers believed and were taught that the harsher the methods, the more effective the discipline. Modern research has shown that what children really learn from harsh discipline is harsh behavior. In the long run, such children tend to be more aggressive and to harshly discipline their own children.

Harsh discipline is successful in immediately stopping younger children from continuing an unwanted behavior, but it does not move the children to become better in the long run. An extreme example is the case of shaken-baby syndrome. Some adults believed that an effective way to stop babies from crying was to give them a good shake. During medieval times, this technique was actually recommended as a good caregiving strategy. The short-term effects of shaking are reinforcing for caregivers: The baby stops crying. But contemporary researchers have found that this effect is the result of stunning the infant, and the consequences can include brain damage and even death.

Modern parents and teachers have moved away from harsh physical punishment and, for the most part, are interested in the welfare of children. They have been taught that it is better to be warm and accepting toward children, rather than cold and rejecting, and that positive discipline in the form of encouragement and rewards is a much better way to get children to move in a desired direction than disparagement and punishment. However, these lessons have been tempered with newer knowledge that being warm and accepting is not enough, because it can be accompanied by a permissiveness that offers no shape to the development of children, and that even positive discipline can undercut some desired outcomes if it becomes too mechanical.

The issue of being too mechanical permeates most of the books devoted to advice about discipline for parents and teachers. These advice books tend to focus on one or another technique—such as time-out, active listening, or logical consequences—as solving all discipline problems. These books are successful with caregivers who want quick answers and simple techniques to make their discipline more effective. What makes this book, *Elements of Discipline*, unique is its holistic approach that offers a variety of techniques for a variety of discipline goals and, even more importantly, a way of thinking about discipline that enables caregivers to go beyond mechanics to a deeper understanding of their role in the successful socialization of children.

Stephen Greenspan shows respect for the intelligence of his readers and offers them much to think about in constructing their own disciplinary strategies. Although most readers are looking for simple techniques, he is convinced that if they are willing to make the effort to understand the theory of discipline and its goals, they will be much more effective in their interactions with children. The main innovation in this book is the effort to discuss the *goals* of discipline as well as techniques. The author shows how three major approaches to discipline—Affective, Behavioral, and Cognitive—can be integrated around the same three domains of discipline and the same three goals.

Parents, teachers, and other caregivers differ in terms of their belief systems and values and should resist any advice suggesting that one size fits all. *Elements of Discipline* presents core principles and leaves it up to caregivers to pick and choose among those principles, and their related discipline methods, in ways that fit with their beliefs and values. Any caregiver who makes the effort to read and understand this book will undoubtedly become more knowledgeable about discipline and more effective in relating to children.

—*Arnold J. Sameroff*

Preface

This book presents what I call the "ABC Model of Discipline," a framework that I developed in outline form more than twenty-five years ago (Greenspan 1985). That being the case, one might ask, "What took you so long to write this book?" There are several reasons, including laziness (an article is much easier to write than a book), but one important reason is that I did not become a parent until my mid-forties, and I dreaded going on talk shows and being asked the question, "How many children do you have, Doctor Greenspan?"

The late Haim Ginott, who is profiled in Chapter 2, answered such questions with various wisecracks, such as "You shouldn't ask personal questions, Lady" (to a workshop participant) and "I have hundreds of children, and they all have problems" (to the host of a morning news show). However, I lack Ginott's chutzpah and prefer to answer questions without evasion. Of course, having children should not have anything to do with the validity of one's ideas (I know several psychologists who are incompetent parents and have little useful advice to offer in the area of child-rearing). Still, I preferred to hold off disseminating my discipline model until I could answer the dreaded question, as I now can, by saying, "I have two college-age sons, and I am not the only one who thinks they are both quite pleasant to be around."

Obviously, my worrying about what to say on a talk show suggests that I did not lack confidence in the potential this book would hold for attracting interest. I have made numerous presentations of the ABC model to parent and teacher groups, and the general response has always been quite positive. Although many new discipline books have been published in the past decade or two, the basic point contained in my book—that there are three major approaches to discipline and that they share certain common elements—continues to apply, as does my belief that there is a need for a book that helps caregivers understand how to integrate the three approaches and how to become more discerning consumers of the discipline literature.

Holding off on writing a book is not always a bad idea. I think my ideas on discipline have become clearer, not least because I have had the rich experience of being a father. (Perhaps the people who asked Ginott how many children he had were not being so inappropriate after all.) I think I am now in a position to write a more realistic book than would have been the case fifteen, or even ten, years ago, and I hope the reader will find this book both informative and challenging.

What Is Meant by "Discipline"?

To many people, the term "discipline" implies punishment, but in this book, I use the term much more broadly to suggest social teaching or direction (getting a child to stop some undesired behavior or to start some desired behavior). Evidence strongly suggests that punishment should play only a small role in the repertoire of effective caregivers and that a discipline style characterized mainly by punishment is highly unlikely to work in the short run (i.e., to achieve compliance and harmony) and even less likely to work in the long run (i.e., to facilitate healthy child adjustment and social competence). Therefore, when I use the term "discipline," I am referring to the process by which adults attempt to change or to maintain the behavior of children and to influence their socioemotional development. Punishment, defined broadly as any adult expression of disapproval directed toward a child, has a definite if limited role in discipline. But discipline, as I use the term in this book, involves the coordinated use of several techniques, most of them involving approval and acceptance rather than disapproval and intolerance.

Who Is the Intended Audience for This Book?

Books on discipline are typically aimed at specific, narrow audiences, such as parents, teachers, or early-childhood specialists. This book is aimed at all of those audiences, which is why I include examples from different settings and generally use the term "caregiver," which refers to any adult who interacts with children from a position of authority and responsibility. Caregivers include people who are unpaid (primarily parents and other family members), as well as people who are paid (teachers, child-care workers, foster parents, youth leaders, group-home workers, babysitters, and so forth). I use a more general term because I believe that the ABC Model of Discipline applies equally to all adults who interact with children and who occasionally need to influence children's behavior.

Although the nine principles contained in the ABC Model of Discipline apply equally to all caregivers, children, and settings, the application of these principles may, obviously, be affected by setting, age, and role factors. Parents, for example, have more freedom in the ways they can discipline their children than do teachers, although new knowledge and concern about child abuse has limited that freedom considerably. For some categories of caregivers, such as babysitters, the emphasis is more on short-term objectives (such as getting a child to bed or preventing him from harming a younger sibling) than on facilitating social development. Similarly, the age of the child may influence which principle a caregiver relies on when implementing one of the domains (e.g., some Behavioral techniques, such as time-out, are appropriate mainly for young children, although the general principles of the Behavioral approach apply across age-groups). The ABC model, thus, provides a framework for dealing with a wide range of discipline situations, child ages, and types of caregivers.

Why Is There a Need for This Book?

Given the dozens of books about discipline that can be found in any library or bookshop, one might ask whether another book about discipline is really needed. My answer is "yes," because the model I espouse is so powerful, yet it is not represented in the popular literature and is not widely known outside academic circles. I hope that making caregivers more knowledgeable about similarities and differences among the various approaches will reduce the confusion many of them currently feel when confronting the discipline literature. I feel that this book will provide caregivers with the opportunity and confidence to choose from the various discipline approaches and to develop a unique approach that suits their own values and personalities.

Although my initial motivation in developing the components of the ABC Model of Discipline was to help parents and other caregivers better understand the discipline literature, it became apparent that nine discipline elements are better than three. Caregivers knowledgeable about all nine principles encompassed in the ABC model are in a position to deal flexibly and effectively with a wider range of child-rearing challenges than would be the case if they were operating within only one of the three major approaches. Thus, in addition to the more theoretically oriented discussions, I provide a tool kit to help caregivers apply the model, along with numerous case studies to show the principles in action.

A third purpose for this book is to immunize caregivers from falling prey to pseudo-experts providing flawed advice. I attempt to do this by stressing that any valid discipline system should emphasize equally the three major domains of Warmth, Tolerance, and Influence. In addition, I illustrate a technique for using the ABC Model of Discipline to evaluate various books on discipline. For the most part, I try to avoid making negative comments about other authors (I make exceptions for John Rosemond and Alfie Kohn in Chapter 1), though I do not hesitate to point out areas where I disagree with the conclusions or advice of others. My basic stance toward the discipline literature is that too many books are unbalanced, because they promote a single discipline domain (typically Influence) with insufficient attention to the other two domains. Such an unbalanced approach, illustrated in the discussion that starts Chapter 1, should be seen for what it is: something grounded in ideology rather than in science or responsible practice. I believe there is a need for a book that allows caregivers to be more discerning consumers of the discipline literature, and I hope this book achieves that purpose.

A Note about the Title

The inspiration for the title of this volume—*Elements of Discipline*—came from *Elements of Style,* by William Strunk and E. B. White (1959). To the extent that I am a competent writer, it is because everything I need to know about writing is contained in Strunk and White's "little book" (as it is often referred to by students of writing). I hope that my own little book will fill the same role for teachers, parents, and other caregivers, who will find in it much of what they need to know about being competent at relating to and influencing children and youth. I realize that comparing myself to Strunk and White may strike some readers as a bit grandiose. Unfortunately (or fortunately), my late mother, Rose Tell Greenspan, did not raise her son to have a low opinion of himself.

What Is in the Book?

The ABC Model of Discipline depicts discipline as a three-tiered framework supporting long-term social competence goals. At the model's foundation are three domains of discipline (Warmth, Tolerance, and Influence). Emerging from each of these domains is a principle for applying discipline. Finally, at the top of the hierarchy are three long-term outcomes (Happiness, Boldness, and Niceness), one arising from each of the domains. Further, the model incorporates three schools of psychological thought—the Affective, Behavioral, and Cognitive approaches—offering a set of three principles for each approach.

Outline of the Book

I begin by addressing the goals and methods of discipline in a somewhat theoretical manner, and then I move to a practical level to illustrate the theory in action and to offer concrete advice for dealing with a wide range of behavioral challenges. I conclude with a discussion of how a caregiver can apply the principles of the ABC model to develop an individualized discipline style.

Chapter 1 argues for a balanced approach to discipline. The chapter describes the derivation of the three discipline domains from research-based factor analysis and discusses desired child outcomes in both the short term (behavior change and system harmony) and the long term (growth in social competence). Chapters 2, 3, and 4 discuss the Affective, Behavioral, and Cognitive approaches, offering theoretical background and describing specific principles designed to link the discipline domains with the desired long-term outcomes while supporting short-term goals as well.

Chapter 5 provides a series of case studies illustrating how each of the approaches would address specific behavioral challenges. Chapter 6 integrates the three approaches to produce the full ABC Model of Discipline, with its complement of nine principles. Chapter 7 reformulates each of the nine principles of the model to generate a set of eighteen concrete techniques—a tool kit—for applying the model; case analyses examine use of the techniques. Finally, Chapter 8 explains how the ABC model can help a caregiver develop his or her own discipline style and discusses the broad applicability of the model across developmental stages, special populations, and cultures.

In addition, two appendixes are provided: Appendix A is a glossary, and Appendix B illustrates how the model can be used to evaluate discipline advice offered by others.

Gender Usage

Rather than repeatedly using the awkward expression "he or she" (or "him or her"), I shall consistently refer to a caregiver as "she" and a child as "he." Obviously, caregivers come in both genders, as do children, and the principles in this book apply to all children and all caregivers, regardless of gender. So, when encountering a "he" or a "she," please simply convert the word in your mind to "he or she."

A Conceptually Challenging Approach

One obvious difference between this book and others in the discipline literature is that I have written this book in a quasi-academic manner, which makes demands on readers that are similar to those they might encounter in a college course. This style may be a turnoff to readers who are intimidated by theoretically dense material or who are reluctant to make the effort needed to truly grasp the model. However, for those who do make that effort, I expect that many will find the book a transformative instrument. Certainly, this has been the experience whenever I have presented the model in workshops, as a few participants always exclaim, "The ABC model has helped me finally understand what discipline and child-rearing are all about."

Acknowledgments

I am very grateful to

- Michael Chandler and Carl Barenboim, my two earliest collaborators
- Art Orgel, who taught me about his mentor, Haim Ginott
- The late Joe Tavormina, whose comparison of discipline models got me started
- A PET workshop trainer, name forgotten, who taught me about Thomas Gordon
- W. Hans Miller, who taught me about the Behavioral approach to discipline
- Robert Shilkret, Mary Cerreto, Jane Goldman, and Gail Kara, who have been huge supporters
- Kenyon Chan, Rune Simeonsson, Bob Emde, and Barbara Keogh, valued mentors
- Mary Fran Flood and Monsignor James Gilg, valued collaborators on teen parents
- Karen Budd and Kathleen Bradley, valued collaborators on marginal parents
- Laraine Masters Glidden, for many things, among them educating me about adoption
- Arnold Sameroff, who taught me that biology is brain damage, not just genes
- Luther Otto, who suggested the upward-flow graphic depiction of my model
- Harvey Switzky, George Woods, Sharon Duffy, and Jim Patton, valued colleagues
- Diane Ossuniyi, whose love of John Rosemond both infuriated and motivated me

- Theresa Bardy Tsuchiya, Christine Loomis, and Stephen Jones, skilled editors
- The late Frank Menolascino and the late John P. Hill, who are both sorely missed
- Alan Taddiken, whose discussions years ago inspired me to think about this book
- Irene Goldenberg, who taught me about family therapy
- Mick Gusinde-Duffy, a very enthusiastic senior editor who believes in this project
- Lynne Frost, a dedicated production editor, who improved the manuscript substantially
- Helen Apthorp, a very supportive spouse who believes in me
- My sons, Alex and Eli, who prove that discipline can produce spectacular results

Elements *of* Discipline

1

In Search of Balance

Domains of Discipline and Long-Term Outcomes

F ew things are more frustrating to adults than being unable to get children to mind them. A feeling of incompetence in developing and maintaining harmonious and satisfactory relationships with children is a major source of parental unhappiness and the main reason why half of all new teachers quit the profession within the first five years. When I became the coordinator of a graduate program in Special Education, I was dismayed to learn that teachers coming out of our combined B.A./M.A. program were receiving almost no training in behavior-management techniques or concepts. This realization was unsettling, because most of these young professionals would be thrust into postgraduation classroom situations where they would be dealing with very challenging behaviors (even in classrooms filled with students assigned the benign-sounding label "learning disabled"). Many of these children or youth likely would find it more enjoyable (and self-esteem-enhancing) to try to drive a teacher to despair rather than try to master academic material they considered difficult or boring. New teachers in general education, many of whom start their careers in urban settings where a large percentage of the students are oppositional and defiant, experience the same challenge. However, even in affluent school districts where the average child or youth is motivated and compliant, a teacher is likely to encounter one or more students in any class who have the potential, whether individually or jointly, to drive her to tears and, eventually, to a different career path.

The need for effective discipline strategies—in both home and school settings—has long been clear. Guidebooks abound, espousing philosophies of child-rearing and discipline regimes that run the gamut from the most rigid to the most permissive. In this book, I offer a more balanced framework—the

ABC Model of Discipline—based on scientific analysis of the characteristics of effective caregivers. The ABC model integrates a variety of psychological perspectives into three major approaches to discipline, which I term "Affective," "Behavioral," and "Cognitive." Each approach employs three core principles to work toward desired outcomes within three domains of discipline. The approaches are described in detail in Chapters 2, 3, and 4.

Unbalanced Discipline: Failure to Emphasize Multiple Domains

The term "caregiver burnout" can be used to describe the demoralization that comes to any parent or teacher who lacks the skills to manage children's behavior. One would like to think that all books on discipline or behavior management try to provide caregivers with such skills, but in reality many books on discipline approach the topic on a global level and never get around to advising caregivers what to do when. The 2006 book *Guiding Children's Behavior: Developmental Discipline in the Classroom*, by Eileen S. Flicker and Janet Andron Hoffman, is a good example of this phenomenon. The book presents a model termed "Developmental Discipline," which, according to the authors, was inspired by the learning theories of Jean Piaget and Lev Vygotsky. Piaget and Vygotsky were certainly great authorities on child development (I consider myself a neo-Piagetian), but they had nothing to say about discipline, as Flicker and Hoffman acknowledge. The idea underlying Developmental Discipline is that "children are active participants in their cognitive and social/ emotional development" (8). That is all well and good, but if you are looking for any idea about how to translate that noble statement into concrete advice regarding how to actually guide the behavior of children, you will not find it in Flicker and Hoffman's book; in fact, they make a point of downplaying the importance or utility of specific discipline techniques.

The core of Developmental Discipline is that classroom misbehavior (a term the authors avoid) presents learning opportunities for the children involved and also for their caregivers. Several problem vignettes are presented, but after discussing various possible caregiver responses—for example, reprimand, encouragement, and ignoring—Flicker and Hoffman assert that the decision regarding what (if any) intervention to make should reflect an understanding of the particular child's temperament, possible lack of readiness, usual pattern of behaviors, and other factors, such as family and cultural issues, caregiver expectations, and poverty. The authors devote a lot of attention to the fact that children's behavior reflects transactions between children and their caregivers, and they urge caregivers to consider how their own attitudes, cultural expectations, or behaviors might contribute to the problems they encounter. Flicker and Hoffman promise to make caregivers more aware and thoughtful about children and their own attitudes, but they do not provide a guide to the core techniques of discipline or how to use those techniques to become more adept at discipline. To me, the mystery is not why such a vague approach would fail to build discipline competence but why anyone would think that it could.

Alfie Kohn also writes about caregiver relationships with children and, like Flicker and Hoffman, is "constructivistic" (i.e., he emphasizes the importance of children's learning from their misbehavior), blames adults (i.e., he asks caregivers to consider their own contribution to child misbehavior), and eschews providing concrete, technique-based advice. However, although Flicker and Hoffman mention some techniques (but then assert essentially that "technique is unimportant, so you choose"), Kohn refuses to do even that much. In his 1996 book *Beyond Discipline: From Compliance to Community*, Kohn—well known for his books aimed at both parents and teachers—basically engages in an extended polemic against the evils of adults trying to tell children what to do. Although his main beef is with punishment, Kohn does not have much use for praise either. In his 1993 book *Punished by Rewards*, Kohn takes umbrage at the concept of positive reinforcement (including praise), because it implies that adults have the right to decide how children should behave. Kohn's basic point is that if caregivers want children to develop into autonomous and happy people, then they should stop trying to control or direct them and shift toward helping them become better decision makers. The way to do that, according to Kohn, is by turning classrooms as well as families into communities where adults are facilitators rather than authority figures.

This approach is fine from a philosophical standpoint, and, in fact, Kohn's position on the importance of avoiding power struggles aligns with much of what I term the Cognitive approach to discipline (summarized in Chapter 4 of this book). Furthermore, many discipline authors caution caregivers to be careful about how they give reinforcement (e.g., it is better to say in a neutral tone of voice, "I'm pleased you cleaned up your room" than to say in a sarcastic tone of voice, "It's about time you decided not to be a slob"). However, few authors other than Kohn are opposed to positive reinforcement *per se*. The real problem is that Kohn's turn-the-other-cheek approach does not tell a teacher what to do (other than "nothing") when a ten-year-old student drops an F-bomb on her in class. Nor does it tell a father what to do when his six-year-old throws a dangerous object at his four-year-old brother. Unlike other Cognitively oriented experts (whom he thinks are cruel for even suggesting how caregivers can and should take charge in such situations), Kohn prefers not to answer such questions and instead blames caregivers for creating the problems in the first place.

Kohn's ideas seem to draw inspiration directly from Jean-Jacques Rousseau's ([1762] 1908) *Émile*, an eighteenth-century novel that is considered to be the first educational philosophy treatise and continues to be the bible for hippie caregivers around the world. Rousseau, who abandoned his own children and had no practical experience as an educator, expresses the view that children come into the world as perfect beings but become messed up by adults and by society in general. His advice, which at one time had great influence, is that the best thing parents or teachers can do for children is to leave them alone, a sentiment that Kohn seemingly shares. In terms of the discipline and competence domains described later in this chapter, Kohn clearly values above all else the discipline domain of "Tolerance" and the child social competence outcome of "Boldness." The problem for me is not that these are bad things to value, but rather that it is impossible to be effective with children, in either the short term (achieving harmony) or the long term (facilitating competence), when adopting such a one-sided emphasis. Even A. S. Neill, the educator whose Tolerance- and Boldness-grounded educational philosophy described in *Summerhill* (1977) also owes much to the philosophy of Rousseau, understands that children need limits; this belief is reflected in the title of Neill's subsequent book, *Freedom, Not License* (1978), in which he criticizes followers who took his previous ideas about child freedom to absurd lengths.

In case the reader has now decided that I am on the "tough" side of the discipline divide, I should point out that many people (including my own kids) would probably consider me a softie. My problem with Kohn is not that he is a gentle soul but rather that (1) his advice is unbalanced, in that he stresses the importance of Tolerance without giving equal emphasis to the discipline domain I term "Influence" and (2) he fails to go beyond rhetoric and does not provide caregivers with a varied tool kit of skills and tactics for dealing successfully with challenging situations. However, this criticism can be applied just as much to discipline authors on the other end of the spectrum, whose sole advice to teachers and parents is to get tough and who fail to give caregivers a tool kit of situation-based techniques for building their skills for dealing with challenging child behaviors. Unlike the overly soft Kohn, who emphasizes Tolerance but fails to emphasize Influence, overly tough authors tend to emphasize only Influence, without attending to Tolerance or another discipline domain I term "Warmth." Like Kohn, however, they also do not provide caregivers what they need in terms of specific techniques and tools for dealing in a differentiated way with various child-behavior challenges.

John Rosemond is an example of an author who espouses get-tough discipline yet eschews a discussion of discipline techniques other than those that emphasize Influence to the exclusion of everything else. He is one of America's best-known discipline experts, having written many books on the topic (almost all involving family discipline), and is the author of a column (some of which addresses classroom discipline) that is syndicated in approximately two hundred daily newspapers. Until a few years ago, Rosemond—who, according to his website, does not possess an earned doctorate—wrote in a secular vein, but more recently he has been couching his discipline advice and lecture topics in more explicitly religious terms. However, I can detect no real change in the basic nature of his message other than, if possible, greater stridency and a single-minded determination to rid America of those he frequently refers to as "spoiled brats."

The essence of Rosemond's message, as reflected in his book *Because I Said So* (1996), is that the modern family has become too child-centered. In Rosemond's view, parents should put their marriage and their own needs first and should demand absolute and unquestioning obedience from children. According to Rosemond, the child has a right to express resentment at this state of affairs, as long as he does so in certain closed-off parts of the house where the caregiver does not have to listen to him. Rosemond views children who are given too much freedom as selfish and self-centered, and he sees the main job of the caregiver as breaking the child's will and making him subservient. He attributes most social ills, such as drug use, to the rise of permissive child-rearing practices that are too concerned with a child's feelings or wishes. He sees himself as having a mission to reverse this trend, which he attributes to liberal authors with their excessive concern about such things as the child's self-esteem and happiness.

Rosemond has a tendency to make statements in a sweeping, authoritative, and non-nuanced manner, with little acknowledgment of individual variation among children or among caregivers. This is reflected in statements such as this one, from a 1994 newspaper column: "Given sufficient nurturing during infancy and early toddlerhood, every child believes the world should treat him as a special case. He believes he should be given what he wants, when he wants it, and please, don't forget the silver platter." Rosemond also justifies his views based on scripture, such as Proverbs 22:15: "Foolishness is bound up in the heart of a child; the rod of correction will drive it from him" (this is often quoted as "spare the rod and spoil the child," but that more famous version is actually from a poem by Samuel Butler). A Biblical analogy Rosemond relies upon to support his views is that Adam and Eve chose to deceive and disobey their "father," but one would hardly be justified in labeling God a bad parent.

Rosemond's message is a variant of the "Tough Love" approach that was developed in the 1970s mainly to encourage parents of drug-using youths to become less enabling. *Toughlove* (York, York, and Wachtel 1982) is based on the justifiable position that caregivers should not continue indefinitely to forgive intolerable and illegal behavior. However, when used as a general discipline framework, it has been taken to absurd lengths and seems to be encouraging parents to think that extreme toughness, including the threat of ultimate "parent-child divorce," is the best stance to take when dealing with all challenging child behaviors.

The ideological underpinnings of Rosemond's "Traditional Parenting" framework, with its exaltation of caregiver authority and its denial of the importance of child feelings or autonomy, can be found scattered throughout "Rosemond's Bill of Rights for Children" and his daily "John Rosemond's Thought for the Day" (both posted on his website, www.rosemond.com). Here is a sampling from his Bill of Rights for Children: "Children have the right to hear their parents say 'no' at least three times a day," "Children have the right to hear their parents say 'because I said so' on a regular and frequent basis," and "Children have the right to learn early in their lives that obedience to legitimate authority is not optional." Here is a representative, and (to me) scary, quote from his Thought for the Day: "If your child accuses you of 'being mean' you must have done something right" (December 1, 2006). Such statements are scary because they turn logic on its head, framing adult rights as children's rights and legitimizing, even glorifying, a mean-spirited and insensitive approach to children, all of whom are portrayed in the same highly negative terms.

It is difficult to find an elaborated statement of Rosemond's discipline framework, as his answer to virtually every discipline situation is the same: an insistence on instant and uncomplaining obedience. In one of his books, Rosemond even goes so far as to say that the task for a caregiver is to make a child her "disciple." Combining advice from various books by Rosemond, I have put together the following list of principles that seem to form the core of his advice to caregivers:

- Parents should be the focus of the family.
- Parents should be firm and authoritative.
- Parents should use the threat of punishment to teach responsibility.
- Frustration and unhappiness are good for children.
- Being right is more important than what works.
- Consequences be damned, expect a child to obey.
- Self-esteem and feelings don't count; praise is bad.
- Having character is more important than being smart.
- Don't try to establish a dialogue with a child.

Although these principles use different words, they all are elaborations on the same core message: The parent is the senior officer, and the child is the lowly private; the parent's job is to give orders, and the child's job is to obey those orders without complaint or discussion. Rosemond makes some effort to justify this state of affairs in terms of eventual benefit to the child in becoming a person with good character, by which he means being a well-behaved conformist. No emphasis is placed on the higher-level form of character as the ability to make thoughtful and autonomous moral decisions, even when others around you are doing the wrong thing.

However, Rosemond's ultimate justification for an authoritarian and highly punitive approach to caregiving is based not on outcome but rather on moral (or what I would consider immoral) considerations. That is, Rosemond has contempt for the idea that it is all right for parents to treat their children as equals or to show concern for their feelings and wishes. Rosemond does not use Biblical justification for such a perspective, but his recent move in that direction does not appear to be much of a leap. Unlike other power-oriented discipline authorities who emphasize Influence but have little or nothing to say about Warmth or Tolerance, Rosemond goes out of his way to denigrate the importance of Warmth and Tolerance. Thus, in his 2005 book *Family Building: The Five Fundamentals of Effective Parenting*, Rosemond writes that "too much praise, as well as praise that is effusive, can create a powerful dependency" (105) and that "a child who receives no praise doesn't go looking for it" (106), which I read as "no praise is better than too much praise." In typical fashion, Rosemond distorts the position of Rudolf Dreikurs (profiled in Chapter 4 of this book) to support his view that too much caregiver warmth directed at children is a bad thing.

Rosemond notes correctly that Dreikurs objected to the use of "evaluative praise" and uses that to support his own position that caregivers should not concern themselves with establishing warm and approving relationships with children. However, Rosemond neglects to point out that Dreikurs advocated a different way of delivering praise, which is termed "encouragement," and that Dreikurs's whole orientation, as is the case with other advocates of a Cognitive perspective—such as the approach espoused in the *Love and Logic* series (Cline and Fay 1990; Fay, Fay, and Cline 2000)—is one in which the tone of the relationship with children is very positive.

In addition to denigrating the importance of caregiver Warmth, Rosemond also denigrates the importance of Tolerance. Rosemond strongly disputes the importance of listening to a child, establishing a dialogue with him, or attending to his feelings. In fact, Rosemond tells parents that they should make it their job to cause frustration and disappointment in their children. He belittles authors who place any emphasis on establishing an affectively sensitive dialogue with children, as Phil McGraw, TV's "Doctor Phil," does in his 2004 book *Family First*. Rosemond also takes issue with McGraw's statement, in referring to family relationships, that "it's not about what's right or wrong. It's about what works." Rosemond responds by writing, "No, it most definitely is *not* a matter of what works; it's a matter of what's right and what's wrong. I, for one, would rather do what is right, even if it doesn't 'work'" (2005, 10).

The problem is that caregivers who turn to authors such as Rosemond definitely *are* looking for solutions that work and are not likely to find them in advice that disparages two of the three pieces of the discipline puzzle. Furthermore, Rosemond's universal advice to "get tougher" fails to recognize that most caregivers who are ineffective at discipline are already being tough, and it is not working for them. There is a paradox operating here, in that caregivers who are struggling to get children to mind them turn to authors like Rosemond for advice, and the only advice they get is to "keep doing what you are already [ineffectively] doing." One of my hopes for this book is that readers will come to understand why such advice—as well as equally unbalanced and ideologically driven advice from authors on the "left," such as Kohn—is badly flawed. In the following pages, I hope to show why, and how, a balanced approach to discipline is the best framework for developing satisfying and effective relationships with children and youth.

Three Domains of Discipline: Basis for a Balanced Approach

My ABC Model of Discipline is grounded to a large extent in scientific research concerning the characteristics of effective caregivers. The three domains of discipline that form the basis of the model emerged from factor analytic studies in which large numbers of caregivers were rated on a number of items and statistical methods were used to group the items into a small number of factors. A limitation of factor analysis is that a factor emerges only if items relevant to that factor are used in the initial measurements. If a domain of discipline has not caught the attention of researchers, they will not include items relevant to that domain in their initial study, and thus a factor reflecting that domain will not emerge in the statistical analysis. This is exactly what happened in the research literature on caregiver discipline, as researchers initially found only two discipline factors. Later work, however, involving reanalysis and the addition of new items revealed that a three-factor model more fully explains the phenomenon of discipline.

The initial two factors were labeled "Warmth" and "Control," the latter of which I prefer to call "Influence." Warmth refers to the extent to which a caregiver overtly expresses love and approval toward a child, while Influence refers to the extent to which a caregiver insists on child compliance and demands behavioral changes from a child. The factors are bipolar, in that a caregiver's scores on these two dimensions can range from one end of a continuum to the other. Thus, on Warmth, a caregiver can range from the midpoint (neither very warm nor very cold) to one end of the continuum (very warm/accepting) or to the other end of the continuum (very cold/rejecting). The same goes for the Influence factor, on which a caregiver can be scored anywhere from very high to very low. As these are independent factors, a caregiver's score on one of the factors does not give any indication of where she will fall on the other factor. Thus, a caregiver could be high on both Warmth and Influence, low on both, or somewhere in between on one or both.

Diana Baumrind, a University of California psychology professor, developed a model of optimum discipline based on the two-factor solution (1967). She postulated four pure, or ideal (i.e., clear-cut), types of caregiver discipline, based on combinations of extreme scores on the two independent factors. She labeled these four ideal types "Authoritarian" (high on Influence, low on Warmth), "Permissive" (high on Warmth, low on Influence), "Authoritative" (high on Warmth, high on Influence), and "Chaotic" (low on Warmth, low on Influence). Baumrind then looked at children whose parents fell in the ideal type categories. She found that four-year-olds whose parents used Authoritative discipline had the best social competence and four-year-olds whose parents used Chaotic discipline had the worst. Both the Permissive and the Authoritarian parents had children who were less socially competent than those of the Authoritative parents, with somewhat different patterns of incompetence emerging. Specifically, preschoolers exposed to highly Permissive parenting were lower on the social competence dimension of "Responsibility" (which I call "Niceness"), while preschoolers exposed to highly Authoritarian parenting were lower on "Assertiveness" (which I term "Boldness"). Preschoolers exposed to Authoritative discipline, on the other hand, were high on both these dimensions of social competence.

In a follow-up study of these children and their parents, Baumrind (1971) found that a subset of the formerly Authoritative parents were not doing very much controlling, while their children were among the most well-adjusted and socially competent in her sample. She termed this discipline pattern "Harmonious" and postulated that these children had become so well-behaved and so attuned to cues from their parents that the parents no longer had much need to set limits; furthermore, when limits were set, they were communicated in a very subtle way (such as the lifting of an eyebrow), and the children picked up on and responded to those subtle cues instantly.

Although there is undoubtedly some truth to this developmental explanation, there is a strong alternative possibility that Baumrind's two-factor model of discipline is inadequate. Specifically, it lacks a situational component, in that no discussion is made of the undeniable fact that competent caregivers do

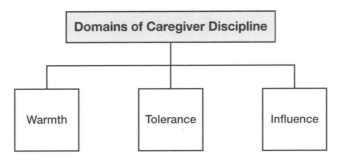

FIGURE 1.1   Research-Derived Domains of Discipline

not set limits all the time; in fact, it is illogical to assume that one could set limits all the time and still be Warm. So, it is very possible that the Harmonious caregiver, whom Baumrind sees as a special exception to her theory, might actually be its most ideal exemplar. Catherine Lewis (1981) made this argument, based on a reanalysis of Baumrind's data. Lewis found that an item Baumrind termed "firm enforcement of rules and standards" actually reflects low parent-child conflict (because of good child behavior) and that the bulk of parents categorized by Baumrind as Authoritative were actually moderate rather than high on Control.

Such a caregiver is one who sets limits when she has to (and thus is more likely to be rated as medium rather than high on Influence), but much of the time she does not set limits, because she understands the importance of giving a child space and not defining everything he does as objectionable. The absence of this discrimination process in Baumrind's model reflects the absence of a third dimension of discipline, which I term "Tolerance." Wesley Becker (1964) identified this third domain of discipline and labeled it "calm detachment versus anxious over-involvement" (I prefer the shorter term Tolerance). It refers to the extent to which a caregiver maintains a boundary between her own needs and values and those of a child, and gives a child room to be himself, without excessive monitoring and intrusion. Figure 1.1 depicts the three-factor model of caregiver discipline.

The domain of Tolerance adds a dynamic, or situational, element to Baumrind's somewhat static and authoritative notion, in that a competent caregiver is not just a limit-setting machine but someone who can discriminate between a situation where a limit is needed (such as breaking a chair) and a situation where a limit is not needed (such as expressing annoyance but not breaking anything). This more laid-back caregiver comes close to what Baumrind termed Harmonious, but the harmony comes not just from having a very well-behaved child but also from making a conscious decision not to treat everything a child does as a problem (a fuller elaboration of this discussion is found in S. Greenspan 2006).

In my own contribution to this research area (S. Greenspan 1978), I identified preschoolers who were unusually high or low on social competence and then used a structured interview to explore the discipline tendencies of their mothers. The interview included various scenarios in which a child was portrayed as engaging in some annoying behavior (such as bouncing a ball in the house) and then responding to a maternal request to stop by complying (one more bounce and then stopping) or not complying (continuing to bounce). The child was also portrayed as either uttering affect (saying, for example, "I don't want to stop") or not uttering affect. The adult subjects were then asked to imagine they were the mom and to verbalize what their response would be after each scenario. What I found was that the mothers of the highly socially competent children were better able to know when they did not have a problem than were the mothers of the children with low social competence. The latter group tended to treat the expression of affect as if it were an act of defiance, even when there was compliance (the one final bounce was also problematic for these moms, who seemed to have little tolerance for anything other than absolute and immediate cessation of the offending activity). These individuals also seemed more likely to hold a grudge, as they made more negative side comments, such as "What a nasty little kid," as the scenarios proceeded from one act of defiance to another. The mothers of the highly socially competent children, on the other hand, were better able to focus on what was actually happening, and when a child was portrayed as complying but only expressing affect, they were more likely to ignore the one more bounce and make a reflective comment, such as "I understand you like to bounce the ball in the house, but thank you for stopping."

The three-factor solution of discipline has support from the research literature, from both "construct validity" (factor-analytic) studies and "predictive validity" (child-adult congruence) studies. Furthermore, I believe this solution makes more intuitive sense than does one that includes only two factors. The three-factor solution also has consensual validation support, as seen in the fact that each of the three major approaches to discipline has a principle that "loads" on one of the three factors (or what I term "domains"). I explore this last point at length in Chapters 2 through 4.

Three Desired Long-Term Outcomes of Discipline

Most of the discipline books that are aimed at parents or teachers emphasize the short-term goal of managing behavior. This involves such things as getting a child to cease an undesirable behavior (e.g., hitting another child) or to initiate some desired behavior (e.g., sharing his toys), as well as restoring the balance in a caregiver-child system (family, classroom, etc.) from one of conflict to one of harmony. The short-term purposes of securing compliance and restoring harmony are very important, because any system—whether a classroom, a family, or a group home—cannot function very effectively if people are causing pain to each other.

One obvious way to maintain peace and harmony is, of course, to always give in to a child and to never set any limits. This is definitely *not* a recommended solution, however. It may make the child happy, but it is also likely to make the adult caregiver very unhappy. The trick to being an effective disciplinarian is to find a method that satisfies the needs of both the child and the adult caregiver. Furthermore, I believe (as do most discipline experts) that adults and children are not equals and that adults have a right to impose their will in certain circumstances. The trick is to do this in a way that does not cause conflict to escalate and that does not damage the child's well-being. Another reason why it is not a good idea to purchase harmony by always giving in is that children need structure and limits, and it is a mistake to think that always giving in will make a child happy. In fact, the opposite is likely to happen. Children who never experience adult limits seem to be always unhappy about something and are more likely to behave in ways that cause peers to reject them (which *really* makes them unhappy).

Most of the nine principles contained within the ABC Model of Discipline are intended to achieve the short-term goal of ending undesirable child behaviors and restoring harmony to a system (family, classroom, etc.). Typically, this involves using two or more of the nine principles in concert. I explore this theme more fully in Chapters 5 and 6.

Important as it is to the restoration of system harmony and the encouragement of short-term behavior change, discipline may be even more important as a means of positively influencing a child's socioemotional development. Obviously, even when exposed to the best caregiver discipline, children can become socially incompetent. We all know families, for example, in which all of the children turn out very well except for one outlier who falls in with the wrong crowd or develops problems for other reasons, such as having a brain-based attention deficit hyperactivity disorder. It is undeniable, however, that caregiving does contribute to healthy child development, in that children exposed to skilled discipline are generally better prepared to deal with life's challenges than are children exposed to inept or chaotic discipline. Thus, effective discipline can be considered a "necessary but not sufficient" condition for the development of socially competent children. What this means is that although it is possible for children exposed to effective discipline to become socially incompetent, it is almost assured that children exposed to inept discipline will become socially incompetent. (But I do not mean to deny that very occasionally, a highly competent "invulnerable" child emerges unscathed from the most chaotic and risk-filled environment.)

In asserting that discipline influences social competence, it is necessary for me to say something about the term itself. Social competence, like many psychological constructs, has proven somewhat difficult to define. One reason is that it can be approached either in terms of outcomes or in terms of inputs, and some scholars get the two mixed up. A socially competent outcome occurs when a child succeeds in a socially valued and age-relevant role. A commonly used outcome index of social competence is popularity and friendships, as measured by peer-nomination methods (such as having everyone in a class rank everyone else, and then summing the rankings). Children who are popular generally have better social skills (such as understanding reciprocity norms) than children who are less popular, and extreme unpopularity can be an indicator that a child needs some form of early mental-health or special-education intervention.

School success or failure can be another good outcome indicator of social competence. This assertion may surprise those who think of school success mainly as a function of cognition, but many social behaviors—such as attendance, effort, work completion, respect for authority, and compliance with rules—contribute mightily to success in school and, later, in adult settings such as the workplace. In fact, given some minimal level of academic potential, it is typically social incompetence rather than low intelligence that causes students to drop out, to be suspended, to be expelled, or to be referred for special services. Ability and social functioning are not unrelated, of course, as in the case of the class clown, who often is diverting attention away from his own sense of academic inadequacy.

Social competence is, of course, just as important for adults as it is for children, and some people believe that the main function of discipline (and even of schooling) is to prepare children to become socially competent adults. Many possible outcome indicators can be used to determine whether an adult is socially competent. One that was used in a long-term evaluation of an early-intervention program that was a precursor to Head Start was whether girls later became pregnant as unwed teenagers. Preschool girls who were enrolled in the program were dramatically less likely to become teen moms (and, consequently, to go on welfare) and thus were much more likely to pursue their studies, to attain a career direction, and to escape from the cycle of poverty in which their own mothers had been trapped (Gray, Ramsey, and Klaus 1982). Although early-intervention programs have pursued the largely unattainable goal of raising intelligence, various commentators have pointed out that the success or failure of these programs should be viewed mainly in terms of whether they prepare their graduates to succeed in adult social roles (such as holding a job and staying out of jail) that, for the most part, depend on social rather than academic skills (Zigler and Trickett 1978).

While social competence outcomes, such as school completion, are important, it is more useful for our purpose to discuss social competence in "input" terms. By inputs, I mean the kinds of behavioral dimensions (such as impulsivity and social judgment) that make one susceptible or invulnerable to a particular social competence outcome, such as becoming suspended or expelled. Many kinds of behaviors fall under the rubric of social competence. Three broad categories have been identified, which my colleagues and I (e.g., S. Greenspan and Driscoll 1997) have termed (1) "Temperament," (2) "Character," and (3) "Social Intelligence."

Temperament refers to one's degree of emotional, motivational, and attentional stability, as reflected in the ability to sustain effort, to take things in stride (without flying off the handle), and to maintain a fairly consistent positive mood. For purposes of the ABC model, I am reframing Temperament as "Happiness." Clearly, Happiness is a major goal of discipline; when asked what she wishes for a particular child, almost any caregiver first answers "to grow up to be a happy person."

Character includes two subtypes. The first refers to the ability to conform one's behavior to societal expectations and to generally behave in a way that others view positively. In this book, I am reframing Character as "Niceness." A nice child is one whom other children, and adults, want to be around, while a "nasty" child is one whom others view negatively and wish to avoid, or worse. Clearly, influencing children to be nice is a major goal of discipline. In fact, it is probably the most explicitly emphasized purpose, given that the dictionary definition of parent and teacher discipline commonly uses phrases such as "maintaining order" and "forming proper conduct."

The other subtype of Character (and the third competence trait depicted in the ABC model) is what I term "Boldness." This trait refers to the ability to assert one's will in situations where to do otherwise would make one vulnerable; it also refers to the development of a unique identity and set of lifestyle preferences. Although excessive Boldness (i.e., when it is not paired with Niceness) could make a person insufferable, there is no question that most of us want children to become adults who are able to assert their needs—but in a nice way. As I articulate in my book *Annals of Gullibility* (2009), it is important for children to develop the ability to say "no" in situations where others would mislead or coerce them down dangerous or undesirable paths, such as engaging in crime, using drugs, or joining a gang or cult.

Becoming non-gullible is an ideal outcome of discipline that has long been implicit in education; for example, the Massachusetts Bay Colony established public schools in North America not to prepare children for work but to keep them from being misled by Satan. Within the secular setting of public education today, discussion of non-gullibility as a goal is not stressed much, except within the context of curricular add-ons, such as saying no to drugs. Families, however, express much concern about the importance of children being able to resist peers who would lead them astray. This was a constant refrain of my late mother, who used to warn me unceasingly about my tendency (as a shy individual) to be swayed by "bad influences." However, this worry is not something emphasized much by discipline experts, whose discussion of "will" is less about the importance of strengthening the willpower of children and more about the importance of strengthening the ability of caregivers to impose their will on the children in their care. Undoubtedly, strengthening the resolve of caregivers is a worthwhile goal, but one should not lose sight of the fact that children who grow up to become weak-willed adults who cannot assert themselves are very likely to be exploited and very *un*likely to become happy or successful. Furthermore, to paraphrase Erik Erikson (1950), it is a sin to crush the spirit of a child.

Social Intelligence, a third input domain of social competence, has been very important in my own research, but I do not stress it in this book. It refers to the extent to which a child or adult possesses an awareness and understanding of people and their behavior. Social Intelligence is obviously a very important contributor to success or failure in various social roles and situations. In terms of the ABC model, however, I prefer to view it as a "mediating variable" and thus do not emphasize it. In calling Social Intelligence a mediating variable, I mean that it operates behind the scenes and is not directly observed.

To illustrate: When a child is in a situation where he could behave nicely or nastily, his level of Social Intelligence (such as judging likely adult responses and taking the perspective of someone who might be hurt by his action) contributes to his ability to behave appropriately. The same could be said for Boldness. For example, when a child is being bullied or otherwise pressured, if he has good Social Intelligence, he is more likely to understand that taking a stand is essential to getting the bullying to end, is more understanding of the true motives of the bully (namely, to test the child's resolve), and is more aware of other options available to him (such as appealing to adults for help). Thus, although I do not talk directly about Social Intelligence within the framework of the ABC model, I nevertheless believe that one of the ways in which discipline contributes to the other social competence outcomes (such as Niceness) is by impacting on a child's Social Intelligence. Of the three

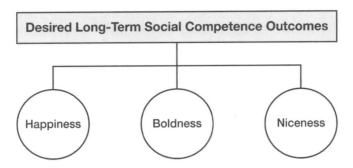

FIGURE 1.2   Desired Long-Term Social Competence Outcomes for Children

discipline approaches in the model, the Cognitive approach most explicitly emphasizes Social Intelligence as a mediator of good behavior.

The outcome of social competence used in the model, as portrayed in various figures in this book, thus has three components: Happiness (emotional stability and positive mood), Boldness (autonomous functioning), and Niceness (kindness and appropriateness). Figure 1.2 depicts this aspect of the model. One obvious thing to keep in mind is that the most socially competent children (and adults) are relatively high on all three components. Thus, although Boldness is a desirable trait for any human being to possess, a child who is very bold but not very nice is ultimately not going to be very socially competent in outcome terms. Similarly, Happiness is a desirable state to which all human beings aspire, but true happiness can only exist in people who also care about the happiness of others (as long as one is not so concerned about others' happiness that he forgets about his own—that is, becomes too low on Boldness).

Logical Links between Discipline Domains and Child Outcomes

At the heart of the ABC Model of Discipline is the idea that the three domains of discipline and the three desired social competence outcomes are logically linked. Figure 1.3 illustrates this linkage. The three discipline domains appear at the bottom of the figure, and the three desired competence outcomes are at the top, connected by arrows pointing upward, suggesting that each discipline domain has a logical causative link with one of the desired outcomes.

By calling this a *logical* link, I am suggesting a commonsense connection rather than one that has necessarily been empirically validated. Human beings differ from machines in that they cannot be perfectly programmed to turn out

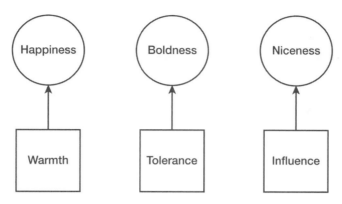

FIGURE 1.3 Logical Links between Domains of Discipline and Outcomes

a certain way. But I think a case can be made for arguing that a child who is exposed to caregiver Warmth is more likely to be a Happy kid, a child who is exposed to caregiver Tolerance is more likely to be a Bold kid, and a child who is exposed to caregiver Influence is more likely to be a Nice kid. I explore these logical connections more fully in the next several chapters, especially in Chapter 6.

2

The Affective Approach
to Discipline

Underpinnings and Three Principles

The Affective approach to discipline grew out of the writings of theorists on adult psychotherapy, particularly Sigmund Freud and Carl Rogers. Although Freud and Rogers did not say much about discipline themselves, their theories certainly had major implications for the way adults disciplined children, and several of their followers did, in fact, develop these ideas into what I am terming the Affective approach to discipline.

Early Freudians, both psychoanalysts and their patients, were somewhat naive and unsophisticated in the way they applied Freudian notions to caregiving. Because patients in psychoanalysis tended (and were encouraged) to spend a lot of time complaining about the intrusiveness and awfulness of their parents, some early enthusiasts of psychoanalysis assumed that the key to becoming a healthy adult was to be raised by very permissive parents. Among these devotees of permissiveness was, early in his career, Doctor Benjamin Spock, the pediatrician whose book *Baby and Child Care* went through many editions and became a fixture in the households of most American families, especially in the third quarter of the twentieth century. This approach, which some have termed "vulgar" (overly simplistic) Freudianism, was later replaced by a more nuanced synthesis, one the later Doctor Spock summarized as "firm but friendly," in which parents were encouraged to be permissive of feelings (no matter what their content) even while setting limits on unacceptable overt acts.

Rogers was a major figure in twentieth-century psychology. He devised a system of psychotherapy that he termed "non-directive therapy," which relied mainly on the use of a technique he called "active" (or reflective) listening. This technique involves a therapist's responding to a patient's comments by serially reflecting back to him, each time with slightly different (and more specific) words, the feeling the therapist believes is being expressed. An example would be the following: A young man named Robert seems upset over a perceived slight from his father. The therapist could say, "It disappointed you that your dad gave your sister a bigger present than he gave you?" Robert might reply, "Yes, it wasn't fair," to which the therapist could reply, "You wish your father loved you as much as your sister?" The purpose of such a sequence of increasingly more focused questions is to give Robert a chance to clarify his feelings (including the chance to say "no" when the therapist misses the mark) and to open him up to exploring feelings that might be somewhat buried and confusing to him.

Rogers also believed in the importance of showing respect for the personhood of the patient, no matter the nature of his past acts or of the feelings being expressed. He termed this concept the principle of "unconditional positive regard," meaning that every human being has the same intrinsic worth, and that worth is not diminished, no matter what thoughts, feelings, or acts have been expressed by the person. The implication of this principle for discipline is that caregivers should never convey to a child any diminished valuation of the child (e.g., through sarcasm or "guilt trips"), even when the caregiver has to set a limit on some unacceptable behavior by the child.

The Affective approach to discipline, expressed in a widely read book by Dorothy Baruch (1949), is based on the idea that unacceptable behavior in a child is always motivated by feelings (affect), and that the way to defuse many conflict situations is to provide an acceptable outlet for those feelings. Helping the child to get in touch with his feelings and to understand that all feelings are acceptable is seen as essential for healthy socioemotional development in the child. A logical flip side of this argument is that caregivers also have feelings that they have a right to express, and children must learn to recognize and respect those feelings. The principle of unconditional positive regard also requires caregivers to always keep in mind that discipline messages must be directed toward the child's specific action and that disrespectful or damaging comments about the child's personhood are to be avoided.

Skilled discipline in the Affective system involves a balancing act. Caregivers have a right and responsibility to communicate disapproval of specific unacceptable actions, but such communications should also (1) acknowledge the legitimacy of the child's feelings (both those that underlie the act as well as those stemming from the imposition of a limit) and (2) address the act but in no way disparage the child or comment on his character or worth.

The two authorities who have done the most to systematize and popularize the Affective approach are Haim Ginott (1965)—who might be considered

Baruch's successor—and Thomas Gordon (1970). Baruch and Ginott were child psychoanalysts, and their work can be considered neo-Freudian in nature. The ideas of Ginott (who died in 1973) have been effectively carried forward in several books written by Adele Faber and Elaine Mazlish, who started out as members of one of Ginott's parent groups and went on to write several books themselves. Their two best-known books, *Liberated Parents, Liberated Children* (1975) and *How to Talk So Kids Will Listen and Listen So Kids Will Talk* (1980), built on Ginott's ideas about discipline. Ginott's 1965 classic, *Between Parent and Child*, was reissued in 2003 in a revised and updated version edited by his wife, Alice Ginott, and a colleague, H. Wallace Goddard.

The late Gordon, whose best-known book is *P.E.T.: Parent Effectiveness Training* (1970), was a nondirective psychotherapist whose books were more explicitly influenced by the writings of Rogers than by the writings of Freud. However, the Rogerian perspective can be considered an offshoot of psychoanalytic theory, and I find that Ginott and Gordon offer very similar suggestions regarding how caregivers should approach discipline. However, Ginott and Gordon differ on the question of the appropriate power differential between caregivers and children: Gordon believed such differences were to be resolved through negotiation, while Ginott encouraged caregivers to assert their will when necessary. I consider this to be a relatively minor difference, and I believe it is appropriate to lump Ginott and Gordon together as proponents of the Affective approach. They agreed on all three of the core principles of this approach, including the third principle, which encourages caregivers to express their needs and expectations regarding what they consider standards of acceptable child conduct.

Gordon's major contribution to the development of the Affective discipline approach is that he developed a workshop format—termed "Effectiveness Training"—in which he systematically taught Affective communication techniques, including active listening, to parents, teachers, and others (administrators, youth, etc.). In these seminars, Gordon used a variety of teaching tools, among them a "decision window" for deciding when a behavior is problematic (described later in this chapter), to make it easier for caregivers to learn how to apply Affective discipline methods.

Gordon expanded on his ideas about discipline in a later book, *Discipline That Works* (1991). This book was partly inspired by the popularity of the conservative *Dare to Discipline* books by Focus on the Family founder James C. Dobson (1977, 1996), which call upon parents to become tougher in imposing their will on children. Gordon marshals powerful arguments against such a message, and he presents his own theoretical position on discipline more fully than in his previous work. In the process, Gordon comes close to carrying out his own integration between the Affective and Cognitive discipline approaches, as he places much more emphasis than he did before on the role of caregivers as teachers and on the cognitive processes that children use when they learn how to become better at controlling their own behavior.

Another area of applied psychoanalysis that has contributed to a surge of interest in the Affective discipline approach involves the notion of "emotional intelligence," or EQ. The term was first coined by two psychology professors, Peter Salovey of Yale University and John Mayer of the University of New Hampshire, but interest in the concept increased dramatically after the publication of the best-seller *Emotional Intelligence,* by science writer/psychologist Daniel Goleman (1995). The term refers to one's understanding of emotion, in oneself and in others, as reflected in the ability to modulate one's emotional reactions to potentially upsetting events. Goleman argues that emotional intelligence is mediated by certain brain structures, particularly the amygdala, small almond-shaped areas on both sides of the mid-brain that have been found to play a role in processing emotionally charged information. However, Goleman finds that family and educational experiences contribute to (or detract from) the development of a child's EQ in important ways and can even affect brain development, a point also made by John Gottman (1998) in his book *Raising an Emotionally Intelligent Child.*

Gottman, known more for his path-breaking research on marital interaction, makes very explicit his debt to Ginott (to whom his book was dedicated), and it is clear that he considers his book to be an extension of the Affective discipline approach pioneered by Ginott and carried on by others, such as Faber and Mazlish. The main innovation Gottman adds to the Affective discipline literature is the notion of "emotion coaching," a practice by which caregivers look for opportunities (such as when a child acts out) to make a teaching intervention intended to help the child better understand and regulate his behavior and the feelings underlying his behavior.

Gottman's understanding of the importance of emotion coaching came during a longitudinal study he was conducting of successful marriages in young adults who were also parents. He found that parents of socially competent four- and five-year-olds were much more likely to engage in emotion coaching—that is, accepting and facilitating the expression of emotion in their children—than were other parents. Specifically, Gottman found that children whose parents were good emotion coaches had better emotional self-regulation and other indicators of social competence than did children whose parents were poor emotion coaches. Gottman attributed this to better "vagal tone" (the ability of the nervous system to handle stress) and suggested that good emotion coaching had a positive impact on the children's developing brain structures and processes. Gottman noted that, to his knowledge, his study was the first to support the empirical validity of Ginott's ideas about child-rearing. Actually, there was at least one earlier study—by me (1978). In that work, I found that mothers of socially competent four-year-olds were much more likely to accept verbal expressions of affect in their children, especially when the expressions were not accompanied by inappropriate behavior.

Lawrence Shapiro (1998) covers some of the same territory in his book *How to Raise a Child with a High EQ: A Parents' Guide to Emotional Intelligence* but extends the discussion of desired child outcomes to include not only emotional self-regulation but also the acquisition of an optimistic outlook on life. Shapiro's interest in optimism is part of a major recent shift within clinical psychology toward what has been termed "positive psychology." This shift has arisen in reaction against the prevailing tendency to view mental health mainly as the absence of pathology or deficit; instead, the objective is to refocus attention on the skills and qualities that make people happy and that enable them to cope better with life's inevitable disappointments.

The leading figure in the positive psychology movement in general, and optimism in particular, has been University of Pennsylvania professor Martin Seligman. He also has written a book for caregivers, titled *The Optimistic Child* (1995). In it, Seligman urges caregivers to make children less susceptible to later depression by coaching them into new, more optimistic ways of thinking about the world. The key to this coaching technique, used not just by parents but also in school settings, is to encourage children to have an internal dialogue in which they become aware of how their own pessimistic beliefs cause them to make ineffective and overly emotional responses to what Seligman terms "adversity." By teaching children to have more optimistic outlooks (in part through a technique called the "brain game," which models rapid-fire disputation of pessimism), Seligman demonstrates that children can be helped to become happier, more stable, and more competent people.

Shapiro uses similar methods to promote emotional self-regulation, offering a version of the brain game termed "mind ping pong." Like Gottman and Goleman, Shapiro puts more emphasis than does Seligman on changes in brain structures (the thalamus and the amygdala, in particular) resulting from caregivers' use of EQ-boosting techniques. Shapiro, in line with the Adlerian/Cognitive approach (see Chapter 4), also emphasizes the benefits to the child not only of achieving better emotional self-regulation but also of becoming more empathic, caring, and morally mature.

A final popular author on child-rearing who can be placed in the Affective camp is recently deceased psychiatrist Stanley I. Greenspan (no relation, though sometimes I did get phone calls intended for him). He was a psycho-

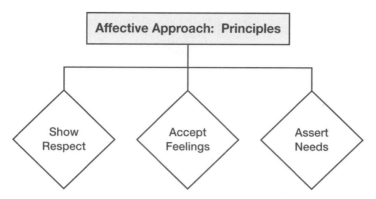

FIGURE 2.1   The Three Principles of the Affective Approach

analyst interested particularly in the emotional development of infants. Like many developmental scientists who consider the first two years of life critical for the development of intelligence, Greenspan considered this period critical also for the development of social competence and mental health. To Greenspan (2003; S. I. Greenspan with Salmon 1993), the key to becoming a socially competent child (and, later, adult) is acquiring the ability to empathize—namely, to understand and to be moved by what others are feeling. Caregivers, particularly parents, play a critical role in helping the child become more empathic by building a strong relationship in which the reciprocal expression and acceptance of feelings is central.

Stanley I. Greenspan developed a core technique, which he termed "floortime," that involves literally getting down on the floor with young children and conversing with them about their feelings about this or that. He promoted the technique as a way for caregivers to help develop empathy in children. As with all the techniques I mention in this book, floortime is something that competent caregivers often do naturally without having a name for it. By naming this action, Greenspan's intention was to sensitize caregivers to children's affective needs and to provide them (much as Gordon and Ginott did with active listening) with a tool for becoming more skilled in speaking the language of emotion with children. Although floortime is a general tool for use with all children, it has become widely used with autistic and at-risk children (S. I. Greenspan and Wieder with Simons 1998), because an inability to empathize or to otherwise recognize the perspectives of others is a core aspect of autistic-spectrum developmental disabilities.

I have distilled this body of literature into three principles that characterize the Affective approach to discipline: Show Respect, Accept Feelings, and Assert Needs (see Figure 2.1).

The First Affective Principle:
Show Respect

One of the curious things about human functioning is that adults are typically much more careful in the way they express annoyance to adult strangers than they are in how they express annoyance to their own children or students. Even the most hurtful and disparaging of comments are routinely directed to young children. Thus, I designate "Show Respect" as the first principle of the Affective approach to discipline. This principle can be stated as follows: "Caregivers should refrain from commenting on a child's character, motives, or overall patterns of behavior, or from otherwise assaulting a child's sense of worth." What this means is that even when setting a limit on a child's behavior, a caregiver should do so in a way that focuses on the desired behavioral change rather than on the child as a person. This principle does not prohibit a caregiver from ever feeling or expressing anger. Rather, it directs caregivers to exercise some degree of care in the manner in which they communicate anger (just as they would with adults) by being constructive in their comments (telling the child what he did that was unacceptable) rather than destructive (tearing the child down with comments about how bad or inconsiderate he is).

Gordon suggested use of what he termed "I-messages" to help a caregiver communicate her disapproval without attacking the child. This widely used technique, when applied correctly, especially in conjunction with active listening, is a powerful tool for setting limits in a manner likely to be effective, rather than ineffective, in influencing the behavior of children.

An I-message is communicated in the following form: "I feel x (e.g., upset) when you do y (e.g., kick the wall), because z (e.g., walls are bothersome to repair)." Such a message focuses on the caregiver and why she has a problem with a particular act of the child. The importance of avoiding a message starting with "you" is that you-messages inevitably lead to a comment about the child's character (e.g., "you are bad"), motives (e.g., "you only care about yourself"), or overall patterns of behavior (e.g., "you never think"). Such you-oriented messages tear down the child's self-regard and can foster resentment and resistance rather than harmony and compliance.

Gordon's I-message formula—"I feel x when you do y, because z" (which Ginott formulated a little differently as "chairs [cats, brothers, etc.] are not for kicking [hitting, painting, etc.]")—has the advantage of reminding the caregiver to keep her comment of disapproval short and to the point. Too often, caregivers engage in a long-winded lecture every time they have to set a limit. Lectures are ineffective because children tune them out, as do adults, especially when they have heard the lecture before. More important, lectures are disrespectful, as they convey the message "I am smart, and you are stupid."

Violations of the Show Respect principle can take other forms in addition to lectures and put-downs. It is important that the caregiver's tone of voice be neutral and respectful, even when communicating displeasure. Sarcasm (a dismissive tone that is typically ironic, as when one says, "You are really smart" with a tone that says, "You are really stupid") is also a violation of the Show Respect principle and can be very hurtful to the child's feelings. Physical punishment, especially when it verges on abuse (as in the use of straps for whipping), is also an extreme form of disrespect that violates the child's sense of worth and serves mainly to teach the child that "might makes right." None of the Affective theorists encourages the use of physical punishment, and the same can be said of most other reputable discipline experts.

It is important to note that poorly delivered praise can also be a violation of the Show Respect principle. This occurs when a caregiver praises by commenting on the child's personhood rather than on a specific act. Although praise (positive comment or reward) is, obviously, a very good thing, inept praise (such as "You are a great piano player") is less effective than adept (and more honest) praise (such as "I liked that particular passage" or "It pleases me to hear you play with so much enthusiasm"). Inept praise, because it involves a heavy dose of evaluation, can often turn an activity done for intrinsic reasons (e.g., enjoyment) into something that is externally imposed and, thus, to be feared, resented, and (all too often) abandoned.

The I-message form ("I feel x about y"), when applied to praise, would sound something like, "It makes me feel good to see you completing your school project on time." This is obviously preferable to a backhanded you-message form of praise, such as "You finally did something without being reminded," or even a less sarcastic form of you-oriented praise, such as "Thank you for doing your work on time." A major difference is that an I-message form of praise leaves responsibility for the good behavior with the child and does not turn it into an accomplishment for the caregiver.

The Second Affective Principle: Accept Feelings

"Accept Feelings" is the principle that is probably most central to the Affective approach. It can be stated as follows: "Caregivers should provide symbolic outlets for the expression of feelings." What this means is that caregivers should make a distinction between overt actions and the feelings that underlie those actions, and allow the expression of those feelings even when setting limits on the overt form in which those feelings are expressed. Thus, if Sam expresses anger toward his younger brother John by punching him, the caregiver's task is to acknowledge the feeling while diverting the expression from an unacceptable overt form (hitting John) to an acceptable symbolic form. This caregiver acceptance, and facilitation, of Sam's feelings extends not just to Sam's feelings toward John but also to his feelings toward the caregiver herself when she seeks to exert discipline over Sam's unacceptable act.

Ginott proposed the following formula to guide caregivers when they enter into a discipline scenario such as the conflict between Sam and John:

1. Reflect the child's underlying feeling: "You're really angry at John for ruining your painting. I understand."
2. Set the limit: "But the rule in this house [classroom etc.] is 'no hitting.' Brothers [friends etc.] are not to be hit, no matter how angry you are at them."
3. Offer an acceptable symbolic outlet for the underlying feeling: "Tell John how you feel in words, or in a note. If you are so angry that you have to hit, why don't you make believe that doll is John and punch it?"
4. Reflect the child's feeling toward the caregiver for setting the limit: "You're really angry at me for stopping you from hitting John. I understand."

One book that addresses the how and why of caregiver acceptance of child anger is *Mom I Hate You!* by Don Fleming with Mark Ritts (2003).

The central technique that Affective theorists have promoted for facilitating child affect is psychotherapeutic reflection, which Rogers terms "active listening." A formula proposed by Gordon in his PET and TET (Parent and Teacher Effectiveness Training) workshops and books goes as follows: "You feel x (angry, sad, disappointed, etc.) about y (John's ruining your painting etc.)." The idea is that this statement will elicit a response (such as "yes," "no," or some elaboration) that can then to be followed by a variation on the caregiver's original reflective comment. This use of successive elaborations is intended to help the child articulate (and understand) what he is actually feeling (as opposed to what the caregiver may think he is feeling). It is recommended for use with children precisely because they lack the self-insight to be able to respond to a more open-ended question, such as "Tell me what you are feeling," with anything other than "I don't know." At the same time, some degree of care and effort needs to be put into the use of active listening, because following a specific formula too obviously is not likely to be effective.

It is important to understand that the Accept Feelings principle does not always require the use of an active listening response. There are times when a child may express a feeling symbolically without engaging in an unacceptable act, such as when a child is working on an art project and expresses frustration over some mistake. The Accept Feelings principle could be satisfied by making an active listening comment (such as "You wish that color was a little different?"); however, it could also be satisfied perfectly well by not making any comment at all and just accepting the child's remark. Either way, the caregiver conveys the message that expressing a feeling is acceptable and does not constitute a problem for the caregiver.

The Third Affective Principle: Assert Needs

The emphasis in the Affective approach on treating a child with respect (the first Affective principle) and on allowing him to autonomously have and express his own feelings (the second Affective principle) may give the mistaken impression that people who promote this approach care only about the feelings and needs of the child and not at all about the feelings and needs of the adult. Nothing could be further from the truth. This balance is reflected in the third Affective principle—"Assert Needs"—which can be stated as "Caregivers should let a child know when he has done something unacceptable."

The Affective approach grew out of a humanistic tradition, and at the core of humanism is the notion that relationships should be mutually satisfying. A relationship that is totally one-sided, such as when the child always wins and the adult always loses, is no more justifiable or healthy from this perspective than is the more traditional approach (against which the Affective approach was a corrective) in which the adult is always the winner. The Affective approach may thus be seen as a composite of two opposite views of the proper power relationship. These two views are summarized by Gordon as "you (child) win, I (caregiver) lose" and its opposite: "I (caregiver) win, you (child) lose." Gordon describes the synthesis underlying his approach as a "win-win" solution, and he justifies it on ethical grounds—namely, that mutual satisfaction of needs is the best and most desirable way to constitute any relationship, even between adults and children. More important for our purposes, however, is that Gordon also asserts that a win-win situation makes for the healthiest child-rearing environment, in that it is more likely to contribute to child compliance, family/classroom harmony, and healthy child development.

As noted earlier, there are subtle and not-so-subtle differences among practitioners of the Affective approach concerning how this win-win philosophy is to be implemented. For proponents of Gordon's Effectiveness Training approach, when a caregiver experiences a problem, she is encouraged to communicate her displeasure by framing it as an I-message focused on her feelings about a child's action. For proponents of Ginott's approach, on the other hand, the expression of adult feelings is described as "setting a limit," which implies a more forceful stance. To me, however, this distinction is not as great as it may seem, in that whether you call it "communicating a feeling" or "setting a limit," both expressions describe what happens when an adult tells a child to "cut it out."

Applying the Affective Approach

The key to being an effective caregiver, within any of the three major approaches, is knowing when to assert needs and when not to. Affectively oriented theorists have suggested decision devices to help caregivers make this important judgment. Ginott constructed a verbal formula for determining when to set a limit, while Gordon devised a visual scheme for the same purpose. As in the case of the guidelines these experts suggested for fulfilling the Accept Feelings principle, their decision devices are also actually quite similar in intent.

Ginott's verbal formula, designed to help caregivers decide when to set a limit, goes as follows: "A caregiver should set a limit when a child does something dangerous or destructive or that violates the caregiver's standards of acceptability." The term "limit" refers to a verbal injunction, which can be either positive (e.g., "I want you to start doing your homework") or negative (e.g., "I want you to stop hitting your brother"). For Ginott, the terms "destructive" and "dangerous" refer to child actions that are universally viewed by caregivers as problematic for the caregivers (any caregiver these days who does not have a problem with a child doing something dangerous can expect a visit from a child protective agency). The last part of Ginott's formula ("violates the caregiver's standards of acceptability") is intended to indicate an awareness that caregivers vary widely in what they are willing or unwilling to tolerate and that there is nothing wrong with that variation as long as individual caregivers (or families) maintain some degree of consistency in their rules and reactions.

Gordon did not specify the types of child behaviors deserving of adult limit-setting, but he did develop an elaborate decision-making visual aid, which he termed a "decision window." Figure 2.2 shows how the decision-window idea works. This illustration is not an exact replica of Gordon's graphic (in fact, the boxes here are labeled differently), but it conveys the general idea. The rectangular box in the figure represents a standard window, with a horizontal sash (solid line) roughly in the middle. Caregivers are instructed to think of the window as their own perception of behaviors engaged in by a hypothetical child. Above the sash are child behaviors that are problematic for the caregiver, while below the sash are behaviors that are not problematic for the caregiver.

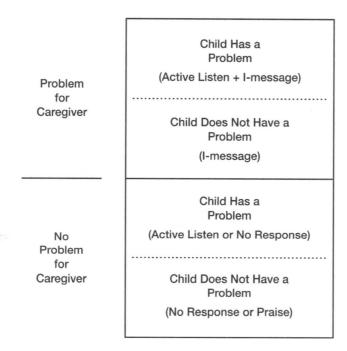

FIGURE 2.2 An Approximation of Gordon's Decision Window

Within each of the two categories, a dotted horizontal line is drawn (again, roughly in the middle of each window pane) to indicate whether the behavior is perceived as indicating that the child is experiencing a problem (e.g., he is unhappy about something). Thus, in the top half of the window (problem for caregiver), the top segment (above the dotted line) represents a behavior that is problematic for the caregiver (e.g., because the child is doing something destructive) *and* is indicative of a problem the child is having (he is being destructive because he is unhappy about something). The next segment down represents a behavior that is problematic for the caregiver but is not indicative of a problem for the child (he is quite happy while doing something destructive or otherwise bothersome, such as bouncing a ball against the wall).

Below the solid sash line are child behaviors that are not experienced by the caregiver as problematic for herself. These behaviors might be quite pleasant, or they might border on unpleasant without being unpleasant enough for the caregiver to feel the situation warrants her intervention. However, just because the child's behavior is not problematic for the caregiver does not mean that it does not signal a problem the child is having. Below the sash, the segment above the dotted line represents a behavior that indicates the child is upset about something (a problem for the child) but also that he is not express-ing that affect in a manner that is problematic for the caregiver. Below the dotted line is the ideal scenario, where both the child and the caregiver are problem-free.

The decision window assists the caregiver in deciding which of the two parties—herself or the child, or both—has a problem, but it also provides a guide for appropriate responses in each case. For the top quadrant, where both the child and the caregiver have a problem, the suggested response (indicated in parentheses in the diagram) is for the caregiver to acknowledge the child's affect through an active-listening response (in line with the Accept Feelings principle) and then to follow up with a limit-setting message about the objec-tionable behavior (in line with the Assert Needs principle). This limit should be conveyed in the form of an I-message (in line with the Show Respect principle).

For the second quadrant down, where the child does not have a problem but the caregiver does, no active-listening response is needed. However, this situation does call for a limit to be conveyed through an I-message.

For the third quadrant down, just below the window sash, the child has a problem but the caregiver does not. Here, there is no need for the caregiver to set a limit with an I-message. However, in keeping with the Accept Feelings principle, the caregiver has two choices: to offer an active-listening comment or to make no response at all.

For the fourth quadrant down, neither the child nor the caregiver has a problem. Thus, no response of any sort is required. However, if the child is doing something that the caregiver *likes* to see, she has the option of making a praise comment. In line with the Show Respect principle, this comment, even though it involves praise, should still be in the form of an I-message (i.e., "I feel *x* about *y* because *z*").

As noted earlier, caregivers vary in terms of what child behaviors they regard as problematic. The intent of the Affective approach is not to tell care-givers what their values or expectations *should* be but rather to help them become more aware of what their values *are* and of how their discipline responses promote or detract from those values. Figure 2.3 uses the decision-window device to illustrate two very different (but equally acceptable) patterns of caregiver "discipline deciding."

The decision window on the left side of the figure portrays a relatively strict discipline pattern. Here, the sash is fairly far down in the window, suggesting that the caregiver tends to perceive a relatively large number of child behaviors as problems that require her to set a limit. The decision window on the right side of the figure portrays a relatively more permissive pattern. In this case, the sash is fairly far up in the window, suggesting that the caregiver tends to per-

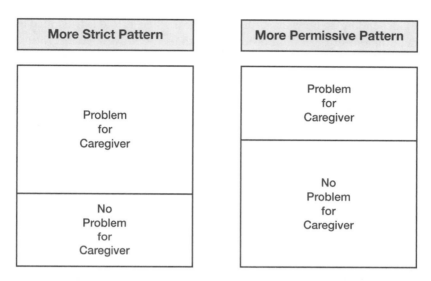

FIGURE 2.3   Two Patterns of Discipline Problem Definition

ceive a relatively small number of child behaviors as problems that require her to set a limit.

Gordon recognized the variation among caregivers in terms of their values and expectations, and he accommodated it in his decision-window scheme by varying how high or low the sash is depicted. Even for an individual caregiver, however, the position of the sash may not be fixed. It is likely that a caregiver who adopts the Affective approach will find her window sash gradually moving up. This is because there is a large class of child behaviors—involving only symbolic expressions of affect—that she will be increasingly less likely to see as problematic the longer she follows the approach. The idea behind the second Affective principle—Accept Feelings—is that limits are set only on overt expressions of affect (assuming that the overt behavior is problematic for the caregiver), whereas symbolic (i.e., verbal) expressions of affect are always allowed. In cases where a child expresses a feeling symbolically but does not actually do anything overt (such as kicking the cat), the caregiver can ignore the expression of affect or can make a reflective comment ("You feel x about y"), but the caregiver does not set a limit (through an I-message) on that expression of affect. Given that many caregivers make the mistake of regarding a child's expression of feelings as problematic, a caregiver who employs the Affective approach will, over time, find that she is less likely to treat everything the child does as a problem than was the case before.

In some cases, however, a symbolic expression of affect alone can take on the quality of an overt act, and a caregiver is certainly free to set a limit in such cases, depending on her values. One example is when a child is frustrated over something and utters a mild obscenity, such as the S-word. A caregiver can choose to treat this as purely symbolic (by ignoring it or by saying something like "It really annoys you that you couldn't get your computer to turn on"), or she can treat it as a problem (by saying something like "I understand you are upset about your computer, but the rule in this house is we don't use words like that"). In either case, she can provide the child with a more appropriate symbolic outlet for the underlying feeling: "Instead of using that word, why don't you say 'Oh, fiddlesticks' whenever you have a problem with your computer?"

Another category of symbolic expression that a caregiver might have trouble tolerating is verbal expressions directed at the caregiver herself (e.g., "I hate you, Mommy" or "Drop dead"). However, it is best to ignore such expressions or to simply acknowledge them reflectively ("I understand that you are angry with me, but you still have to turn off the TV and come to dinner").

One key to being effective in asserting needs is to use a tone of voice that is emphatic enough to get the child's attention and that conveys the idea that the caregiver means business. Pleading or whining is a weak posture for a caregiver to take and should be avoided. One reason why some caregivers do not use sufficiently emphatic language is because they do not want to appear angry or emotionally abusive. However, one can be emphatic while still being quite calm and nonabusive, and being emphatic does not necessarily equate with displaying anger (not that anger is an inappropriate emotion for a caregiver to feel or to show, as long as it is expressed in a controlled and legally acceptable manner).

I am reminded of one client I worked with: the mother of an out-of-control four-year-old son. This mom was unusually quiet and nonassertive. In spite of quickly mastering the elements of effective discipline, she communicated in such a passive manner that her child had trouble knowing when she was setting a limit. My intervention with this mother focused mainly on helping her use a more emphatic tone of voice, so that when she asserted disapproval (or approval, for that matter), it was possible for her son to recognize what she was doing.

Myths about the Affective Approach

One reason I wrote this book was to clear up certain misconceptions that readers might have about the three discipline approaches. These myths can cause caregivers to misapply or even abandon an approach. With respect to the Affective approach, two misconceptions are common: (1) the caregiver has to become a therapist and (2) every feeling equals anger. I discuss these myths briefly on the next two pages.

The Myth of the Caregiver Having to Become a Therapist

The Affective approach grew out of the counseling psychology literature and borrows some techniques—such as active listening—used by therapists. For that reason, some caregivers assume wrongly that the intent of authors operating within the Affective approach is to turn them into psychotherapists. Because some parents and teachers prefer not to take on that role, they may find the Affective approach a little off-putting.

The intent of the Affective approach is to make caregivers more sensitive to a child's feelings and more careful about how they express their own feelings. This is something that almost all competent caregivers do as a matter of course in dealing with children, and one does not have to be a therapist or use therapeutic methods to accomplish these goals.

Affectively oriented discipline authors provide model phrases for dealing with situations in which the caregiver or the child might have a problem. Model phrases that can be used when the child has a problem include forms of the reflection formula suggested by Gordon (e.g., "You feel angry that Johnny took your truck") and Ginott (e.g., "It really bothered you when Johnny took your truck"). Examples of responses that can be used when the caregiver has a problem are Gordon's I-message (e.g., "It made me worried when I saw you hit Johnny, because I don't like to see anybody get hurt") and Ginott's limit-setting formula (e.g., "But children are not for hitting. The rule in this house [classroom etc.] is 'no hitting.'"). These formulas are useful teaching tools but are not meant to be followed slavishly.

A caregiver once told me, "Ginott's approach isn't right for me, because I don't feel comfortable using the expression 'Chairs are not for kicking.'" Unfortunately, she had missed the underlying principles (in this case, Assert Needs combined with Show Respect) that Ginott's expression was meant to illustrate. My main objective in writing this book, in fact, was to make the underlying principles clearer and, thus, to free caregivers from feeling locked into specific therapeutic or other verbal formulas or techniques.

The Myth That Every Feeling Equals Anger

One of the hardest things to get a caregiver to do when learning the Affective approach is to talk about feelings other than anger. It is a little easier to use non-anger-related words (e.g., "You were sad when . . .") in using reflective listening with the child, but there is an almost universal tendency for the caregiver to fall back on the A-word when setting limits or using I-messages (e.g., "I am really angry that you came in two hours late"). It is not that anger is necessarily a taboo feeling for a caregiver to have or to express, but constantly telling a child how angry one is will eventually prove ineffective. An even more important reason for finding other emotion words to use is that a caregiver's anger is usually a smokescreen for some other emotion, and expressing the other emotion is likely to be more honest. In response to a child coming home two hours after he was supposed to, a more honest caregiver expression would be something along the lines of "I was really worried . . ." or "I am so relieved. . . ."

One of the exercises that Affectively oriented discipline educators use with caregivers is to increase their vocabulary for non-anger affect words. Even when anger is the emotion they are feeling, caregivers are encouraged to delve deeper to see what feeling preceded or accompanied the anger. Caregivers are reluctant to use affect terms, such as "scared" or "sad" or "hurt," when talking with children out of concern that they will appear weak or non-adult-like. But in my experience, kids are much more likely to take a limit seriously when an adult says, "It really hurt my feelings . . ." than when she says, "It made me really angry. . . ." Furthermore, children who constantly express anger, especially in trivial situations, are typically not very socially competent or happy. Caregivers who rely on anger as their emotion of choice are, therefore, modeling socially incompetent behavior to children.

3

The Behavioral Approach to Discipline

Underpinnings and Three Principles

The Behavioral approach to discipline reflects the behaviorist perspective in psychology, a worldview that has been very influential in academic psychology but even more so in applied settings—including schools, clinics, and residential programs—and with exceptional populations. To save on words in the discussion that follows, I shall sometimes use the term "behaviorists" in lieu of the more awkward expression "adherents of the Behavioral approach."

Behaviorism includes many different subtheoretical strands, but two in particular have influenced the literature on caregiver discipline: (1) classical conditioning, as exemplified in the work of early-twentieth-century psychologist John B. Watson, and (2) operant (or instrumental) conditioning, as exemplified in the work of mid- and late-twentieth-century psychologist B. F. Skinner. The recent popular Behavioral child-rearing literature has been much more heavily influenced by Skinner than by Watson, but some brief discussion of Watson's work is included here to provide historical context and because that work was extremely popular at one time.

An excellent summary of Watson's ideas about child-rearing is contained in a book by Ann Hulbert (2003) titled *Raising America: Experts, Parents, and a Century of Advice about Children*. Watson was a professor of psychology at Johns Hopkins University until he was fired in a sex scandal; he later went on to become a successful Madison Avenue advertising executive, specializing in the use of fear to sell products.

Watson was a follower of the ideas of the great Russian physiologist Ivan Pavlov, who demonstrated the phenomenon of conditioned reflexes by training dogs to produce digestive juices upon hearing a bell. Watson applied Pavlov's ideas to child-rearing, as in an infamous experiment in which he trained a young child ("Little Albert") to have a phobic response to the sight of a bunny rabbit and, later, white fuzzy objects. Watson, who denied any place for heredity in the development of children, promoted the theories of the emergent field of behavioral psychology as a way for parents to attain complete control over the course of a child's life. Based on zero empirical evidence, Watson made this famous boast: "Give me a dozen healthy infants, well-formed, and my own specified world to bring them up in, and I'll guarantee to take any one at random and train him to become any type of specialist I might select—a doctor, lawyer, artist, merchant-chief and, yes, even into beggar-man and thief, regardless of his talents, penchants, tendencies, abilities, vocations and race of his ancestors" (quoted in Hulbert 2003, 119).

Using his considerable celebrity, Watson promoted some truly bizarre ideas about child-rearing, most of them having to do with the notion that any expression of love, such as kissing a baby, is to be avoided. Although Watson claimed a scientific basis for his ideas, they were actually polemics reflecting his own negative view of human nature, as in the following claim: "Mothers just don't know, when they kiss their children and pick them up and rock them, caress them and jiggle them upon their knee, that they are slowly building up a human being totally unable to cope with the world it must later live in" (quoted in Hulbert 2003, 142). (The reader may be struck here with the similarity between Watson's promotion of caregiver coldness and the ideas expressed by John Rosemond, profiled in Chapter 1.)

The Behavioral approach to caregiver discipline grew mainly out of the work of Skinner and his followers and actually had no connection to the ideas of Watson. Although initially interested in Watson, Skinner (by all accounts, a very loving father to his two children) quickly took Behaviorism in a very different direction and promoted a view of the ideal parent-child relationship that was as warm and accepting as Watson's had been cold and rejecting. Unfortunately, a major misunderstanding arose when Skinner invented a Plexiglas box that was intended primarily as a safer nighttime alternative to a crib. The device was mistakenly assumed to be a Watsonian implement to enable caregivers to raise infants without ever handling them.

Skinner's theories were heavily grounded in experimental data, while Watson's ideas, as noted, were grounded in his own prejudices. The main thread that tied Watson and Skinner (along with other proponents of behaviorism) together, however, was the notion that the proper subject for psychology is not what goes on inside an organism's head but rather the overt observable behaviors engaged in by the organism. Where Skinner departed from Watson is that Skinner believed that an organism's behavior is influenced most by the consequences that follow the behavior, while Watson believed that an organism's behavior is influenced most by the stimuli that precede it.

Skinner's theory was dubbed "operant conditioning" (to differentiate it from Pavlov's and Watson's "classical conditioning"), and the field he developed became known as "the experimental analysis of behavior." The applied fields of "behavior modification" and "applied behavioral analysis," which address practical issues in raising children (and helping needy caregivers become more effective), grew out of Skinner's ideas but were actually initiated by some of his devoted students and followers. Skinner himself dedicated relatively little attention to matters of child-rearing, except to some extent in his novel *Walden Two* (1948), which describes a utopian community in which positive child-rearing methods produce a happier and better-adjusted society of humans.

So many authors have written discipline books reflecting the Skinnerian perspective that to single out any particular author as the best exemplar of the Behavioral approach to discipline is very difficult. Three outstanding promoters of this perspective are Gerald Patterson (Patterson and Gullion 1968), Wesley Becker (1971), and Rex Forehand (Forehand and Long 2002). The basic idea underlying the Behavioral approach is that the future actions of children are heavily affected by the "contingencies" (positive or negative responses) dispensed by caregivers immediately following past child actions. To understand a child's conduct, according to Behavioral experts, all one has to know is the child's "reinforcement history."

The most powerful method in the Behavioral discipline tool kit is reinforcement. Skinner has been quoted as saying that one can shape the behavior of a child (even one with a severe behavior disorder) quite successfully without often, if ever, having to resort to punishment. Reinforcement can take two forms: positive and negative. Positive reinforcement is the most common form and can be defined (somewhat circularly) as "any response by a caregiver that has the effect of increasing the frequency of a particular behavior in the child."

Negative reinforcement, which is sometimes mistakenly confused with punishment, is somewhat less common, in that it does not involve the dispensing of something that is desired but rather involves the removal of something that is undesired. An example is removing some prohibition (e.g., against watching TV) if the child receives a good report card. Negative reinforcement is considered a form of reinforcement because it serves to increase a target behavior. Punishment, on the other hand, which involves making some kind of undesired response, differs from negative reinforcement in that it has the effect of decreasing, rather than increasing, a target behavior. In fact, punishment can be defined as "any response by a caregiver that has the effect of decreasing the frequency of a particular behavior in the child."

The reason reinforcement and punishment are defined in terms of their effect rather than more directly is because children differ in terms of what kinds of consequences they will experience as reinforcing or punishing. For example, verbal criticism is generally experienced as punishment—that is, it has the effect of decreasing the behavior criticized. However, for some children, especially those who get very little praise or positive attention, the attention received through criticism may actually be reinforcing, even if it has aversive aspects. That is one of the reasons why caregivers are counseled by behaviorists to use punishment sparingly.

Positive reinforcers are of two types: "primary" and "secondary." A primary reinforcer is something material, such as a piece of candy or money. A secondary reinforcer is something symbolic and typically has a social component, such as verbal praise, a smile, or affection from a caregiver. As a rule, secondary reinforcers are the most frequent and powerful tools used by caregivers, especially with older children. For this reason, the term "praise" is typically used, instead of the more scientific term "reinforcer," in many behaviorist discipline manuals, such as W. Hans Miller's *Systematic Parent Training* (1975).

A key feature of behavioral theory is that reinforcement is effective in shaping a child's behavior only when skillfully paired with ignoring. This is because improving a child's conduct involves two things: increasing the rate of some desired behavior and decreasing the rate of some incompatible, undesired behavior. In Skinnerian psychology, the way to decrease an undesired behavior is not to punish it (except in rare circumstances) but rather to "extinguish" it. The way to extinguish a behavior is to not reinforce it through attention, praise, or any other form of acknowledgment. Then, at the first appearance of a desired behavior (particularly one incompatible with the behavior to be extinguished), the caregiver praises and otherwise reinforces the heck out of it. In fact, the importance of *not* reinforcing bad behavior is so central to the Behavioral discipline approach that the most widely used mild punishment technique behaviorists recommend for young children is "time-out." This term is shorthand for "time out from reinforcement," and although it has punitive aspects (e.g., making a child sit in a designated time-out chair), it is actually a form of enforced ignoring.

The rule of thumb that Behavioral discipline authors use to carry out extinction of a behavior is that a caregiver should "ignore things that she doesn't like but can live with" and that she should only "punish things that she doesn't like and cannot live with." This leaves room for individual variation among caregivers, who obviously differ considerably in terms of what they can or cannot live with. This rule, in fact, overlaps somewhat with the Affective Tolerance principle Accept Feelings, because the kinds of behaviors that one does not like but can live with often involve symbolic expressions of affect, such as whining, complaining, diversionary tactics (intended to throw a caregiver off her stride), and the like. However, behaviorists choose not to specify the kinds of behaviors that one should ignore, and they generally avoid talking about affect. Some behaviorists would even take exception to active (reflective) listening as a response to whining, as they would interpret it as a form of secondary (attentional) reinforcement. I disagree with that criticism, however, because in my view, reflection is a very neutral accepting response and thus has much of the same quality as ignoring.

For Behavioral discipline authors, the function of discipline is to foster social learning in children. Discipline affects the development of children, both positively and negatively, by the learning that results from the pattern of caregivers' consequences. Thus, a child whose behavior is maladaptive has been taught by caregivers who have inadvertently shaped bad behavior and extinguished good behavior through an inept pattern of responses. Conversely, the way to build a pattern of positive adjustment in children is through the systematic application by caregivers of operant principles. The key is for a caregiver to reinforce good behaviors and extinguish bad behaviors by responding to child actions in a skilled and consciously motivated manner.

Although this sounds more than a little Watsonian in that the emphasis is on the engineering of certain child outcomes by a caregiver who is seen as controlling the child's development, in practice the Skinnerian approach is much more humanistic (i.e., friendly and nondomineering) than it seems. The emphasis is not so much on being able to control all aspects of a child's development as it is on imparting to caregivers the skills to manage conflict and create a harmonious and effectively functioning classroom or family setting. Although emphasis is placed on the caregiver as someone who is in charge, the idea is not to produce a perfectly programmed robot but rather to achieve short-term goals (such as a child sitting at his desk or going to bed on time) in a predictable and effective manner. In fact, behavioral psychologists are very reluctant to talk in terms of long-term goals of discipline, and prefer to use the term "control" or "influence" in a much more limited sense, meaning "getting a child to do what you want him to in a particular situation."

The Behavioral approach to discipline thus shares with the Affective and Cognitive approaches the fact that it is an attempt to describe and to systematize what effective caregivers already do rather than to re-engineer (as Watson thought he was doing) a radically new type of human society. The essence of the Behavioral approach to discipline is that there are three categories of caregiver response—praising, ignoring, and punishing—and that being skilled at discipline is merely a matter of a caregiver's emitting these three contingencies intelligently and immediately in response to three classes of child behavior: behaviors that should be praised, behaviors that should be ignored, and behaviors that should be punished.

Behaviors that should be praised are acts that the caregiver likes and wants to see more of. Behaviors that should be ignored are acts that the caregiver does not like but can live with. Behaviors that should be punished are acts that the caregiver does not like and cannot live with. Caregivers are encouraged to do far more praising than punishing and to do far more ignoring than punishing. Punishment (defined broadly as any undesired consequence, including merely saying, "Stop it") is, thus, something that is to be used infrequently and only when necessary. The best way to transform a child from a pain in the neck into someone who is a pleasure to be around is through extinction of most undesirable child behaviors by the coordinated use of ignoring and praise. This is achieved by giving an undesired behavior no attention and then giving positive attention to a subsequent desired behavior, especially if the desired behavior is one that is incompatible with the undesired behavior.

The Behavioral approach is, thus, based on "differential reinforcement," where a caregiver shapes good behaviors through a combination of ignoring and praising. Skinner, in fact, wrote that one can be an effective behavior manager, even with children who pose severe behavior challenges, almost entirely through the use of positive methods, and that strong punishment (such as spanking) is almost never necessary or desirable. In short, caregivers who follow the Behavioral approach to discipline are very encouraging, positive, and tolerant people. This hardly jibes with the drill-sergeant image associated with the writings of Watson, which many critics (including myself at one time) have mistakenly assumed to be the core message disseminated by advocates of behavior modification.

Nevertheless, Behavioral theorizing has a mechanistic dimension that stems from the image of the child as a hedonistic being (seeking to maximize pleasure and minimize pain), with no emphasis on internal cognitive or affective processes. More recent theorizing by "social learning theory" behaviorists, such as Albert Bandura, has emphasized internal cognitive processes, such as modeling and self-evaluation, much more than in the past.

Skinner's own experiments were carried out almost entirely with rats and pigeons, and some critics have pointed out the inappropriateness of designing a method for managing and relating to humans that is derived from a theory worked out initially by studying the behavior of animals. In addition, the ideal caregiver portrayed by behaviorists is a technocrat who pulls levers and pushes switches, much as an engineer might do in managing a hydroelectric plant. Such imagery does not give much credit to the role of freedom and dignity in the process of becoming a competent human being. In fact, one of Skinner's best-known late works is a book titled *Beyond Freedom and Dignity* ([1971] 2002). All this said, the Behavioral approach to caregiver discipline is very

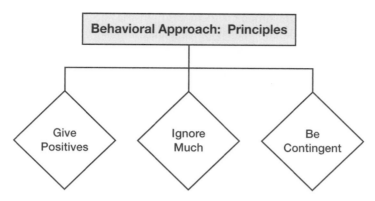

FIGURE 3.1   The Three Principles of the Behavioral Approach

widely used and respected, and it provides a simple but powerful conceptual framework for becoming more effective at the game of discipline.

Here I delineate three principles that characterize the Behavioral approach to discipline: Give Positives, Ignore Much, and Be Contingent (see Figure 3.1).

The First Behavioral Principle:
Give Positives

The first principle—"Give Positives"—can be stated simply as "Caregivers should do a lot more praising than punishing." This reflects the position of Skinner and other operant conditioning theorists that by far the best way to build desirable patterns of behavior in a child is through positive reinforcement—that is, by responding to the child's desirable acts with approval and other forms of reward.

Many studies have shown that in families or classrooms where children are happy and well-behaved, there is almost always a great deal of positive adult responding going on. In contrast, where children are acting out and conflict and unhappiness exist in both children and adults, there is almost always a relative absence of such positive responding. Such a situation has been termed "praise deficit," and behaviorists maintain that it is essential that a praise deficit be turned into a praise surplus if an ineffective caregiver is to become effective.

Ineffective caregivers have praise deficits for a number of reasons, most often because they have a limited repertoire of responses (perhaps modeling how they were raised or taught); consequently, they think that responding harshly is the only way to get a child to shape up. This belief is illusory, however, because punishment works mainly in the short term (i.e., it gets a child to stop some offending behavior for a few minutes). Thus, often a circular pattern develops, where a child acts out, a caregiver yells, the child stops for a few minutes, the caregiver does not respond to the positive change, the child then does something else that is offensive, and so on, *ad infinitum*. The caregiver thinks the yelling (sometimes called "nattering") works, because it does stop the offending behavior momentarily, but if one steps back and looks at the situation from a distance, it is clear that the caregiver's nattering does not ultimately build a positive behavior pattern in the child.

The key to reducing a praise deficit is to help a caregiver recognize opportunities to praise and to convince her of the importance of doing a lot more praising. Many caregivers do too little praising because they have excessively high standards regarding what they consider to be a child behavior that deserves to be praised. They wait to praise the ultimate child behavior (which may rarely occur) but meanwhile miss dozens of opportunities to praise acts that fit the criterion of being behaviors that one likes and would like to see more of.

The fact is that even the most behaviorally disordered children behave offensively only some of the time. For a child to be seen as "emotionally disturbed," it is only necessary that he do something seriously bad once or twice a day; during the rest of the day, he is either not bothering anybody or is doing something that deserves to be encouraged and reinforced. Caregivers with a praise deficit respond with only negative attention to acts that should be punished or, often, ignored. But they tend not to respond with positive attention, even to behaviors that are quite deserving of praise (including sitting quietly and not bothering anyone). Given such a pattern of caregiver response to negative acts only, it is little wonder a child would continue to misbehave.

When behaviorists use the term "praise," they are referring to any caregiver behavior that might be considered positive. Praise could involve verbal approval (what we normally consider praise), as well as physical affection (smiles, hugs, etc.), rewards (treats, gold stars, etc.), and encouragement. Thus, praise is another word for what behaviorists term a "positive reinforcer." A reinforcer is usually defined less in terms of its inherent quality than in terms of its actual effect on a child's behavior. Thus, a reinforcer is any response that causes a child to increase some target behavior.

Because the Give Positives principle is framed in terms of both praise (do lots) and punishment (do much less), it is also necessary to define the term "punishment." According to the behaviorist definition, it is the opposite of a reinforcer; that is, punishment is any behavior that has the effect of reducing the frequency of a target behavior in a child (at least in the short term). Here, I am using the term somewhat more broadly to mean any form of negative attention or indication of disapproval. Thus, punishment can take many forms, ranging from a verbalization (such as "no" or "stop that"), to a hard stare, to (never recommended) a physical act, such as a slap or a spanking.

Punishment is often confused with "negative reinforcement," but there is a major difference between them. Negative reinforcement, as discussed earlier, involves the removal of something undesired by the child in response to his doing something desirable (e.g., removing a restriction when the child gets As on his report card). Punishment, also experienced as aversive, is intended to stop a behavior rather than to increase it.

One reason caregivers are urged to do less punishing is because, as noted, in a setting where a praise deficit already exists, negative attention can become a form of positive reinforcement. This has to do with the fact that adult attention itself is a very powerful reinforcer for children, and in a situation where attention is given only for misbehavior, that attention may paradoxically be sought as the only attention that is available. Misbehavior can also become a way for a child to exert some power over the caregiver, if the caregiver always responds in a predictable fashion to the child's misbehavior. If the caregiver is able to pay less attention to misbehavior (by doing less knee-jerk punishing), then when she does praise the child (gives positive attention to his good behavior), this attention is likely to be that much more effective and powerful.

This pairing of ignoring mild forms of misbehavior followed immediately by praising good behavior is termed "differential reinforcement" and is at the heart of the Behavioral approach to discipline. (The nature and importance of caregiver ignoring—the "Ignore Much" principle—are explored in the next section.) So how much praising should a caregiver do? There is no hard and fast rule, but in every family or classroom where the adults are effective in influencing children, there is always at least twice as much praising as punishing going on (in any time period, such as a day) and typically much more. Even ten times as much praise as punishment is fine, as long as the praise is not for misbehavior (i.e., it does not violate the third Behavioral principle, "Be Contingent").

In an early stage of building certain target behaviors (as when a socially incompetent child is starting to become more socially competent), a caregiver is advised to praise almost all the time—including a child's efforts at and "successive approximations" of target behaviors—to build certain child behavior patterns. When these patterns have become more established, caregivers are encouraged to fade to more of an "intermittent reinforcement" schedule, where targeted good behaviors (never to be punished) are praised often but not all the time. There are two reasons for this fading from continuous to intermittent praising. The first is that intermittent reinforcement has been found to be more effective in maintaining target behavior patterns, in part because constant praise, especially if done ineptly, can become too obviously manipulative. The second reason is that intermittent praise is more natural and comfortable, and the intent is for discipline to become easy for the caregiver rather than something that she has to work at constantly. The main point of the Give Positives principle is not that a caregiver should become a constant praise-giving machine but that she should praise often, that she should do a lot less punishing, and that her praise (positive attention) should always be for a behavior that she likes and would like to see more of.

A technique that behaviorists sometimes use to systematize the dispensing of positive reinforcement is termed a "token economy," a system by which a caregiver rewards a child for good behavior by awarding points that can be traded in for items or treats of his choosing. A token economy can take many different forms, from gold stars posted on a chart for younger children to points entered into a book for older children. Points can be awarded every time a good behavior occurs or, more typically, at the end of each day. Because a token economy is a reinforcement device rather than a punishment device, points should never be taken away for bad behavior, although practice in that regard varies. Similarly, a token economy should never be used as a basis for receiving items to which every child has a legal and moral right, such as meals, sleep, clothing, or shelter.

Token economies are most typically used to build competence in children who are severely lacking in competence, and for that reason token economies are frequently found in institutional settings, such as residential treatment centers. Once a child attains a certain threshold of competence, he usually graduates to a more natural reinforcement schedule, even in treatment centers. In home or school settings, token economies are typically not needed if a parent or teacher is using reinforcement in a more naturally occurring manner. However, for some populations (e.g., a special-education class) or when a caregiver is in the initial stages of trying to get a child to become more compliant, some form of token system can be effective in ensuring that (1) children are given tangible incentives for good behavior and (2) caregivers are reminded of the need to give positives.

The Second Behavioral Principle: Ignore Much

The second principle of the Behavioral approach is termed "Ignore Much" and can be stated as follows: "Caregivers should do a lot more ignoring than punishing." This principle flows logically out of the other two Behavioral principles—Give Positives (a caregiver should do more praising than punishing) and Be Contingent (do not praise bad behavior or punish good behavior). The reason for this is simple math: If a caregiver is going to increase her praise-to-punishment ratio, and she is not going to praise undesirable behaviors, then the only alternative is to do more ignoring of behaviors, including some of those that in the past would have been met with negative attention.

In a situation such as the earlier example of the circular pattern of adult nattering both preceding and following child misbehavior, ignoring can help transform an ineffective (and unhappy) caregiver into a more effective (and happy) one, because the home or classroom can be transformed from a place of noncompliance and disharmony to one of compliance and harmony. This kind of "perpetual motion mutual punishment pattern," termed a "coercion cycle" by Patterson (1982), is almost universal in dysfunctional family or classroom settings and goes somewhat as follows: A mother is in a supermarket with her young child. He suddenly grabs a piece of candy off a shelf, and the mother responds by yelling something like, "Put the candy back on the shelf." The child does that, and the mom does not respond with any form of praise. A minute or two later, the child grabs a toy off the shelf, and the mom again yells, "Put the toy back on the shelf." The child complies, the mom does not praise, and a minute or two later the child does something else that gets a rise out of his mother.

What is going on here, according to Patterson, is that the attention associated with the punishment (the mom's saying "no") is actually reinforcing to the child (because he never gets attention for good behavior). The initial "no" serves to stop the child momentarily, because that is what punishment typically does in the short term. The child's temporary stopping of the object-grabbing behavior serves as negative reinforcement of the mother's nattering (her constant "no") pattern, because it solidifies her belief that the way to stop child misbehavior is to yell at the child. This increases the likelihood that the mom will respond with nattering the next time the child grabs something off a shelf or does something else to get her goat. Meanwhile, the mom's responding with "no," although intended as punishment, becomes positively reinforcing to the child because it is the only attention he receives. The poor result of this cycle is reflected in the fact that the child always responds with another aggravating behavior a few minutes after the mother has uttered her most recent "no." Thus the pattern is coercive, because both adult and child are causing mutual pain to each other, and each is causing the other to respond in a predictably dysfunctional manner. The child's negative reinforcement of the mom's response (by stopping momentarily) and the mom's consequential inadvertent positive reinforcement of the child's misbehavior (by giving attention) creates a form of perpetual motion machine that can operate for hours or even—as a dysfunctional family or classroom pattern—for years.

Punishment is adopted by an adult caregiver as an Influence mechanism, a way for her to feel in control of the child. But, paradoxically, as this example shows, the child is actually in control, because he decides when and how the adult will behave. Thus, ignoring is actually a necessary mechanism in breaking such a cycle and putting the adult in control by allowing her, rather than the child, to determine when and how she will behave.

"Ignoring" is a general term used by Behavioral discipline experts to refer to any caregiver response of a neutral nature—that is, one that does not involve either praise or punishment. Because both praise and punishment always involve some degree of adult attention directed at the child, the rule of thumb in ignoring is to avoid giving any attention to the child. Thus, the caregiver does not look at him, smile at him, frown at him, or give any indication that she is noticing a particular behavior. Sometimes, this can even take the form of the caregiver's turning her back on the child or walking away from him.

From a theoretical standpoint, caregiver ignoring comes out of the Skinnerian notion of "extinction." In operant conditioning theory, the best way to reduce a particular behavior pattern is to withhold any form of reinforcement. Sooner or later, an unreinforced behavior pattern will die out, especially when behaviors that are more desirable are reinforced. Thus, ignoring rather than punishing is the recommended method for eliminating an undesired behavior pattern, particularly when used in combination with immediately reinforcing (praising) a more acceptable type of child response.

So, what kinds of behaviors are caregivers urged to ignore rather than to punish? Specific guidelines have not been developed, but a general formula sometimes used is that caregivers should punish behaviors that they do not like and cannot live with but should ignore behaviors that they do not like and *can* live with. Obviously, caregivers differ in terms of what they decide they can live with (especially when it involves young children), but certain kinds of child behaviors are universally viewed as not able to be lived with. Such behaviors include aggression (hitting a sibling or peer), destructive action (breaking furniture or other objects), and dangerous action (touching a hot stove or darting out into a busy street).

One class of child behaviors that caregivers are explicitly urged to ignore involves what have been termed "diversionary tactics," child behaviors intended to distract a caregiver from following through on some punishment. An example: A mother and child are in a doctor's waiting room, and the child is doing something that bothers other children. The mom tells him to stop, but halfway through her limit-setting, he asks her to read him a headline in a magazine or explain the meaning of a picture mounted on a wall. Because such diversionary tactics may involve desired behaviors (the mother may highly value the child's development of an interest in literature and art), it is easy for her to mistake the diversion for a positive behavior and praise (pay attention to) it. In this way, the child is changing his mother's agenda, and she would have been better served if she had ignored the questions and finished her punishment intervention, saving the encouragement of art and reading for later.

Behaviorists do not treat affective expressions as any different from other behaviors, but it is obvious that attention-seeking immature child behaviors—such as whining, tattling, crying, and pleading—are kinds of behaviors that most Behavioral experts would urge caregivers to live with even if they do not like them. Because the class of disliked child behaviors that one can live with is typically larger than the class of disliked child behaviors that one cannot live with, it is easy for a caregiver who follows this rule to cut down dramatically on the amount of punishing that she does. This is not necessarily easy to stick to, as a child is likely to test a caregiver's resolve by increasing his rate of obnoxious behavior. This approach is termed the "burst of extinction," and it involves the common phenomenon of a child's increasing his rate of obnoxious behaviors during the initial stages of a caregiver's attempt to extinguish those behaviors. But a caregiver who sticks to her ignoring guns and offers increased praise for desired behaviors will soon find that differential reinforcement works, and there will be fewer forms of undesired behaviors to ignore in the future.

The Third Behavioral Principle: Be Contingent

Saying that a caregiver should do more praising than punishing and more ignoring than punishing does not mean that she should never do any punishing. I have already noted that a caregiver should punish an action that is both undesirable and something she cannot live with, while ignoring an undesired act that she can live with and praising a desired act that she likes and wants to see more of. Knowing when to praise, when to ignore, and when to punish involves a perceptual and cognitive activity known as "discrimination," which is sometimes anything but easy to carry out.

Caregiver discrimination among various classes of child behaviors is at the heart of the Behavioral approach and constitutes the core of the third Behavioral principle, which I have termed "Be Contingent." I describe this principle as follows: "Caregivers should not punish behaviors they like and should not praise behaviors they dislike." The reader might wonder why I have not worded it more positively (e.g., "A caregiver should praise a behavior that she likes and should punish a behavior that she dislikes"), but the answer is fairly obvious if one keeps in mind the other two principles.

If a caregiver punishes a behavior that she dislikes every time it occurs, then she is violating the first Behavioral principle (Give Positives), because her praise-to-punishment ratio suffers. Ditto for the second principle (Ignore Much) as she is not doing enough ignoring. The critical thing is not that a caregiver must punish disliked behaviors but rather that she must never praise them. The same logic extends to praiseworthy behaviors: Caregivers have a great deal of latitude as to when they choose to praise a desired behavior, especially as they move from early-stage continuous reinforcement to later-stage intermittent reinforcement.

Obviously, caregivers should do a lot of praising, but this does not require them to praise an acceptable child behavior every time it occurs. Remember, it was noted that after a while, intermittent (frequent but not continuous) reinforcement has been found to be more effective as well as more comfortable and natural. The important point here is not that a caregiver praise a desired behavior every time it occurs but that she never praise a behavior that is better responded to with ignoring or punishment.

For the same reason that I frame the third Behavioral principle as a negative statement, I use the word "contingent" here rather than the more widely used "consistent." Consistency implies that one has to respond to a child behavior in exactly the same way every time (i.e., always praise a behavior that one likes and always punish a behavior that one does not like). But a caregiver does not always have to praise a liked behavior (again, intermittent reinforcement implies praising it often but not always) and may on occasion choose to ignore a disliked behavior, even if it is one that has been punished in the past. The important thing here is that a caregiver not feel obligated to maintain a rigid adherence to how she has responded in the past (one is reminded of Emerson's famous declaration: "A foolish consistency is the hobgoblin of little minds"). Rather, the important thing is not to cross over categories by praising bad behaviors or punishing good behaviors.

I chose the term "contingent" for one other reason: the Behavioral notion that a caregiver's reinforcers are "contingencies" that are dispensed immediately after the child behavior that the caregiver wishes to reinforce. Whether praising or punishing, a caregiver needs to remember that her response has to be contingent upon a child's action—that is, it must be dispensed almost immediately. Waiting for a few minutes or hours to praise or punish a child's action is not an effective teaching tool.

Applying the Behavioral Approach

At this point, the reader might ask, "How likely is it that a caregiver would be dumb enough to praise a disliked behavior or punish a liked behavior?" It is more common than one might think. Adult alcoholics, for example, report that when they were quite young, family members would call them "cute" and give other forms of positive attention whenever they would take a sip of wine or beer. Although many other factors undoubtedly contribute to a person's becoming an alcoholic, some experts believe that having received early parental approval of alcohol consumption is a frequent contributing factor. Many other examples show a caregiver knowingly or unknowingly reinforcing a behavior that she really should not.

An example from my own life is that, for some unknown reason, I developed a game with my youngest son when he was a toddler where I would stick my finger in front of his face and then pull my finger away just as he tried to bite it. This seemed like harmless fun until his preschool teacher took me aside one day to report that Eli was biting other children and that, unless he stopped, they would have no choice but to expel him. Needless to say, I hoped the teachers had not suspected my own role in teaching this maladaptive behavior, and I worked very hard over the next couple of weeks to break Eli of his dad-induced biting habit.

These two examples involve undesired behaviors (or behaviors that became undesired at a later date) that caregivers praised intentionally, under the mistaken impression that the behaviors were desirable. More common, however, is a situation where a caregiver knows a behavior to be undesirable but praises it anyway. An example can be seen in an early episode of the TV show *Supernanny*. The mom being observed by Jo Frost (the star of the series) is trying to get her rambunctious young son to stop doing something, but at one point she smiles, as if thinking to herself, "What a cute little rascal he is." Such a mixed response (trying to stop a behavior while at the same time smiling at it) is confusing to a child and constitutes intermittent reinforcement rather than the punishment that was intended.

The opposite mistake—punishing a desirable behavior—is even more common, making it very difficult for a caregiver to be effective. This typically happens when a caregiver is overly perfectionistic and fails to recognize when a child is making an effort to comply with her wishes. I saw this in a research study when I presented some hypothetical situations to parents and asked them to role-play what they would do and say in response. In one story, a four-year-old child was depicted taking a bath: "He is splashing and getting water all over the bathroom floor. You ask him to stop splashing, and he does one more splash and then stops." When I asked caregivers what they would do if this were their child, I received two categories of response. One group of caregivers would praise the child by saying, "Thank you for stopping," while the others would punish him by saying something like, "I told you to stop. Why don't you ever listen to me?"

The first group, which I would consider more competent, recognized that the child had stopped and that they should praise this compliant action. Although they might have recognized that the child committed a minor act of defiance (making one more splash), they considered this something they could live with and chose to ignore that brief prelude to his stopping. The second group, which I would consider less competent, was enraged by the minor defiance (the additional splash) and lost sight of the fact that the child actually had complied by stopping. Even if they did recognize that the child had stopped, they did not seem to consider the act worthy of praising, as it was done in a less than perfect and immediate manner. Thus incompetent caregivers miss many opportunities to praise; instead, they treat lots of child behaviors as problems when in fact the behaviors could be viewed as steps on the path to good behavior.

When a behavioral psychologist works with a parent who needs to improve her discipline skills, the first step is typically to assess and to sharpen her discrimination skills. After briefly teaching the three classes of adult response—praising, ignoring, punishing—and explaining the kinds of situations in which each response is to be used, the psychologist then reads a story or shows a video recording in which an adult and a child are interacting. Various acts of minor or major undesirable behavior are depicted, as well as various acts of compliance and good behavior. At various points in the story or video, a bell goes off, and the subject is asked to say what kind of response should be given to the child behavior depicted in the segment immediately preceding the bell. This exercise is used repeatedly as a teaching tool until the caregiver's discrimination scores approach 100 percent correct hypothetical responses.

The next stage in the intervention involves helping a caregiver make accurate discriminations in the laboratory (*in vitro*) and in the real world (*in vivo*). A common laboratory exercise is to have the caregiver interact with a child in a room that has a one-way mirror. The caregiver wears a small earpiece (termed a "bug in the ear"), and the discipline educator on the other side of the mirror talks to her through a microphone. The educator's feedback consists of praising her when she makes an appropriate discrimination, prompting her when she misses a chance to reinforce or to set a limit, and correcting her when she offers noncontingent praise or punishment.

In the real world, caregivers are encouraged to keep a number of charts (a staple of the Behavioral approach) on which they record child behaviors as well as their own responses. Initially a caregiver charts child problems and good behaviors, then later charts the frequency of her own praising and punishing during a similar period. The intent of this exercise is to open the caregiver's eyes to the frequency of both problems and nonproblems, and to give her a benchmark for evaluating the growth of her own skills as a dispenser of effective discipline.

Myths about the Behavioral Approach

Two misconceptions about the Behavioral approach are held by many caregivers who are otherwise attracted to it: (1) caregivers need to become praise machines and (2) discipline equals frequent use of time-out. I discuss these myths briefly below.

The Constant Praise Myth

The Give Positives principle is wrongly interpreted by many caregivers as meaning "Give positives all the time." Caregivers have told me, "It is a strain to have to praise everything a child does that is praiseworthy." In response I tell them, "I agree, but I think you are mistaken in thinking that all behaviorists expect you become constant praise-dispensers. What they are really asking you to do is a lot more praising, especially if you have a praise deficit, and to use praise wisely rather than foolishly."

Two of the three Behavioral discipline principles touch on the dispensing of praise, but neither of them requires constant praise. The first principle, Give Positives, merely encourages caregivers to do considerably more praising than punishing, in order to turn a potential praise deficit into a praise surplus. The third principle, Be Contingent, merely requires that when a caregiver does praise a child, it is only for a behavior that she likes and would like to see more of.

The only time that a caregiver is encouraged to give praise constantly (what behaviorists term "continuous reinforcement") is during the initial stages of getting a child to attain some new skill. Once that skill begins to fall into place, caregivers are encouraged to move away from continuous praise, both because intermittent reinforcement is more effective in maintaining the skill and because it is a much more natural and comfortable mode for caregivers. Thus, caregivers who turn away from the Behavioral approach because they find it unnatural to give praise constantly are missing an important point. Behavioral discipline educators tell caregivers to praise a lot more than they punish and to use praise only for behaviors that they like. That is hardly the same thing as saying that one should never pass up an opportunity to praise something.

The Myth That Time-out Defines the Behavioral Approach

If I were to ask a random group of caregivers to sum up the Behavioral approach to discipline, probably more than half would say "time-out." To me, the notion that the Behavioral approach equals time-out is as much a myth as the notion that the Affective approach requires use of the expression "Chairs are not for kicking" or that the Cognitive approach requires use of family or class councils. Time-out is just one of many techniques used by Behavioral discipline experts, especially with young children. But it is hardly their only (or even central) technique and, like any technique, time-out should never become an end in itself. In fact, caregivers who rely excessively on time-out are typically ineffective (as they would be if they used any form of punishment excessively), and it is entirely possible for a caregiver—even one who adheres to a Behavioral philosophy—to be very effective without ever once resorting to time-out.

4

The Cognitive Approach
to Discipline

Underpinnings and Three Principles

The Cognitive approach to discipline owes much to the work of Alfred Adler, one of the first founders of psychoanalysis to break with Sigmund Freud. Adler was a major psychotherapy theorist whose work is considered to be a precursor of the (currently very popular) cognitive-behavioral emphasis in psychotherapy. He was one of the few early psychiatrists to work directly with children and is considered the father of the child-guidance movement in Europe and America. He contributed many important concepts—including self-esteem, sibling rivalry, and birth order—to the field of personality psychology.

Adler's break with Freud, as was the case with other pioneers of psychoanalysis, was ostensibly over what he saw as Freud's excessive emphasis on sexuality as the core motivational drive explaining human behavior and psychopathology. For Adler, a better candidate for such a core drive was the need to feel important and valued as part of a social unit. The mark of mental health, Adler believed, was not healthy sexuality but, rather, healthy relationships with other people—that is, achieving a balance between autonomy (self-definition and actualization) and empathy (being a kind person who avoids using people and who cares about others and about society).

Unhealthy adult social patterns, often found in persons who are cruel and antisocial or who care excessively about power, reflect an imbalance that probably stems from an inability as children to learn that feeling good about oneself and obtaining approval from others, including parents, does not have to be obtained at the expense of others (e.g., siblings). As with the theoreticians (Freud, Rogers, Skinner) whose work provided inspiration for the Affective and Behavioral discipline approaches, Adler himself did not, to my knowledge, have much to say directly about discipline. Rather, implications of the Adlerian framework for discipline were worked out mainly by his followers, with the biggest contribution coming from Rudolf Dreikurs, whose many books, including *Children: The Challenge* (Dreikurs with Soltz 1992) and *A New Approach to Discipline: Logical Consequences* (Dreikurs and Grey 1968), are widely known. Don Dinkmeyer and Gary McKay's *STEP Program* (1976; Dinkmeyer, McKay, and Dinkmeyer 1998) is another example of a widely used discipline curriculum that is primarily grounded in the Cognitive framework, although these authors appear to have incorporated elements from the Affective approach as well.

The basic idea underlying the Cognitive approach, and the reason why I call it "Cognitive," is that the development of child social competence occurs when the child learns to consider the perspective of others, peers as well as adults. Helping a child become someone who is well-behaved hinges on his acquiring mature moral judgment—namely, an ability to take the feelings, needs, and rights of others into account. Development of such "perspective-taking" in a child is not likely to be fostered by discipline that is arbitrary or that is justified by the superior strength or status of the caregiver. Saying "Do it because I say so" may work in the short term, but it does not help a child become self-regulating; instead, this tactic merely teaches him that it is all right for the strong and powerful to dominate the weak and less powerful.

Within the Cognitive discipline approach, a great deal of emphasis is placed on helping a caregiver avoid getting caught up in a power struggle with a child when setting limits on the child's behavior. Power struggles are counterproductive for several reasons: (1) They foster resentment and cause a child to focus more on justifying his own position (and plotting revenge) than on taking the caregiver's perspective; (2) they typically lack an educational component, and thus are less likely to help the child develop an understanding of the need for certain kinds of conduct; and (3) they encourage the child to develop a habit of blaming or using others rather than taking responsibility for his own behavior. For these reasons, a caregiver is encouraged not only to avoid engaging in her own power struggles with a child but also to resist efforts by the child (such as through tattling) to ensnare her in his power struggles with peers or siblings. Caregivers are also strongly discouraged from comparing children, whether favorably or unfavorably, to others, and they are advised to treat every child as an individual with his own talents, needs, and interests.

Elements of the Cognitive approach to caregiving and positive mental health can be found in books for parents and teachers by two best-selling authors: H. Stephen Glenn and William Glasser. Because neither of these authors (along with most other authors of books for caregivers) explicitly identified the theoretical antecedents of their prescriptions, I am uncertain about the extent to which they were directly influenced by Adler's ideas or considered themselves to be Adlerians. However, their work includes enough similarities in emphasis to the ideas of Adler (particularly on the central importance of developing autonomy, self-reliance, and good judgment in the child) for me to feel comfortable in assigning them to the Cognitive discipline camp.

Glenn is the founder of the "Developing Capable People" movement, and he coauthored a book with Jane Nelson titled *Raising Self-reliant Children in a Self-indulgent World: Seven Building Blocks for Developing Capable Young People* (1989). In their book, Glenn and Nelson emphasize several concepts that are very central to the Adlerian perspective, including use of encouragement to build a sense in the child of "internal locus of control" (belief that he can perform difficult tasks on his own), use of logical and natural consequences instead of arbitrary punishments, family meetings, respect for the child's own perceptions and choices, avoiding directing and doing too much for children (because it undermines self-reliance), developing a sense of purpose through full participation, fostering the development of good interpersonal judgment and skills, and movement from "loving control" to "loving autonomy."

Glasser is a psychiatrist who developed a well-known approach to conducting psychotherapy with acting-out youths that he originally termed "Reality Therapy" (Glasser 1965). He later elaborated the theoretical rationale underpinning Reality Therapy, and he termed that rationale "Control Theory," a name he later changed to "Choice Theory." To my knowledge, Glasser's only book that deals exclusively with caregiver discipline is *For Parents and Teenagers: Dissolving the Barrier between You and Your Teen* (2003), but he has written at least two other books—*The Quality School Teacher* (1998) and *Choice Theory in the Classroom* (Glasser and Dotson 1998)—that address some of the implications of Control/Choice Theory for discipline in school settings.

The key to Choice Theory and Reality Therapy is to help the child understand that his actions, such as those that habitually get him into trouble, are not automatic reactions to external events (or to the actions of others) but are conscious choices that are influenced by his own thoughts and the things he tells himself about those events. In this respect, Reality Therapy is very similar to another Adler-inspired intervention: Albert Ellis's "Rational Emotive Behavior Therapy," known as REBT. For Glasser, the key to being a quality caregiver is making an effort to help a child become more knowledgeable about what motivates his own behavior (namely, his efforts to control his world and to make things happen as he would like them to happen), about how his behavior can be self-destructive, and about how he can choose behaviors that are more likely to work for him.

Destructive interpersonal incidents (e.g., fights among children) should, therefore, not be responded to with caregiver impositions of power, such as punishment, but rather should be used as teaching opportunities. Recommending the use of such Dreikurs-like participatory methods as class councils, Glasser offers tips on how all the children in a class, and not just the two fighters, can learn from such an incident—about Choice Theory and about how they can become more effective at controlling their lives and making choices that are more likely to lead to success.

Another source of theoretical, as well as empirical, support for the Cognitive approach to discipline comes from the writings of developmental psychologists, particularly those who have examined the development of social cognition and moral judgment. This work, much of it influenced by Swiss developmental psychologist Jean Piaget, has painted a picture of the developing child not as a passive vessel into which adult influences are poured but rather as someone who processes those inputs through his own cognitive activity. Such a worldview, sometimes termed "constructivistic," has been applied to research on discipline by scholars interested in the child's moral development (which is another name for character).

Martin Hoffman, a psychology professor at the University of Michigan, studied children whose parents used one of three kinds of discipline, which he termed "power assertive," "guilt-oriented," and "inductive." Parents who use power assertion tend to say such things as "Do this because I told you to," while parents who are guilt-oriented tend to say such things as "If you loved me, you would do this" or "Do this because it will make me happy" (and its opposite, "If you don't do this, I'll get cancer and die, and then you'll really feel sorry," as one mother I know once said to her child). Inductive parents, on the other hand, attempt to help children understand the interpersonal consequences of their behavior; an example is telling a child who is making noise outside late at night, "Sound carries at night, and I am afraid that you are disturbing people in the neighborhood who are sleeping."

The essence of inductive (and Cognitive) discipline is, thus, an appeal to reason rather than power or guilt in attempting to influence a child to do the right thing. Hoffman (1975; Hoffman and Salzstein 1967) found that children exposed to inductive (also termed "victim-centered") discipline had more advanced moral development—in other words, were nicer and more altruistic—than were children exposed to more coercive discipline styles.

Although not explicitly mentioned as a source of inspiration by Cognitively oriented discipline experts, their approach and the ideas expressed share some similarities with some Asian religious philosophies (not that all Asian caregivers necessarily follow those philosophical tenets; many of them are into guilt-tripping and blurring parent-child boundaries, as are many Western caregivers). In the Cognitive approach, caregivers are encouraged to understand that effective discipline requires them to avoid getting into power

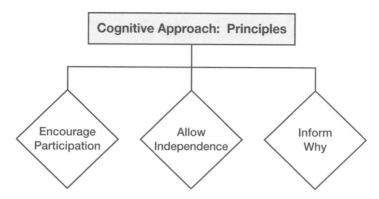

FIGURE 4.1   The Three Principles of the Cognitive Approach

struggles with children and that the best way to avoid a power struggle is to step back and not respond to all provocations. Switching over from treating many child behaviors as problems to treating all but a few of them as non-problems is a shift that can be difficult, because it calls for something in the nature of a personality transformation. One source of inspiration for undergoing such a transformation may be found in the Eastern philosophy of Taoism, in which it is repeatedly emphasized that "letting go" of a desired end is often the best means of achieving it. In his book *The Parent's Tao Te Ching: A New Interpretation—Ancient Advice for Modern Parents* (1999), William Martin explores how Taoism can help a caregiver become more tolerant. An example can be found in his poem "Doing Nothing": "Doing nothing while your child fails / requires great courage / and is the way of wisdom. / . . . "Do not succumb to / . . . controlling / your child. / Let your gentle presence / teach all that is necessary" (74).

The objective of developing social competence in children by modeling perspective-taking and avoiding power struggles can be pursued through application of the three principles that characterize the Cognitive approach to discipline: Encourage Participation, Allow Independence, and Inform Why (see Figure 4.1).

The First Cognitive Principle: Encourage Participation

The first principle of the Cognitive approach is "Encourage Participation," which can be explained as follows: "Caregivers should allow a child to participate in making and following rules." Collaboration between adults and children is desirable as a way of helping a child put himself in the shoes of others and, thus, develop a better understanding of how his actions impact others' needs and values. A collaborative approach also increases the chances that rules will be accepted and followed, because the child played a part in developing those rules. Finally, such an approach makes for a happier and more harmonious unit, as everyone feels that his or her needs are being taken seriously, even when they cannot be met.

Any number of methods and techniques allow caregivers to encourage a greater degree of participation, although the main objective in applying this principle is to encourage a mind-set in caregivers that is more respectful and accepting of the ability and willingness of children, even at an early age, to attain some degree of control over their environment. One obvious way for this attitude to be put into practice is to be willing to consider face-saving compromises with a child rather than always seeking complete surrender on his part. Setting a limit could include giving the child some opportunity to choose from among a range of alternative forms of compliance. For example, when telling a child that the TV is so loud it is hurting her ears, a caregiver could offer the child the options of turning it down, watching in a different part of the house, or doing something else. Offering such options is a way of letting the child participate in a problem-solving exercise rather than arbitrarily forcing a solution upon him.

A participatory technique that is widely associated with the Cognitive approach, particularly as espoused by Dreikurs, is the family or class "council." This is a deliberative body made up of every member of the family or class unit—including even very young children—and it meets on a regular basis (preferably weekly). In the council, a particular issue of concern to one or more members is discussed, and possible rules as well as consequences for violating those rules are fully discussed, with every person having the opportunity to be heard. An interesting twist in the running of a council is that the rules that are developed are generally applied to everyone in the unit, adults as well as children.

I know one family in which the father is himself a Cognitively oriented parenting psychologist. This family had a problem getting the kids to pick up toys and other objects. The family council discussed this problem, and a rule was generated stipulating that any items left in the family room at the end of the day would be put into a box that could not be accessed for a week. The father discovered that an important document that he needed for his work wound up in the box, but he respected the rule by waiting a week to retrieve it. The father told me this story with pride, but I think he missed the opportunity to teach his children another important lesson—namely, that specific circumstances sometimes mandate exceptions to rules.

Another technique by which caregivers can abide by the Encourage Participation principle is by engaging a child in a problem-solving conversation. Such problem-solving is central to what happens (collectively) in a class or family council, but it can also be used in one-on-one conversations between a caregiver and a child. When a caregiver conveys that she has a problem—say, when a child keeps coming out of his room after bedtime—it is always best to give the child an opportunity to generate or to choose from a list of alternatives (e.g., leave a night-light on, leave the door open, have the caregiver rub his back, etc.) rather than just give an ultimatum. Letting the child participate in finding a solution makes it more likely that conflict will cease quickly and helps the child understand that the best solution is one in which all parties have their needs met.

The notion of encouragement is a central element within the Cognitive approach. Dreikurs (with Soltz [1964] 1990) wrote, "Encouragement is more important than any other aspect of child-rearing. It is so important that the lack of it can be considered the basic cause for [child] misbehavior" (36). Adler wrote that one of the goals of psychotherapy is to convert people from pessimists (who are unhappy and see the negative in every situation) to optimists (who are happier and see the positive in situations). Dreikurs was a disciple of Adler, and he coauthored with Dinkmeyer a book on child learning that they subtitled *The Encouragement Process* (Dinkmeyer and Dreikurs 1963).

Dreikurs and Dinkmeyer see encouragement as critical for helping children become optimistic (i.e., possessing the courage to face challenges) rather than becoming discouraged pessimists. Dinkmeyer has coauthored several books dealing with the importance of the technique of encouragement, including *The Encouragement Book* (Dinkmeyer and Losoncy 1980) and *The Skills of Encouragement* (Dinkmeyer and Losoncy 1996).

In the STEP curriculum, described in their book *Systematic Training for Effective Parenting*, Dinkmeyer and McKay (1976) make an important distinction between praise and encouragement: Praise involves making a positive comment about a child's performance (e.g., "You are playing the piano really well"), while encouragement involves making a positive comment about a child's efforts (e.g., "You really seem to be trying to master that difficult piano passage"). Both praise and encouragement (which could be considered a more adept form of praise) are much better than punishment, but encouragement is better than praise, in the view of Dinkmeyer and his colleagues, because the goal of Cognitive discipline is to foster "intrinsic motivation."

Intrinsic motivation is motivation that comes from within—from the child's own values and desires—while "extrinsic" motivation comes from without (in the case of praise, from the caregiver). Encouragement is more likely to respect and to foster intrinsic motivation (in this example, playing the piano because it pleases the child). Praise, on the other hand, emphasizes extrinsic motivation (playing the piano because it pleases the caregiver). Children, and adults for that matter, are more likely to stick with a task if they feel that the motivation to do the task comes from within themselves. This attitude is reflected in the common example of talented young musicians who abandon their instruments because they feel too much pressure to meet the expectations of their parents or teachers. Edward Deci (a former teacher of mine) and Richard Ryan are the cofounders of "self-determination theory," which has demonstrated the superiority of "autonomous" over "controlled" motivation in facilitating behavior change and improvement in many spheres, including education and child development (Deci and Ryan 1985; Ryan and Deci 2000).

Encouragement is a type of caregiver communication style that is descriptive and empowering (imparting courage) but leaves the locus of power and motivation in the child. It is seen as preferable to punishment, because punishment has the effect of discouraging a child (i.e., communicating that he lacks the competence to be cooperative). Changing one's behavior requires effort. It also takes courage, because any new initiative carries the possibility of failure. Encouragement imparts to the child the sense that the caregiver believes that the child has the courage to change. It also communicates the idea that what counts is not perfection but an effort to do better. Encouragement thus fosters a willingness to take risks. Punishment, on the other hand, undermines a willingness to take risks by indirectly, and probably unintentionally, communicating doubt about the child's ability or willingness to improve.

Dinkmeyer and McKay thus view behavioral changes as based not only on understanding what needs to be done but also on possessing the courage to change, including the courage to be imperfect. In the Cognitive approach, frequent encouragement is seen as critical to motivating children to change their behaviors and to accept who they are and to become happier human beings. One discipline book that features this dimension is *The Encouraging Parent*, by Rod Wallace Kennedy (2001).

The Second Cognitive Principle: Allow Independence

The second Cognitive discipline principle is "Allow Independence," which can be explained as follows: "Caregivers should not interfere with the efforts of a child to solve his own problems and to develop his own lifestyle preferences." Two issues are involved here. The first is that a caregiver should help a child develop self-acceptance, the idea that it is all right for him to be the person that he is. The second issue is that a caregiver should help a child develop self-efficacy, the sense that he can tackle various challenges successfully. If a child is to become both happy and effective, it is important for his caregivers to encourage him to solve his own problems and to define his own personhood.

One obvious outgrowth of this principle is that caregivers are advised not to get involved in "triangulation" or other power games. Triangulation occurs when one child tries to recruit a caregiver as an ally in his campaign against another child. This is done covertly, of course, and its most usual tactic is through tattling. When Johnny comes to the teacher and says, "Billy broke your rule regarding _____," and the teacher falls for it and punishes Billy, she is responding in a knee-jerk fashion to the reported offense and failing to understand that Johnny has used her to gang up on Billy. In this example, the teacher should have said, "Johnny, I do not respond to tattling. Please do not do that again." In addition to not responding to tattling, Cognitively oriented child-rearing experts counsel caregivers to not intervene in peer disputes, except, of course, when they involve physical violence or danger. Thus, siblings should be encouraged to work out their disputes in a spirit of compromise and fair play without expecting a parent to step in and decide a winner and a loser.

As part of the need to always keep in mind children's individuality, caregivers should never make comparisons among children, whether invidious or otherwise. Saying, "Sam, why can't you get a report card like your sister Holly?" implies that Holly is better or more valued than Sam. Such a message is discouraging and can undermine a child's sense of self-worth. A more constructive way for the caregiver to communicate her concern would be for her to sit down with Sam and ask him how he feels about his report card and whether he is interested in raising any of his grades. If Sam says "yes," then he and the caregiver can discuss some ways of doing that, while always keeping in mind that for Sam to turn his grades around, he needs to take ownership of both the problem and its possible solution.

In fostering a sense of independence in children, it is important that caregivers use methods that are encouraging rather than discouraging. Comparisons among children are discouraging to children, precisely because comparisons convey the sense that the adult does not think that one child is as good as the other. More often than not, such comparisons cause a child to get the idea that there is no point in even trying to change. The important thing for caregivers to convey is that a child has to do things for reasons that are important to him and not simply to fulfill someone else's expectations. It is important to let a child know that he has equal value to everyone else in the class or family and that the important thing is to become the best person he can be. One way that Cognitive discipline experts suggest doing this is by having a caregiver spend some time alone with each child on a weekly or other regular basis, doing things that are important and interesting to that child.

In avoiding making comparisons among children, caregivers need also to keep in mind that children are independent entities and should not all be expected to share the same values, preferences, and lifestyle choices as each other, or as the caregiver. Although caregivers have a right to point out that a lifestyle choice can have undesired consequences (e.g., dressing like a hoodlum will likely not go over well in a job interview), it is preferable that a caregiver give a child the maximum amount of space to explore and to define who he is. Many of the fights that caregivers get into with children and youth could be avoided if a caregiver had a clearer understanding of what is and is not a problem for her. Even relatively young children have the capacity to show preferences and should be allowed and encouraged to make decisions (e.g., about what outfit to wear) whenever possible.

The Cognitive approach, thus, has a core emphasis on maintaining clear boundaries between the caregiver's values, feelings, and perceptions and those of the child. A common discipline style that blurs or obliterates these boundaries has been termed "enmeshed" and is often seen in many first- or second-generation immigrant families. In an enmeshed system, the caregiver acts as if the child were an extension of herself, and whenever the child makes a lifestyle choice or expresses an opinion that diverges too much from her own, there is a strong possibility that the act will be treated as a betrayal and responded to with hurt, outrage, or rejection. Such a caregiver response can be termed "guilt-inducing" and, in more extreme forms, may include "love withdrawal."

Love withdrawal involves responding to what a child has done by giving him a very cold shoulder for an extended period, warming up only after the child apologizes or changes his behavior. A somewhat less toxic, but still harmful, form of this reaction occurred in a family in which an adolescent son was beginning to show an interest in politics and expressed a positive opinion about a political leader of whom his parents disapproved. Instead of asking their son to clarify his opinion or respectfully pointing out why they disagreed with his opinion, the parents reacted with strong outrage, indirectly conveying the message that only a fool could hold such views. The unintended consequence of such a response (repeated many times, of course) was that the son came to the conclusion that it would be better to keep his opinions about important matters to himself rather than risk subjecting himself to ridicule and verbal abuse.

A guilt-oriented discipline style, in which the boundaries between the business of the child and the business of the caregiver are unclear, conveys to the child the burden of thinking that he is responsible for the emotional equanimity and happiness of the caregiver. The child develops the idea that he must avoid adopting courses of action that will disappoint the caregiver or cause her to reject him. Needless to say, such guilt induction or love withdrawal is destructive to the child's development of an autonomous identity and can undermine his ability to function as a happy and independent human being. Of course, this does not mean that a caregiver should avoid telling a child that she disagrees with a particular behavior or opinion. But Cognitive discipline theorists would urge caregivers to always keep in mind that it is possible—indeed, necessary—to be effective at discipline without undermining the child's autonomy.

The Third Cognitive Principle:
Inform Why

The third Cognitive discipline principle is "Inform Why," and can be explained as follows: "Caregivers should help a child understand the reasons underlying rules and expectations." This principle is based on the notion that the purpose of discipline is not just to secure immediate compliance but to build self-regulatory capacity in the child. The child is most likely to develop the capacity to regulate his own behavior if he acquires an ability to consider other perspectives and an ability to reason about morality and the need for family and classroom rules and expectations. Developing in the child an ability to think about others and to conform his behavior to notions of good conduct is central to the Cognitive approach, as reflected in its name.

One obvious way to inform a child of the reason for a limit or rule is to explain it to him. This does not mean that a caregiver should give a long-winded lecture; that approach is usually counterproductive and causes a child to tune the message out. Verbal explanations should be short and sweet and stated in terms of a consequence that is hurtful to someone (including possibly the caregiver, the child, or others). A general principle covering such a class of behavior can also be included in this brief communication. An example is a child hogging the TV remote control; a good way for a caregiver to respond to this behavior is to say, "I was enjoying that program, and then suddenly you switched the channel. When other people are watching the TV with you, it is important to ask how they feel about it before you change the channel."

Another example is when two kids are horsing around in a school hallway and accidentally slam an innocent bystander into a locker; the teacher or principal could say, "The reason why we don't allow horseplay or running in the hallways is because someone could get hurt. What just happened here shows why this is an important rule to have. Students walking in the hall or standing in front of their lockers should not have to worry about getting run over by other students." Under no circumstances should a caregiver justify a punishment by a power-assertive statement, such as "Because I said so." There should always be an opportunity for children to learn something from the caregiver's intervention that has the potential to make the young person think more deeply about what he is doing when faced with a similar situation in the future.

Applying the Cognitive Approach

A unique feature of the Cognitive approach is to advise caregivers, when setting a limit, to choose a punishment that itself—even without any accompanying verbalization by the caregiver—teaches the child a lesson. This result has been termed "natural consequences" or "logical consequences." An example of a natural consequence is when a child misses his school bus and is then made to walk to school rather than being driven by his parent. If that is not safe or feasible, then a logical consequence would be for the child to stay home but not watch TV or play video games, instead to stay in his bed as if he were sick (which is the only justifiable excuse for a child's not going to school). Another example of a natural consequence of a child's not picking up his clothes and putting them in the hamper is that the clothes will not be washed, and he will not have clean clothes when he wants them.

The beauty of the natural/logical consequences technique is not only that it has some educational value but also that it puts responsibility on the child for taking an action that is in his interest. By linking the consequence naturally or logically to a child's failure to act responsibly, the caregiver lets the child know that the violated rule was for his own benefit and was not being arbitrarily imposed. Another benefit of the use of such consequences is that it removes the element of power struggle from discipline. Avoiding and eliminating power struggles is central to the Cognitive approach's philosophy, because the core message in this approach is that one does not have to defeat others in order to have one's own needs met.

In that regard, it is important for discipline to be imbued with a sense of fairness and justice. It is not fair to have one set of rules for one child in a classroom or home and another set of rules for everyone else. It is not fair to use collective punishment, whereby one child's failure to perform adequately causes other children to be punished. It is not fair to select an enormous consequence for a minor infraction. If discipline is intended to teach a sense of justice and fairness to children, then it is essential that caregivers demonstrate justice and fairness in the way they treat the children in their care.

Myths about the Cognitive Approach

Many caregivers believe two misconceptions about the Cognitive approach, even when they are otherwise attracted to it: (1) caregivers never give verbal feedback and (2) caregivers never intervene in peer or sibling disputes. I discuss these myths briefly below.

The Myth That Caregivers Never Give Verbal Feedback

Because Cognitive experts promote verbiage-light logical and natural consequences in lieu of moral castigation forms of punishment, some caregivers interpret this as being told that they should never give verbal feedback. That, in fact, is not the case. As a rule, punishment should teach a moral rule (such as "Don't leave toys out where they can be rained on"), and a good way to convey such a lesson is to arrange for the child to figure it out for himself. But the larger issue here is not the method one uses but the internalized learning one wants to take place. Obviously, verbal feedback is necessary and unavoidable at times, but the point Cognitive discipline experts are making is that caregivers should try to keep power struggles out of the process. As with the other two discipline approaches, the Cognitive approach must be understood not so much as a set of specific techniques but through the domains of caregiver and child competence those techniques are intended to enhance.

The Myth That Caregivers Never Intervene in Disputes

The Cognitive discipline approach was inspired by the writings of Adler, the psychiatrist who first wrote about sibling rivalry, low self-esteem, and the will to power as being key factors in the development of mental illness. Reflecting Adler's influence, the Cognitive approach to discipline is based on the idea that healthy child development involves developing cooperation, feeling empathy, and caring for others rather than trying to dominate others. Therefore, adult caregivers should avoid being used in power struggles involving a child's siblings or peers and should let children work out compromises among themselves without caregiver intervention. In other words, caregivers should not let themselves get sucked into taking sides (e.g., by responding to tattling).

Some caregivers have wrongly assumed that this means that Cognitive experts are telling them to never respond to peer disputes. That is a mistaken interpretation, in my opinion. Obviously, common sense dictates that there are occasions when not intervening in a peer dispute would equate to child neglect. Such situations would be, for example, when an older child is tricking a gullible younger, or disabled, child in some way; when one child is hurting another child; or when a group of children are tormenting a single child. The key aspect of the Cognitive approach is not that a caregiver should not intervene but that she should always look for an opportunity to make an intervention (or nonintervention) educational for the children involved. Thus, when a caregiver overhears two children planning a cruel trick on another child, she can use it as an opportunity to help the children try to take the perspective of the other child and understand how they would feel if they were the ones being tricked. Similarly, when one child tattles on another, the caregiver can use the opportunity to teach the child some skills for communicating his needs and working out compromises on his own.

5

Case Studies in Discipline

Using the Three Approaches
to Address Behavioral Challenges

To illustrate the similarities and differences among the three major discipline approaches—Affective, Behavioral, and Cognitive—it is necessary to bring the discussion to a more practical level. In this chapter, I present three hypothetical case studies (compiled from typical real-world experiences)—two involving families and one involving a classroom—and describe the kinds of advice the caregivers in these stories would receive if they consulted with a psychologist or other discipline expert operating within each of the three approaches. First, I provide a synopsis of each case, and then I discuss how each would be addressed from the standpoint of the Affective approach, the Behavioral approach, and the Cognitive approach. In subsequent chapters, I break down the distinguishing features of the three approaches by demonstrating how they are, in fact, highly congruent and how they can be combined in a mix and match fashion to suit any family or classroom circumstance.

The point I want to make in discussing these and other cases is this: Competence at discipline, or any other adult activity for that matter, is a function less of the precise actions one engages in (such as how much active listening one does) than of when and how effectively one engages in those actions. Thus, I ground the discussion of the cases as much as possible in concrete examples of effective and ineffective caregiver responses to specific child behaviors.

One thing that becomes apparent from examining the cases in this chapter, and again in the two chapters that follow, is that the *framework* therapists and discipline educators communicate to caregivers does not change from case to case, though the *emphasis* might. Within the Affective approach, for example, all caregivers are taught the same three principles—Assert Needs, Accept Feelings, and Show Respect—but the emphasis might be a little different from case to case, depending on a caregiver's strengths and weaknesses across the three discipline domains. Thus, for one family (such as the first one discussed here) the obvious starting point might be to convince the parents of the importance of asserting needs, while the starting point might be a little different for another set of parents, whose main problem might not be an unwillingness to set limits but perhaps an inability to accept feelings or to show affection.

Finding the starting point can be the first challenge in a discipline intervention. The discipline profile is a tool that can be used to identify a caregiver's strengths and weaknesses in discipline. The profile is a simple graphical plot displaying a caregiver's relative skill in applying specific principles of discipline; performance on each is rated as low, medium, high, or excessive. Caregiver discipline is regarded as competent when scores for all principles plotted are close to high (or on the medium side of high) without being *too* high (i.e., excessive). Although the Affective, Behavioral, and Cognitive approaches all have principles corresponding to the Warmth, Tolerance, and Influence domains, the principles are not identical across approaches, and it is possible that the same caregiver's discipline profiles for the three approaches will differ somewhat. Any discipline educator will emphasize all three of the domains, but an individualized discipline profile (or series of profiles, to cover the three approaches) can help the educator as well as the caregiver get a better handle on the areas that need particular attention. Discipline profiles constructed for each approach illustrate the case analyses that follow, highlighting areas where improvement is needed for each caregiver.

Three Challenging Discipline Cases

Case 1: An Overly Weak Parent of Young Kids

Kathy Berne is a thirty-year-old single mother who lives with her two young children, Peter, age five, and Sarah, age three. Kathy's husband moved out of the home a year ago, and the change has been difficult for the children, especially Peter. Wanting to make up the loss to her kids and keep them happy, Kathy sets very few limits. This practice fits in with Kathy's values overall, as she grew up in a very strict and cold household, and she is determined to raise her kids in a more permissive and warm environment. Thus, Kathy's postdivorce permissiveness is not new but rather is an exaggeration of a tendency she already had.

Kathy was forced to seek help from a discipline expert when the head of her son's preschool told her that Peter's disruptive and aggressive behavior would cause him to be expelled unless something was done. Although the initial focus of the intervention was on five-year-old Peter, it became apparent that the root of the problem lay in the family dynamics, particularly Kathy's inability to set firm and effective limits. This became apparent from a video recording that was made of Kathy and Peter in the therapist's waiting room. Peter continually touched artwork and other objects, kept running out into the hallway, and consistently ignored his mother's responses, which ranged from ignoring to weak pleas to occasional nervous laughs. In failing to comply with his mother's pleas to settle down, Peter would argue with her, saying things such as "You're a mean mommy" and "I hate you." Kathy's response would be to argue back, making comments such as "I am not mean" and "You're very naughty to say that."

At an initial session with the discipline expert, Kathy admitted that she was very frustrated and unhappy about Peter's unruly behavior and also was concerned that Sarah, the three-year-old, was beginning to exhibit similar behaviors. The household was in a state of constant uproar, the children followed no set routines, and Kathy's efforts to redirect her children's behavior—on even simple issues, such as not drawing on the walls or getting ready for bed—were met with resistance and conflict. Especially upsetting to Kathy was Peter's occasional physical aggressiveness toward his sister, because on a few occasions serious injury to the younger child was only narrowly averted.

Case 2: An Overly Harsh Teacher

Ann Stark is a forty-year-old woman who has been a fifth-grade teacher in a suburban community for the past ten years. She has a reputation for being very strict, but one would never know it from looking in the door of her classroom. Students are constantly running around the room, leaving the classroom without permission, yelling and making wisecracks while she is speaking, throwing things, and ignoring most of the rules posted at the front of the room. Mrs. Stark's reputation for strictness stems mainly from the fact that she is constantly screaming at the students, constantly threatening (and occasionally imposing) punishment, and constantly taking one student or another to task for some act of misbehavior. When she reprimands students, it is usually in a very demeaning tone of voice and with comments such as "You have a lot of nerve," "Only a stupid person could behave like that," and "When are you finally going to grow up?"

Although Mrs. Stark sends more students to the principal's office than any other teacher in her school, little or no improvement has been made in her classroom's atmosphere. Mrs. Stark was encouraged to seek assistance from a discipline consultant after an incident in which several of her students, including one who is usually well behaved, approached and backed her against the blackboard while making mocking comments and cursing at her. This incident so shattered Mrs. Stark's confidence that she started to consider whether she ought to leave the teaching field.

Case 3: Guilt-Tripping Parents of an Unhappy Teenager

Betty and Stan Green are in their early forties and have one child, a fifteen-year-old daughter named Heather. She is an outstanding student, getting mostly As at the local high school, is well behaved in school and other settings, and has several close friends in spite of a tendency toward shyness. The incident that precipitated the Greens' decision to seek professional help occurred when they told Heather she could not go to a long-planned sleepover birthday party at the home of her best friend, Sue. Furthermore, they told Heather that they would no longer allow her to be friends with Sue because they disapproved of her parents, who lived a lifestyle that was too bohemian and fun-loving for the Greens' tastes.

When Heather was given this news, she reacted with a very uncharacteristic outburst, telling her parents that she hated them. They responded by telling her that she was very bad to express such a sentiment and sending her to her room. A couple of hours later, Mrs. Green went into Heather's bedroom to discuss the situation and was alarmed to find Heather unconscious, with an empty pill bottle on her nightstand.

The Greens called an ambulance and Heather was taken to a hospital, where her stomach was pumped. Although she recovered fully, Heather was checked into a psychiatric ward for observation. A psychiatrist met with her, and she shared with him her despair over her parents' unwillingness to allow her the freedom of behavior and expression that was the norm in the families of other teenagers. The psychiatrist also met with Heather's parents and discussed with them the events that led up to their daughter's suicide gesture. Although he did not think Heather had deep-seated emotional problems, the psychiatrist suggested that she receive professional counseling. In addition, he strongly recommended that the Greens avoid future episodes of this sort by retaining the services of someone who could help them evaluate their discipline practices.

On the surface, this case seems very different from Cases 1 and 2, in that while the previous cases are marked by rampant child misbehavior, in this case the child in question is very well behaved—in fact, quite in excess of what is considered typical for a teenager. Furthermore, while in the two preceding cases the adult caregivers have become quite unhappy as a result of their inability to achieve adequate control over the children in their care, in this case the adults feel very little discomfort about their discipline effectiveness. Rather, whatever unhappiness Heather's parents feel toward their child is less a reflection of her actual misbehavior than of their own strict and excessively critical standards. Thus, it seems unlikely that these parents would ever have sought the help of a discipline expert had it not been for the hospitalization of their daughter and the suicide gesture that precipitated that hospitalization.

How an Affective Consultant
Would Approach the Three Cases

Let us assume that an Affectively oriented discipline expert, "Dr. Fred Jones," was hired to assist the caregivers in all three of these cases. In each case, after a session in which he met with the caregivers to learn about their discipline problems, he would explain to them the basics of the Affective approach. Those basics are discussed and illustrated in Chapter 2, and Figure 5.1 provides a consolidated portrayal of the approach. In this figure (and in Figures 5.5 and

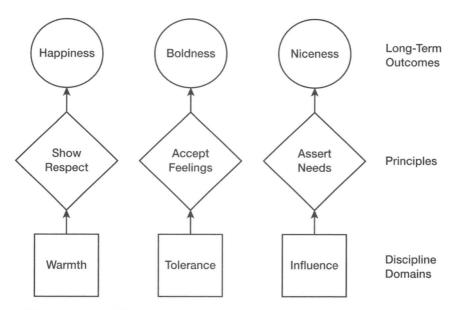

- **Show Respect**—The Affective principle for the domain of Warmth
   Objective: Fostering the child outcome of Happiness
   Statement of principle: Caregivers should refrain from commenting on a child's character, motives, or overall patterns of behavior, or from otherwise assaulting a child's sense of worth.

- **Accept Feelings**—The Affective principle for the domain of Tolerance
   Objective: Fostering the child outcome of Boldness
   Statement of principle: Caregivers should provide symbolic outlets for the expression of feelings.

- **Assert Needs**—The Affective principle for the domain of Influence
   Objective: Fostering the child outcome of Niceness
   Statement of principle: Caregivers should let a child know when he has done something unacceptable.

FIGURE 5.1   The ABC Model Showing Only Affective Principles

5.9, which illustrate the Behavioral and Cognitive approaches), arrows point from each of the three discipline domains along the bottom of the diagram, upward toward the related discipline principle in the middle, and from there up to the desired child social competence outcome at the top. The features of the discipline principles are outlined below the diagram.

Dr. Jones most likely would simply present the three Affective principles (the row of diamonds in the figure): Show Respect, Accept Feelings, and Assert Needs. In the clinical setting, he would not discuss the more theoretical aspects of three domains (Warmth, Tolerance, and Influence) or three outcomes (Happiness, Boldness, and Niceness). In the course of evaluating each situation, Dr. Jones would create a discipline profile for the caregivers to highlight strengths and weaknesses in their application of the three Affective principles. This profile would help focus the subsequent discussions and assist the caregivers in understanding why their current methods were not achieving the goals they held, whether for themselves or for the children in their care.

Affective Take on Case 1: Kathy Berne

In attempting to understand the discipline style of single mother Kathy Berne, Dr. Fred Jones, an Affectively oriented discipline expert, asked her to articulate her child-rearing philosophy. That philosophy appeared to have been taken straight out of Rousseau's *Émile* (the bible for permissive parents and educators), consisting of the notion that children are inherently good and can only be messed up by adult direction, and maintaining that the way to help a child grow into a happy and competent adult is to give him maximum freedom to behave as he wishes.

Dr. Jones was able to get Kathy to admit that this approach was not working and that, in fact, the opposite was happening. Peter was not a very happy child, in part because peers avoided him and in part because he was always upping the ante with additional demands that could not be instantly met. He also was not socially competent, as reflected in the fact that he was in danger of being expelled from his preschool because of his lack of age-appropriate skills for taking adult direction and for getting along with other children.

Analysis. Kathy's discipline profile for the Affective principles is shown in Figure 5.2. She scores high on Show Respect (the Affective principle for Warmth), medium on Accept Feelings (the Affective principle for Tolerance), and low on Assert Needs (the Affective principle for Influence). Kathy clearly does not have a problem being warm toward her children, as indicated by her high score on that domain. Nor for the most part, does she need to do much work on being tolerant. The reason she received a medium, rather than a high,

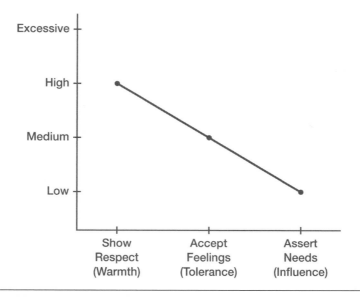

FIGURE 5.2   Discipline Profile for Kathy Berne: Affective Principles

score on that domain mainly reflects the fact that she sometimes takes expressions of anger or other affect personally. However, her low score on Assert Needs (Influence) indicates that the main focus of any intervention with Kathy must be to get her to become much more able to communicate her needs and expectations to her children.

Intervention. While discipline educators applying any of the approaches (Affective, Behavioral, or Cognitive) address all three domains (Warmth, Tolerance, and Influence) as an integrated package, it is often the case that one area or another will require extra attention. It was apparent to Dr. Jones that Kathy's biggest problem was in the domain of Influence, and in his intervention he placed great emphasis on the corresponding Affective principle: Assert Needs. Specifically, he helped Kathy understand that an adult's setting of limits is necessary not only to meet the adult's needs but also to give children the structure they need (and seek out) if they are to become competent and happy individuals. Kathy learned that by failing to set limits, she was failing to meet her children's need for order and, consequently, was impeding their social development.

The Assert Needs principle states, "Caregivers should let a child know when he has done something unacceptable." Kathy could easily determine limits on activities that were dangerous or destructive, but she needed some help in establishing her bottom-line standards of general behavioral acceptability. Dr. Jones used Thomas Gordon's decision-window device to help Kathy think about the kinds of child behaviors that she needed to start responding to with firm limits.

The decision window is described in detail and illustrated in Chapter 2. Briefly, it is an imaginary window through which a caregiver views the behavior of a child. The window is divided into four segments representing four combinations of potential problems in behavior. Behaviors are characterized as:

- No problem for the child and no problem for the caregiver. *Caregiver response:* Do nothing or offer some form of encouragement or praise.
- No problem for the child but problematic for the caregiver. *Caregiver response:* Set a limit in the form of an I-message (possibly followed by active listening if the child resists the imposed limit).
- Problem for the child (i.e., indicative of a problem the child is experiencing) and problematic for the caregiver. *Caregiver response:* Make a reflective comment, followed by an I-message, followed by active listening.
- Problem for the child and no problem for the caregiver. *Caregiver response:* Make an active listening comment or offer no comment.

Kathy came up with the following list of behaviors that she would consider problematic for her and that she would respond to with a limit: (1) destructive behaviors, such as knocking over furniture and defacing walls; (2) dangerous behaviors, such as running into the street; (3) aggressive behaviors, such as Peter's striking his little sister; (4) use of very disrespectful language to Kathy or to other adults; and (5) excessive resistance to daily routines, such as bathing or going to bed.

Dr. Jones modeled for Kathy the use of the I-message technique ("I feel *x* when you do *y* because *z*") for setting limits, and Kathy was asked to practice this technique until she was comfortable with it. Dr. Jones also attended to Kathy's tone of voice, encouraging her to sound less pleading and more authoritative.

Kathy worried that her children, particularly Peter, would test her new resolve by throwing tantrums, crying, and unleashing verbal attacks. In other words, it was difficult for her to imagine doing anything that would not create a "problem for the child." In the past, Kathy had responded to such verbalizations by getting into long-winded arguments or by acting hurt, but she was told to resist being sucked into these kinds of responses. Dr. Jones taught her the importance of dealing with "problem for the child" responses by applying the Accept Feelings (Tolerance) principle: "Caregivers should provide symbolic outlets for the expression of feelings." Thus, when Peter responded to a limit by crying or expressing some other emotion, Kathy was encouraged to respond with a brief verbalization along the lines of "I understand that you are mad at Mommy for taking away that toy, but the rule in this house is 'Toys are for playing with and not for throwing.'"

By stating the limit in very succinct form, with emphasis on the act rather than on Peter's character, Kathy was also implementing the Show Respect (Warmth) principle: "Caregivers should refrain from commenting on a child's character, motives, or overall patterns of behavior, or from otherwise assaulting a child's sense of worth." In doing this, Kathy learned to avoid playing the game of repeated arguing and recrimination that had previously characterized her occasional half-hearted efforts at setting limits.

Affective Take on Case 2: Ann Stark

Because the discipline situation in Mrs. Stark's fifth-grade classroom had gotten so far out of hand that she had begun to question her career choice, she consulted Dr. Fred Jones, an Affectively oriented discipline expert, for advice. In attempting to understand Mrs. Stark's discipline style, Dr. Jones asked her to articulate her child-rearing philosophy. In reply, Mrs. Stark emphasized the importance of being tough and assertive and never letting misbehavior go unpunished. She showed no appreciation of the importance of creating a warm classroom environment in which children felt encouraged or appreciated. Although the end product of Mrs. Stark's classroom management was not too different from Kathy Berne's result—namely, an unhappy adult and unruly and out-of-control kids—Dr. Jones's analysis revealed that the discipline style responsible for the mess was quite different.

Analysis. Mrs. Stark's discipline profile for the Affective principles is shown in Figure 5.3. She scores low on Show Respect (the Affective principle for Warmth), medium on Accept Feelings (the Affective principle for Tolerance), and excessive on Assert Needs (the Affective principle for Influence). Her plot is the opposite of Kathy Berne's, as seen in the upward slant of Mrs. Stark's line versus the downward slant of Kathy's line. The only point of commonality is that both received medium scores on Accept Feelings (Tolerance). Although Tolerance is a domain that needs attention for Mrs. Stark, this minor deficit does not go to the core of why she is so ineffective a teacher from a discipline standpoint.

The two biggest areas that Mrs. Stark needs to work on are raising her low score on Show Respect (Warmth) and lowering her excessively high score on

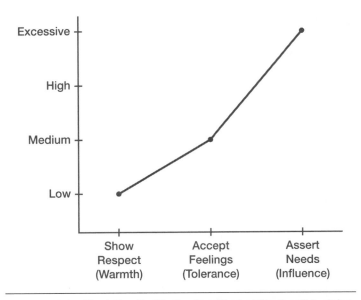

FIGURE 5.3 Discipline Profile for Ann Stark: Affective Principles

Assert Needs (Influence). The striking thing about Mrs. Stark's classroom, apparent to any knowledgeable observer after about ten minutes, is how negative the vibes are. There is hardly a minute when Mrs. Stark is not attempting to set a limit, usually with words that are disrespectful and hectoring. This creates a disharmonious and unhappy classroom, one that is marked by Mrs. Stark's constantly inflicting pain on her students and by the students' reciprocating. The amazing thing is not that Mrs. Stark is beginning to think about leaving the teaching field but that it took ten years for her to get to this point or for her supervisors to try to do something about the situation in her classroom.

Intervention. Once again, Dr. Jones taught all three Affective principles, but he concentrated primarily on what he viewed as Mrs. Stark's biggest problems: her tendency to set entirely too many limits and her use of disrespectful and antagonistic language when doing so. The starting point for this intervention, therefore, was to get Mrs. Stark to become much more focused in her limit-setting efforts and to become more positive, and much less disparaging, in the tone of her interactions with students. In essence, she would be working to reduce her score on Influence and increase her score on Warmth. The approach was also designed to raise Mrs. Stark's score on Tolerance by teaching her to tell the difference between what was really problematic for her and what was not. Thus, unlike the intervention for Kathy Berne, where the goal was to get her to place more things in the "problematic for the caregiver" category, Dr. Jones worked with Mrs. Stark to get her to place fewer behaviors in the "problematic for the caregiver" category, including, of course, expressions of affect.

Affective Take on Case 3: The Greens

The situation in the Greens' household differed from the first two cases in that the child in question (fifteen-year-old Heather) was, if anything, *too* well behaved. A suicide attempt by Heather, which had been preceded by an uncharacteristic verbal outburst in response to restrictions imposed by her parents, prompted the Greens to seek the advice of Dr. Fred Jones, an Affectively oriented discipline expert. Dr. Jones started off by interviewing Heather and her parents, both separately and together, and concluded that the caregiving style of the Greens was too controlling and restrictive. He helped them realize that they would have to loosen their tight grip on their daughter if she is (literally) to grow up into a happy person.

Analysis. The Greens' discipline profile for the Affective principles is shown in Figure 5.4. They score medium on Show Respect (the Affective principle for Warmth), low on Accept Feelings (the Affective principle for Tolerance), and

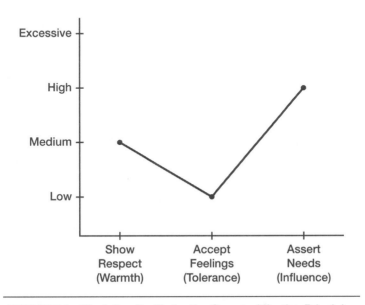

FIGURE 5.4   Discipline Profile for the Greens: Affective Principles

high on Assert Needs (the Affective principle for Influence). This profile is somewhat mixed; it combines some elements of Kathy Berne's overly weak profile and some elements of Mrs. Stark's overly harsh profile. Like Mrs. Stark, the Greens have no trouble stating their expectations, although their rating is merely high rather than excessive on Assert Needs (Influence). Like Kathy, and unlike Mrs. Stark, the Greens are not terribly disrespectful toward their child, as reflected in their rating of medium on Show Respect (Warmth).

The area in which the Greens are unique is Accept Feelings (Tolerance), where they score low. In fact, it was the Greens' ongoing unwillingness to allow Heather to have her own perceptions and feelings, as much as or more than their denying her a much-anticipated outing, that contributed to her emotional meltdown.

Intervention. Dr. Jones quickly concluded that the basic problem in the Green household was the parents' insensitivity to their daughter's emotional life, which extended even to an unwillingness to allow her to have and to express feelings of which they disapproved. The intervention focused, therefore, on helping Mr. and Mrs. Green to understand that every person, including a child, is entitled to have and to express feelings, including anger directed against parents, and that although it might be appropriate to set limits on behavior (such as attending a sleepover with a disapproved-of friend), it is never appropriate to treat a feeling (in this case, the wish to go to the slumber party and resentment at the parents for preventing it) as a problem. The Greens were taught active listening skills ("You wish you could go," "You're very angry at us," etc.) for implementing this newly acquired insight. Furthermore, they were taught to avoid using evaluative terms such as "bad" (the reason for their score of medium on Show Respect) when responding to their child's behavior or affective expressions.

Regarding the limit itself (preventing Heather from attending the party), the Greens were encouraged to reflect on why they felt that such an activity was a violation of their standards. Although most Affectively oriented experts would be reluctant to impose their own standards on a client, Dr. Jones emphasized that the Greens should have clear reasons they could articulate, and the reasons should not be arbitrary or simply an exercise in adult authority. After reflection, the Greens came to the realization that a big part of their problem was their fear of their fifteen-year-old daughter growing up and their desire to protect her from contamination by contact with peers who were interested in dating and such. In light of how unhappy they had made their daughter, they concluded that they needed to revise their standards to take into account that she is no longer a little girl and to trust that she can handle her newly attained freedom in a responsible manner.

How a Behavioral Consultant
Would Approach the Three Cases

Let us next assume that a Behaviorally oriented discipline expert, "Dr. Ruth Smith," was hired to assist the caregivers in the three cases. After a session in which she met with the caregivers to learn about their discipline problems, she would explain to them the basics of the Behavioral approach. Those basics are discussed and illustrated in Chapter 3, and Figure 5.5 provides a consolidated portrayal of the approach.

In the clinical setting, Dr. Smith would focus on the three Behavioral principles (the row of diamonds in the figure): Give Positives, Ignore Much, and Be Contingent. There would be little or no explicit discussion of how those principles fit into a theoretical framework of discipline domains (Warmth, Tolerance, and Influence) and outcomes (Happiness, Boldness, and Niceness). As part of each evaluation, Dr. Smith would create a discipline profile for the caregivers to highlight strengths and weaknesses in their application of the three Behavioral principles. This profile would serve as a starting point for the subsequent discussions of how the caregivers could improve their situations.

Behavioral Take on Case 1: Kathy Berne

Dr. Ruth Smith, a Behaviorally oriented discipline expert, started off with a preliminary discussion with single mother Kathy Berne about her problems with her son, Peter, but she also observed Kathy interacting with Peter in the laboratory (watching from an adjoining room, through a one-way mirror). In addition, she had Kathy keep daily charts (a staple of the Behavioral approach) noting the frequency of certain critical behaviors of Peter as well as her own responses to those behaviors. What Dr. Smith learned from these methods was that Peter engaged in many problem behaviors and that, although Kathy made many positive verbalizations (praise) and loving physical responses (hugs), these were not used in a contingent or skilled manner in any effort to bring about behavioral change in Peter.

Analysis. Kathy's discipline profile for the Behavioral principles is shown in Figure 5.6. Kathy scores high on Give Positives (the Behavioral principle for Warmth), medium on Ignore Much (the Behavioral principle for Tolerance), and low on Be Contingent (the Behavioral principle for Influence). Kathy's strength in behaving warmly toward her children is reflected in her high score on Give Positives. Although she does not have a major problem in the domain of Tolerance, the reason she receives only a medium score there is that she

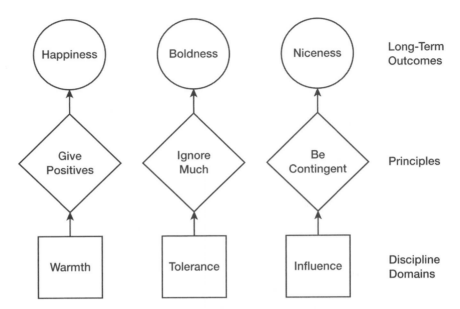

- **Give Positives**—The Behavioral principle for the domain of Warmth
    Objective: Fostering the child outcome of Happiness*
    Statement of principle: Caregivers should do a lot more praising than
    punishing.

- **Ignore Much**—The Behavioral principle for the domain of Tolerance
    Objective: Fostering the child outcome of Boldness*
    Statement of principle: Caregivers should do a lot more ignoring than
    punishing.

- **Be Contingent**—The Behavioral principle for the domain of Influence
    Objective: Fostering the child outcome of Niceness*
    Statement of principle: Caregivers should not punish behaviors they like and
    should not praise behaviors they dislike.

* Objectives for the individual principles of the Behavioral approach have been
inferred from the actions advocated. From a strict behaviorist standpoint, the differential reinforcement specified for each principle has the same goal: influencing
behavior change.

FIGURE 5.5 The ABC Model Showing Only Behavioral Principles

needs to start ignoring diversionary tactics and other forms of resistance,
such as whining and other verbalizations. (Unlike the Affective advice to make
reflective comments in response to such verbalizations, Behavioral experts
suggest ignoring them altogether.) It is her low score on Be Contingent (Influence) that provides the main focus for any intervention with Kathy. If she is

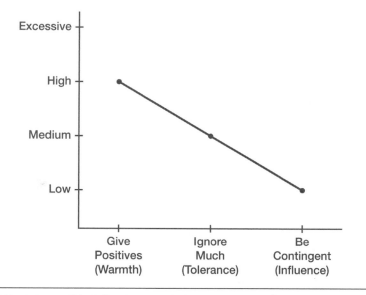

FIGURE 5.6 Discipline Profile for Kathy Berne: Behavioral Principles

to be effective in shaping more compliant and socially competent behavior in her children, she must become better able to set limits for them.

Intervention. The starting point in an intervention designed to increase a caregiver's effectiveness in limit setting is "discrimination training." Dr. Smith began by teaching Kathy the three major Behavioral discipline responses—praise, punish, and ignore—and then helping her improve her ability to recognize when to engage in these responses.

Specifically, Kathy was taught (1) to be aware of opportunities to use praise (any form of positive behavior, including attention) when a child does something that she likes and wants to see more of, (2) to use punishment (any behavior, including verbal disapproval) aimed at stopping an action she dislikes and wants to see less of, and (3) to use ignoring (complete absence of any response, including attention) when she sees something she dislikes but is able to live with. With this discrimination training method (using verbal and videotaped scenarios portraying other adults and children), Kathy was able to approach 100 percent accuracy in her ability to recognize when to use these different kinds of responses. Learning to use them in her real-world home environment was, obviously, a much bigger challenge.

Kathy first had to decide which behaviors she liked and which she disliked, and then to subdivide the latter category into behaviors she could and could not live with. She placed in the "could not live with" category the following: (1) aggressiveness toward other children, including Peter's sibling; (2) disrespectful language toward adults, including Kathy herself; (3) dangerous behaviors, such as running into the street; and (4) excessive resistance to daily routines, such as bathing and going to bed.

Among the behaviors that Kathy decided she did not like but could live with were Peter's whining, crying, and making accusatory comments (e.g., "You're a mean mommy"). Kathy was taught to ignore these behaviors rather than to get defensive. In this way, behaviorists integrate the Ignore Much (Tolerance) principle with the Give Positives (Warmth) principle, as Kathy was taught to follow an ignore response for a disliked (but not punishable) behavior with praise for the first appearance of a desired behavior.

As part of the training process, Dr. Smith used a bug-in-the-ear communication system. The technique involved having Kathy wear a receiving device in an earplug through which she could hear comments that Dr. Smith made into a microphone from the opposite side of a one-way mirror. By observing Kathy and Peter engaging in some task (such as cleaning up or making something), Dr. Smith could shape Kathy's discipline behaviors either with praise and encouragement whenever she gave an effective and contingent response or by giving her a prompt (e.g., "praise now") when she missed an opportunity to use these skills. The charting system that Kathy had used as part of the assessment process was continued for awhile to provide evidence of outcome effectiveness in bringing about desired behavior changes in Peter. In addition, Kathy was encouraged to develop a token economy as an additional method for praising desired behaviors in Peter. This involved doing daily charting of a few desired behaviors, such as putting away his clothes, and giving Peter stars that he could later convert into desired rewards.

Kathy's biggest need was to learn how to limit undesired behaviors, so Dr. Smith helped her develop some effective punishment responses for those (decreasingly frequent) occasions when Peter engaged in behaviors that she disliked and could not live with. Given Peter's young age and the inappropriateness of using spanking or other physical punishment (which is disapproved of by all reputable discipline experts), Kathy was taught to use time-out as an effective response tool.

Time-out is a form of mild punishment recommended by Behavioral discipline experts because it involves a brief period of enforced ignoring and, thus, removes the possibility of the caregiver's inadvertently reinforcing bad behavior by attending to it. By keeping charts of her discipline behaviors, Kathy became contingent in responding with punishment, such as time-out, while at the same time doing more ignoring than punishing and more praising than punishing. In this way, Dr. Smith's Behavioral approach combined all three principles into one package while addressing Kathy's biggest deficiency, which was an inability to impose her will on the behavior of her children.

Behavioral Take on Case 2: Ann Stark

Behaviorally oriented discipline expert Dr. Ruth Smith spent quite a bit of time observing Mrs. Stark's fifth-grade classroom, which was beset with discipline problems. She used a charting method in which she broke each observation session into ten-minute blocks and checked off the numbers of praises, punishes, and ignores. For feedback purposes, and to put Mrs. Stark's responses in context, Dr. Smith videotaped several thirty-minute segments. She also used a structured interview method to help her better understand Mrs. Stark's attitudes toward discipline issues and her grasp of Behavioral principles.

The observations revealed that Mrs. Stark had a profound praise deficit. Although most effective teachers have a ratio of praise to punishment of at least three or four to one, in Mrs. Stark's case the ratio was 0.25 to one. In other words, within any given block of time, Mrs. Stark made four negative responses for every positive one. It is possible that her habitual ratio was even lower, because, with an observer in the room, Mrs. Stark (not to mention the students) likely made an effort to keep things less negative and confrontational than usual.

In the interview, Mrs. Stark stated that she felt her negative style was justified by the unruly behavior of her students. Although there is some truth to the notion that children influence adults, as well as the other way around, Mrs. Stark could not understand or accept that she had the power to break that cycle by choosing what and when to ignore or not ignore and by bringing into the mix a positive way of reinforcing behavior that she liked and wanted to see more of. As is the case with a large percentage of ineffective caregivers, Mrs. Stark tended to take good behavior for granted and to focus only on bad behavior, for which her habitual response was punishment. Using the videotaped sessions, Dr. Smith was able to point out to Mrs. Stark that in a class that she saw in totally negative terms, there were many examples, even among her most difficult students, of perfectly acceptable behaviors that could have been praised and reinforced.

Analysis. Mrs. Stark's discipline profile for the Behavioral principles is shown in Figure 5.7. She scores low on Give Positives (the Behavioral principle for Warmth) and medium on Ignore Much (the Behavioral principle for Tolerance) and Be Contingent (the Behavioral principle for Influence).

Although the Affective, Behavioral, and Cognitive approaches all have principles addressing the same three domains of discipline (Warmth, Tolerance,

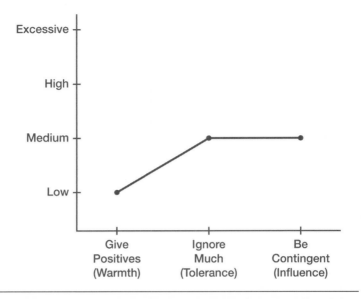

FIGURE 5.7   Discipline Profile for Ann Stark: Behavioral Principles

and Influence), those principles are not identical across approaches. Thus, as discussed earlier, the shapes of the discipline profiles for any one caregiver may vary from approach to approach. That is the case for Mrs. Stark's Affective and Behavioral profiles. The dramatic difference in the shapes of the profiles stems from the fact that Mrs. Stark receives different scores on the domain of Influence: excessive on Assert Needs (the Affective principle; Figure 5.3) and medium on Be Contingent (the Behavioral principle; Figure 5.7). Neither of these is good, but they are bad in different directions.

Mrs. Stark receives a medium score on Be Contingent (Influence) because she appropriately applies the letter of the principle ("Caregivers should not punish behaviors they like and should not praise behaviors they dislike"). As a rule, her punishments are in response to behaviors she does not like, and she does not praise undesirable behaviors. However, she is not fully successful on Be Contingent (which would yield a score of high) because she often makes threats that she fails to follow through on. Because Mrs. Stark punishes so many student offenses, even of a minor (and thus ignorable) nature, her punishment responses to significant misbehaviors do not stand out and thus are not taken seriously by her students. The students' lack of concern about any potential consequence culminated in the grievous offense of backing her up against the blackboard while taunting her. And this time, in an ultimate breakdown of disciplinary effectiveness, Mrs. Stark did nothing in response (other than have her own private meltdown), possibly because she was embarrassed to have the school's administration become aware that such an outrageous thing had occurred in her classroom.

Mrs. Stark also receives a medium score on Ignore Much (Tolerance), although one could justify scoring her as low. Regardless of the exact rating, it is obvious that Mrs. Stark needs to make more of an effort to differentiate between not-liked behaviors that she can or cannot live with, because her tendency to punish everything causes her students to tune her out.

As Dr. Smith observed, Mrs. Stark's biggest problem is her failure to praise good behaviors—her praise deficit—which is reflected in her low score on Give Positives (Warmth). Although Mrs. Stark needs to work on all three Behavioral principles, the most serious challenge for her, in the eyes of Dr. Smith, is to understand the importance of changing the atmosphere in her classroom from one that is completely negative to one that is much more positive.

Intervention. With Mrs. Stark, Dr. Smith followed the standard practice of the Behavioral approach of providing training in all three discipline principles (the same is true, for the most part, with Affective and Cognitive discipline training). Thus, Mrs. Stark was taught the importance of Ignore Much ("Caregivers should do a lot more ignoring than punishing") and of Be Contingent ("Caregivers should not punish behaviors they like and should not praise behaviors they dislike"). Because a profound praise deficit was Mrs. Stark's biggest problem, however, Dr. Smith made a special effort to impress upon her the importance of recognizing and rewarding behavior that she likes and wants to see more of.

Using discrimination training methods, with both printed and videotaped materials, Mrs. Stark gained an understanding of the three Behavioral principles and eventually became quite good at knowing, in the abstract, when to use each and why. Videos of competent caregivers, both teachers and parents, were shown to Mrs. Stark to help her focus on specific microsituations (praiseable, punishable, and ignorable) and how she could deal with them. Because a bug-in-the-ear method is not feasible in most classrooms, Dr. Smith videotaped several hours of Mrs. Stark in the classroom and then met with her on a regular basis to go over situations seen in the videos and discuss the ways in which she did or did not take advantage of opportunities to do more praising.

At the same time as Mrs. Stark was learning to become more positive, she was helped to narrow her list of student behaviors that could not be tolerated by learning to become much more tolerant of minor annoying behaviors. This left her with a small list of things that would never be tolerated and would be responded to with swift and consistent punishment. At the end of several months, Dr. Smith was confident that Mrs. Stark would no longer be a teacher who would not tolerate students' occasional talking and standing but would do nothing when students backed her against the blackboard. She was even more confident, however, that such an extreme form of student rebellion would be unlikely to happen in the future.

Behavioral Take on Case 3: The Greens

When the Greens' fifteen-year-old daughter, Heather—who, by all outward appearances, was well adjusted and well behaved—was hospitalized after taking a pill overdose following a conflict with her parents, the hospital psychiatrist encouraged them to examine their discipline practices. They consulted with Dr. Ruth Smith, a Behaviorally oriented discipline expert. Dr. Smith started off with a preliminary discussion with Heather's parents about their child-rearing practices, and she observed them interacting with their daughter both in the office and in the home setting. After this initial assessment period, Dr. Smith concluded that some changes were in order.

Analysis. The Greens' discipline profile for the Behavioral principles is shown in Figure 5.8. They score medium on Give Positives (the Behavioral principle for Warmth) and Be Contingent (the Behavioral principle for Influence) and low on Ignore Much (the Behavioral principle for Tolerance). Despite the

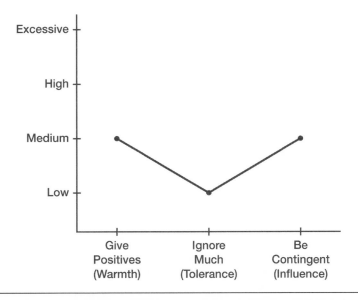

FIGURE 5.8 Discipline Profile for the Greens: Behavioral Principles

dramatic nature of Heather's suicide gesture, she is a well-adjusted and well-behaved child whose upbringing is within normal limits.

The Greens' score of medium on Give Positives (Warmth) indicates that they could probably do more praising than they currently do. They also score medium on Be Contingent (Influence), which reflects the fact that they (appropriately) generally do not discourage good behavior or praise bad behavior. The fact that they are not rated higher on this principle is because of their unfortunate tendency to flip-flop. That is, they decide one week that a behavior is praiseable, or at least tolerable/ignorable, and then the next week decide it is something that calls for punishment (this is what precipitated the incident with Heather). Such extreme disciplinary inconsistency is one of the hallmarks of "toxic parenting" (Forward with Buck 1989) and can be considered "crazy-making" because it can contribute to emotional disturbance in children.

The one area where the Greens stand out as clearly deficient is Ignore Much (Tolerance), where they score low. They simply treat too many of Heather's behaviors as things they do not like and cannot tolerate. This would be a problem at any age, but it is particularly troublesome when the child in question is fifteen years old. Dr. Smith concluded that a big part of the difficulty in this family stems from the Greens' propensity to include too many things in the "punish" category and too few in the "ignore/tolerate" category. This is especially true in the case of purely affective outbursts, such as the "I hate you" comment whose punishment precipitated the crisis that caused this family to seek professional assistance.

Intervention. Because the Greens were below the optimal level on all three discipline domains, Dr. Smith had them work on improving their performance on all three Behavioral principles (the typical approach, given that the three principles form a comprehensive and coordinated system). However, the main priority for the intervention was to bring up the Greens' low score on Ignore Much (Tolerance). Mr. and Mrs. Green were encouraged to loosen the reins on their daughter quite a bit and to become aware of the need to shorten the list of behaviors that they viewed as not liked and cannot be tolerated and to increase the list of behaviors that are not liked but can be tolerated. At the same time, they were encouraged to be somewhat quicker to use praise when their daughter did things they approved of and much less inclined to flip-flop (i.e., to change their minds about things they had once regarded as acceptable).

Because Heather is an adolescent, Dr. Smith suggested the use of "behavior contracts," a device often suggested by Behavioral discipline experts. Such an agreement clearly specifies responsibilities and consequences for violating terms of the contract. In the case of an event (such as the slumber party) about which the parents would have concerns, they could specify conditions such as "no alcohol, no boys, and responsible adults must be present in the home," with the consequence that violating any of these terms would result in the inability to engage in future such events. If Heather demonstrated a willingness to abide by these terms, then the Greens could feel comfortable in relaxing their oversight over time. In this way, Heather would be given the chance to demonstrate competence in the hope that such a demonstration would be rewarded with greater freedom in the future.

How a Cognitive Consultant
Would Approach the Three Cases

Finally, let us assume that a Cognitively oriented discipline expert, "Dr. Jane Arens," was hired to assist the caregivers in the three cases. After a session in which she met with the caregivers to learn about their discipline problems, she would explain to them the basics of the Cognitive approach. Those basics are discussed and illustrated in Chapter 4, and Figure 5.9 provides a consolidated portrayal of the approach.

In the clinical setting, Dr. Arens would focus on the three Cognitive principles (the row of diamonds in the figure): Encourage Participation, Allow Independence, and Inform Why. There would be little or no explicit discussion of how those principles fit into a theoretical framework of discipline domains (Warmth, Tolerance, and Influence) and outcomes (Happiness, Boldness, and Niceness). For each case, Dr. Arens would create a discipline profile for the caregivers to highlight strengths and weaknesses in their application of the three Cognitive principles. This profile would serve as a starting point for the subsequent discussions of how the caregivers could become more effective.

Cognitive Take on Case 1: Kathy Berne

Cognitively oriented discipline expert Dr. Jane Arens spent time observing single mother Kathy Berne and her two young children, and she interviewed Kathy extensively regarding her child-rearing beliefs and attitudes. It became apparent to Dr. Arens that Kathy expected her children to learn good behavior by osmosis and did not understand the critical role played by parents and other adults in helping children acquire the values and self-control needed to function competently in the social world.

Analysis. Kathy's discipline profile for the Cognitive principles is shown in Figure 5.10. She scores medium on Encourage Participation (the Cognitive principle for Warmth) and Allow Independence (the Cognitive principle for Tolerance) and low on Inform Why (the Cognitive principle for Influence).

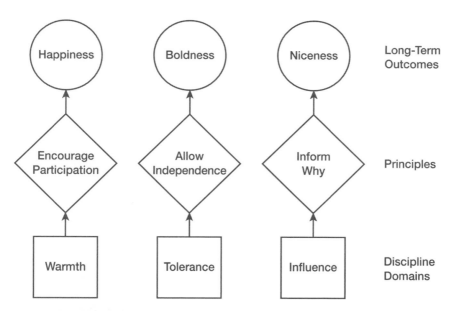

- **Encourage Participation**—The Cognitive principle for the domain of Warmth
  Objective: Fostering the child outcome of Happiness
  Statement of principle: Caregivers should allow a child to participate in making and applying rules.

- **Allow Independence**—The Cognitive principle for the domain of Tolerance
  Objective: Fostering the child outcome of Boldness
  Statement of principle: Caregivers should not interfere with the efforts of a child to solve his own problems and to develop his own lifestyle preferences.

- **Inform Why**—The Cognitive principle for the domain of Influence
  Objective: Fostering the child outcome of Niceness
  Statement of principle: Caregivers should help a child understand the reasons underlying rules and expectations.

FIGURE 5.9   The ABC Model Showing Only Cognitive Principles

Thus, Kathy could use some help on all three Cognitive principles but most needs to work on the Influence domain.

Kathy is generally a warm and loving parent who does encourage her children, especially in the area of intellectual development. Thus, her medium score on Encourage Participation (Warmth) is not indicative of a gross deficiency. The reason the score is not higher is less a reflection of an unwillingness to share decisions about rules than it is a reflection of the lack of any rules to discuss and, thus, the lack of any forum for discussing them.

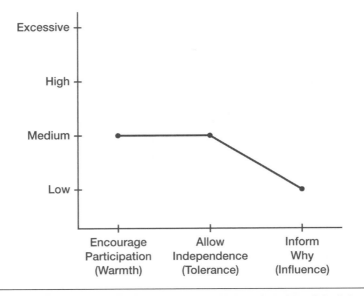

FIGURE 5.10   Discipline Profile for Kathy Berne: Cognitive Principles

The medium score on Allow Independence (Tolerance) may also be a little misleading, given that Kathy is not one to intrude excessively into her children's lifespace. But she does tend to get a little defensive and hurt when her kids argue with her, a response that is quite normal but still something that she could work on.

Clearly, Kathy's area of greatest deficiency is her inability or unwillingness to assert her will on her children's behavior, except in the direst of circumstances. The Cognitive principle for Influence—Inform Why—can be stated as: "Caregivers should help a child understand the reasons underlying rules and expectations." Typically, this takes the form of verbally pointing out the impact of the child's behavior on the interests and feelings of others. One example is explaining to the child that damaging a wall, a piece of furniture, or a toy will cost someone (such as Kathy) money and effort to fix or will make the object unusable. But an equally important impact will be on the child himself, as others (such as peers) will be angry at him and will not be inclined to be nice to him. Kathy's failure to impose a coherent set of rules has left her unable to convey to her children the rationale for such standards.

Intervention.   In all three discipline approaches, experts—whether in consultations or in workshops—encourage caregivers to tap into the extensive discipline literature that is available for parents and teachers. This is even more likely to be the case for experts working within the Cognitive approach. Thus, Dr. Arens encouraged Kathy to read books by leading Cognitive discipline authorities, such as Rudolf Dreikurs. One technique that Dreikurs has written about extensively is the family or class "council" meeting. Dr. Arens felt that such a council, meeting on a weekly basis, would be especially useful in Kathy's family, despite the relatively young age of her two children (especially her daughter, who was only three). At such a meeting, each of the family members could discuss concerns, and rules could be generated for addressing those concerns, which everyone, including Kathy, would be expected to follow.

Such council meetings serve several functions: (1) helping a child acquire empathy (an understanding of the feelings and perspectives of others), (2) helping a child understand that rules are meant to help people meet their mutual needs and are not just exercises in adult power, and (3) helping a child feel that he has a stake in the running of the home (or classroom). Dr. Arens also suggested that Peter's preschool consider establishing a class council, as many of Peter's maladaptive behaviors occur there, and it would be helpful for him to acquire a better understanding of why he is being shunned by peers and having disapproving letters sent home by his teachers.

Kathy was guided by Dr. Arens in acquiring skills for providing corrective feedback to her children when they behaved in ways that were unacceptable to her. One technique she was urged to consider was "natural consequences" or "logical consequences." These are forms of punishment that largely remove the power element from the equation, and they have a teaching function in that a child will learn from the consequence (rather than from exhortation) why the behavior that precipitated the consequence is wrong.

The two types of consequences can be illustrated by considering what would happen if Peter left his tricycle outside the house in spite of repeated requests to bring it inside. A natural consequence would be to let the tricycle remain outside, where it would get rained on and become so rusty that it would eventually be unusable. Such a consequence, assuming Kathy did not run out and buy a replacement, would teach Peter why leaving the tricycle outside was a bad idea. Because most caregivers are unwilling to allow such a destructive outcome to occur, the next best thing would be a logical conse-quence of locking up the tricycle and not letting Peter use it for a few days.

Although there is some element of power use here, the method still serves a teaching purpose and cuts down on the waste of verbiage that otherwise might ensue (and is likely to be unsuccessful). Natural or logical consequences are often the way rules that are generated in a family or class council are imple-mented. Thus, if a family council generates a rule that all papers, toys, and books left in the living room before bedtime will be placed in a box that cannot be accessed for one week, that would quickly teach the lesson that such things are not to be left lying about, while avoiding the fights and arguments that would otherwise accompany noncompliance with such a rule.

Kathy received a score of medium on the Allow Independence (Tolerance) principle. This was less for any tendency to run too tight a ship than for a tendency to become overly defensive when her children cried or complained. In addition, Kathy tended to get sucked into settling fights between her children, and she would always respond to tattling and other "triangulation games" (where one child uses an adult to gain leverage in exerting power over another child). Obviously, Kathy should intervene whenever one of her children (especially the younger one) becomes physically hurt or endangered, but Dr. Arens advised her to try as much as possible to let her kids work things out on their own. When this was not possible, her role was less to take sides than to model for her children ways of seeking compromise and considering all perspectives.

Cognitive Take on Case 2: Ann Stark

Fifth-grade teacher Ann Stark was always directing verbal abuse at her students and sent many to the principal's office, but she was still unable to maintain control of her classroom. After a frightening incident in which she was physically confronted and verbally abused by her students, Mrs. Stark asked for help from Dr. Jane Arens, a Cognitively oriented discipline expert.

Dr. Arens spent some time observing the classroom and was struck by the degree to which Mrs. Stark became involved in power struggles with her students. She would attempt to impose her will on students and they would fight back, often in subtle ways, typically by stopping the offending behavior for a while and then defying her later. Mrs. Stark's style was very autocratic, and she expected students to ask her permission before they did almost anything.

Analysis. Mrs. Stark's discipline profile for the Cognitive principles is shown in Figure 5.11. She scores low on Encourage Participation (the Cognitive principle for Warmth) and Allow Independence (the Cognitive principle for Tolerance) and medium on Inform Why (the Cognitive principle for Influence). The low scores speak for themselves, in light of Mrs. Stark's steady stream of autocratic and demeaning reprimands and punishments for even minor infractions. Because she does set limits, Mrs. Stark receives a higher score on Inform Why (Influence). The score on this domain is only medium, rather than high, because much of the time her punishments are arbitrary, without any justification beyond "Because I said so."

This profile indicates that working with Mrs. Stark will be something of a demolition project, because she needs a pretty radical overhaul in her whole

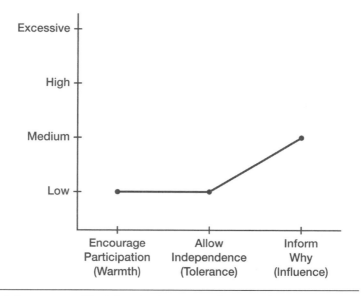

FIGURE 5.11 Discipline Profile for Ann Stark: Cognitive Principles

approach toward interacting with students. Given the disastrous history of mutual acrimony with the current class, one wonders if it would not be better for her to just get through the current school year as well as possible and then begin work in earnest during the summer, with an eye toward implementing a totally new approach during the next school year.

Intervention. For Mrs. Stark to become a successful teacher in the realm of discipline, it was clear she would need to radically change her attitude toward children and her ideas about how to maintain authority and respect in her classroom. The biggest challenge for Dr. Arens was to get Mrs. Stark to buy into the notion that the best way to achieve her goal of having control over her students is to give up trying so hard to control them. In other words, Mrs. Stark would have to come to understand that she cannot win a continual power struggle with children (as her recent experience with her class should have taught her).

Dr. Arens hoped that Mrs. Stark would come to understand that a more relaxed and democratically run classroom is the key to gaining the respect and compliance of her students. So the task for Dr. Arens was basically to win Mrs. Stark over to a different philosophy of child discipline. Obviously, that was a tall order, given that being tough and confrontational toward children was so ingrained in Mrs. Stark's personality and value system.

Dr. Arens suggested that a weekly class council meeting would be a good way for Mrs. Stark's students to feel less alienated in her classroom and to achieve a better understanding of her needs and perspectives, and vice versa. Such a meeting should be run democratically, without fear of criticism or punishment of opinions expressed. Rules developed by consensus (except any that would violate state laws or school policies) would be adopted and enforced, with any needed changes in implementation saved for the next council meeting. Such an approach would go far toward raising Mrs. Stark's low score on Encourage Participation (Warmth).

Another way of bringing up Mrs. Stark's score on the Warmth domain would be for her to do less discouraging and much more encouraging, not just through participation in rule setting but in general. Rather than always seeing the glass as half empty, Mrs. Stark was urged to start seeing it as half full and to do far more to create an atmosphere in which her messages could be characterized as positive rather than negative.

To create a happier and more open atmosphere in the classroom (as well as an environment more conducive to learning), Dr. Arens urged Mrs. Stark to think of some creative ways of implementing the principle of Allow Independence (Tolerance). Mrs. Stark came up with several ideas, most of which involved a shift from the top-down teaching methods she had been using exclusively. Among these ideas were (1) greater use of team and cooperative learning projects, (2) "curriculum compacting" (where students could test out of some lessons, using the freed-up time for individual learning contracts), (3) having students take responsibility for teaching some of the curriculum (e.g., through tutoring other students), and (4) allowing much freer movement around the classroom and the school building.

These changes in her classroom management, along with her personal attitude adjustments, would enable Mrs. Stark to reduce the need for punishment responses and allow her to focus more on matters that are really important. When engaging in corrective feedback, Mrs. Stark was encouraged to always give brief reasons (but not lectures), thus using "induction" rather than "power assertion," and to keep the tone more encouraging of good behavior and less discouraging of bad behavior.

Cognitive Take on Case 3: The Greens

Although most parents would be delighted to have a fifteen-year-old as well behaved as Heather Green, her own parents often found fault with her and sometimes changed their rules in a capricious and arbitrary fashion. When Heather attempted suicide after a conflict arising out of one of these rule

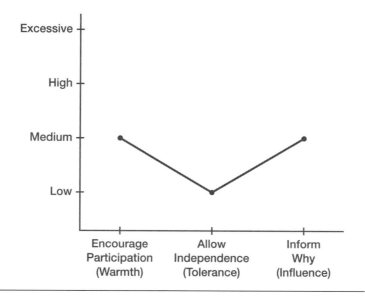

FIGURE 5.12   Discipline Profile for the Greens: Cognitive Principles

changes, the Greens were forced to consult with Dr. Jane Arens, a Cognitively oriented discipline expert.

Dr. Arens interviewed the family in her office and arranged to spend some time in their home. What was striking about this family was the degree of what family therapists call "enmeshment," a fuzzing of the boundaries between family members such that few areas of functioning are considered private or off-limits for other members to comment on.

This lack of respect for the autonomy of family members was especially noticeable with respect to Heather, the Greens' only child. Her political opinions, lifestyle choices (hairstyle, clothing, music, etc.), friends, and career interests were considered fair game for comment by her parents, and much of that commentary was of a disapproving nature. When Heather would resist, her parents would often act hurt, talk about how disrespectful she was being, and give Heather the impression that she was a selfish child for talking back to them. It was apparent to Dr. Arens that this enmeshment was very damaging to Heather's sense of well-being and needed to be the focus of her work with the family.

Analysis. The Greens' discipline profile for the Cognitive principles is shown in Figure 5.12. They score medium on Encourage Participation (the Cognitive

principle for Warmth) and Inform Why (the Cognitive principle for Influence) and low on Allow Independence (the Cognitive principle for Tolerance).
Thus, while they are more or less within the normal range (but needing a little
work) on the domains of Warmth and Influence, they are clearly deficient on
Tolerance. The low Tolerance score supports Dr. Arens's opinion that the family is enmeshed, as enmeshment describes a family pattern characterized by a
lack of respect for the autonomy and independence of one or more members.

The Greens' discipline profile, in conjunction with Heather's suicide gesture, suggests that the task for these parents (unlike the caregivers in the other
two cases) is not so much to socialize their daughter into becoming a well-
behaved person as it is to moderate their own actions as her caregivers. In fact,
Heather is quite well behaved, which suggests that the Greens have done a
good job in terms of helping her understand and accommodate to the needs
of others. Rather, the task for the Greens is to become more attuned to Heather's needs, particularly her emotional needs, and to loosen the strings and
allow her greater freedom to become her own person.

The case of the Green family also offers some cultural lessons, as there are
societies (e.g., some Asian and Middle Eastern countries) where adolescent
and adult children, particularly if they are female, are expected to abide completely by parental expectations, however unfair they might seem to the child.
I am not attempting to pass judgment on such cultures, but I do wish to state
my belief that positive mental health, even in very restrictive societies, cannot
develop if a child is treated solely as if his interests or desires do not matter. If
Mr. and Mrs. Green love their child, as they obviously do, then they need to
learn that Heather's emotional (and even continued physical) well-being
requires them to factor her need for autonomy into their discipline equation.

Intervention. As is always the case with the Cognitive approach (and with the
Affective and Behavioral approaches), Dr. Arens gave the Greens the full discipline curriculum, involving an emphasis on all three principles. This is partly
because these principles are coordinated systems, and challenging discipline
situations cannot typically be addressed adequately with emphasis on only one
domain. Another reason is that few parents or teachers need help in only one
area, and that was certainly true of the Greens. Although their most dramatic
deficiency was with respect to the Allow Independence (Tolerance) principle,
their medium scores on Inform Why (Influence) and Encourage Participation
(Warmth) suggested that they could benefit from information about those
principles as well.

Dr. Arens encouraged the Greens to institute a weekly family council as a
way to provide a forum in which Heather's needs and feelings, as well as those

of her parents, could be put on the table in a spirit of compromise and mutual listening. Gradually, Mr. and Mrs. Green accommodated to the fact that their daughter was no longer a little girl and that they would have to trust her good judgment rather than try to act themselves to protect her from all risks, real or imagined, that she would eventually have to face in becoming a competent adult.

Summary

This chapter demonstrates that the Affective, Behavioral, and Cognitive discipline approaches—as illustrated in the analyses and interventions by Drs. Jones, Smith, and Arens—share many similarities. A competent therapist, working (as is typically the case) within only one of the approaches, could achieve very positive changes for the effectiveness of the caregivers, for the happiness and comportment of the children, and for the health and harmony of the family (or classroom) system. While the three discipline principles within each approach are designed to work together as a complete package, the intervention agent must take into account the caregiver's skill in applying each of the specific principles. The discipline profile is an effective tool for identifying these individual strengths and weaknesses. With a two-pronged approach—applying the complete package, along with particular attention to specific areas of weakness—a well-executed discipline intervention can be highly effective in bringing about needed improvements.

The real strength of the ABC Model of Discipline, however, lies in showing how the three approaches can be integrated fully, thus allowing the caregiver to draw from all nine of the principles. In the remainder of this book, I demonstrate how the three approaches can be combined, and I illustrate how caregivers can use the entire ABC model in addressing a wide variety of discipline situations.

6

The ABC Model of Discipline

Linking Domains, Principles, and Outcomes

I n the chapters leading up to this one, I have systematically built the framework of the ABC Model of Discipline—from its foundation in the Warmth, Tolerance, and Influence domains of caregiving to its ultimate goals in fostering long-term social competence outcomes of Happiness, Boldness, and Niceness in children. I have described in detail the ABCs of the model: the Affective approach, the Behavioral approach, and the Cognitive approach. For each approach, I have reviewed psychological underpinnings and elucidated three principles designed to link the discipline domains with the desired long-term outcomes while promoting harmony in family and school settings along the way. Through numerous case studies, I have illustrated the approaches in action.

In this chapter, I begin with an overview of the foregoing discussions of the components and go on to describe the full extent of the ABC Model of Discipline as a framework supporting effective discipline in the short term and development of socially competent adults in the long term. In the next chapter, the integration process continues, as the principles are recast in the form of a set of specific techniques for applying the model.

Nine Critical Elements

The existing discipline literature—both popular and scientific—draws on three schools of psychological thought, which I term the "Affective," "Behavioral," and "Cognitive" approaches. Most discipline guidance falls into one of these categories, though proponents do not always make their theoretical underpinnings clear. The central premise of this book is that the most effective discipline can be achieved through a *combination* of these approaches, hence the "ABC" in the name of the model I present—the ABC Model of Discipline. I believe that each of the three approaches can be understood in terms of three core principles, and that application of these principles supports a caregiver in performing competently in each of three key domains of discipline, which I call "Warmth," "Tolerance," and "Influence." Further, these core principles foster three desired long-term goals for development of social competence in children—outcomes I term "Happiness," "Boldness," and "Niceness."

The nine principles in the ABC model are portrayed in Figure 6.1, grouped under their associated discipline approaches. Later figures in this chapter will group the elements of the model in various other ways designed to help the reader fully understand the connections among domains, principles, and outcomes. These diagrams illustrate the integrated and coherent nature of the ABC Model of Discipline.

The Three Affective Principles

The Affective approach to discipline is described in detail in Chapter 2. Case studies in application of the approach are provided in Chapter 5, along with a summary figure (Figure 5.1) listing the three principles of the approach and showing how those principles link discipline domains with social competence outcomes. The Affective principles—Show Respect, Accept Feelings, and Assert Needs—are intended to help caregivers become more sensitive to the emotional tone of the child-caregiver relationship. These principles can be described as follows:

- *Show Respect:* "Caregivers should refrain from commenting on a child's character, motives, or overall patterns of behavior, or from otherwise assaulting a child's sense of worth." In other words, caregivers should focus on the specific behavior that is the problem and avoid tearing down or denigrating the child.
- *Accept Feelings:* "Caregivers should provide symbolic outlets for the expression of feelings." The child's behavior may or may not be a problem, but feelings themselves are never a problem. Limits should apply only to overt behaviors stemming from feelings; the child's verbal (i.e., symbolic) expression of displeasure with a situation generally does not qualify as an overt behavior in need of correction.
- *Assert Needs:* "Caregivers should let a child know when he has done something unacceptable." Limit are set on acts that are dangerous or destructive, as well as on those that violate the caregiver's standards of acceptability. The concept of respect is a two-way street that involves not only respecting the child's feelings and needs but also insisting that the child do likewise toward the caregiver.

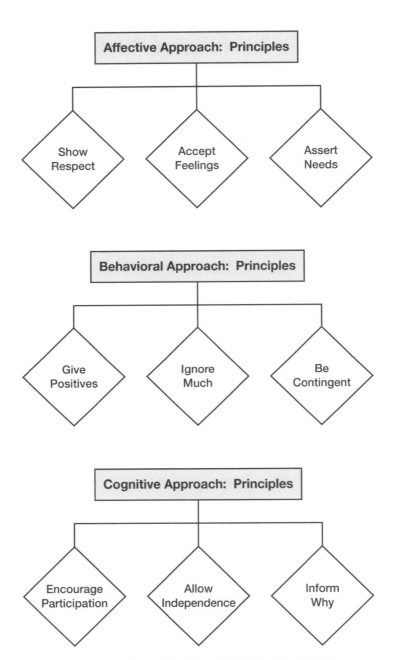

FIGURE 6.1 Principles of the ABC Model of Discipline

The Three Behavioral Principles

The Behavioral approach to discipline is described in detail in Chapter 3. Case studies in application of the approach are provided in Chapter 5, along with a summary figure (Figure 5.5) listing the three principles of the approach and showing how those principles link discipline domains with social competence outcomes. The Behavioral principles—Give Positives, Ignore Much, and Be Contingent—are intended to help caregivers become more skilled in responding to various classes of child behaviors. These principles can be described as follows:

- *Give Positives:* "Caregivers should do a lot more praising than punishing." In quantitative terms, the principle applies in the context of a relatively large unit of time (such as a day), and "a lot" means a ratio of three to five praises (positive utterances or gestures) for each punishment (negative utterances or gestures). A healthy and effective caregiver-child relationship is one in which the atmosphere is decidedly positive.
- *Ignore Much:* "Caregivers should do a lot more ignoring than punishing." In other words, caregivers should ignore things they do not like but can live with and should only punish that relatively small class of behaviors they cannot live with. Again, the principle applies in the context of a relatively large unit of time (such as a day).
- *Be Contingent:* "Caregivers should not punish behaviors they like and should not praise behaviors they dislike." The idea here is not to be slavishly consistent, because caregivers can ignore some disliked behaviors (those they can live with) and are not obligated to praise every desirable behavior every time it occurs (this is a major misunderstanding by many caregivers, who mistakenly think they are supposed to become "perpetual praising machines"). Rather, caregivers need to be aware of whether the child's behavior falls into the desirable or undesirable category, and they need to avoid crossing categories with their responses. Any nonpunishment acknowledgment (such as a stern look) in response to an undesired behavior can be construed by the child as praise, because he has succeeded in getting the caregiver's attention.

The Three Cognitive Principles

The Cognitive approach to discipline is described in detail in Chapter 4. Case studies in application of the approach are provided in Chapter 5, along with a summary figure (Figure 5.9) listing the three principles of the approach and showing how those principles link discipline domains with social competence outcomes. The Cognitive principles—Encourage Participation, Allow Independence, and Inform Why—are intended to avoid top-down power struggles and to help a child take responsibility for his own moral development. These principles can be described as follows:

- *Encourage Participation:* "Caregivers should allow a child to participate in making and applying rules." This is typically done through democratic arrangements, such as family or class councils, as well as techniques such as encouragement.
- *Allow Independence:* "Caregivers should not interfere with the efforts of a child to solve his own problems and to develop his own lifestyle preferences." Caregivers need to resist being drawn into disagreements between children by responding to tattling or participating in other triangulation games (where one child uses an adult to help him exert power over another child). In addition, caregivers should treat each child as an individual who, over time, must be allowed to develop his own ideas.
- *Inform Why:* "Caregivers should help a child understand the reasons underlying rules and expectations." Practical educational techniques such as logical or natural consequences (in which the punishment demonstrates the ramifications of the offense) are often more effective than lectures, particularly with younger children.

Integrating the Principles around the Domains of Discipline

The three domains of discipline that represent the foundation in the model's hierarchy of elements emerged from academic research studies. In these studies, large numbers of caregivers were rated on a number of items in their conduct of discipline, and statistical methods were used to group the items into a small number of factors. Three factors—the domains of discipline— were thus identified: Warmth, Tolerance, and Influence (sometimes termed "Control").

Linking Warmth with Three Principles

The Warmth domain encompasses caregiver actions that create an atmosphere for children that can be described as loving, friendly, and approving. Each of

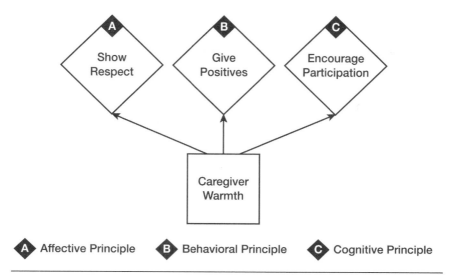

FIGURE 6.2   ABC Principles Associated with the Warmth Domain

the three discipline approaches offers a principle that helps a caregiver maintain discipline in an environment that is rich in Warmth. These principles are shown in Figure 6.2. The Warmth domain is portrayed at the bottom of the figure with arrows radiating upward to the three principles (one from each of the three approaches) above it. The arrows are intended to indicate that the three principles are direct outgrowths of highly effective caregiver performance in the domain of Warmth.

Show Respect and Warmth. The connection between the Affective principle of Show Respect and the discipline domain of Warmth has less to do with encouraging caregivers to be warm than it has to do with discouraging them from being cold or hostile. A setting in which caregivers very rarely make sarcastic, disparaging, or rejecting comments may or may not display an abundance of Warmth, but it is very unlikely to suffer a deficit of it. Thus, the first Affective principle does contribute to the goal of helping caregivers operate competently in the Warmth domain.

Give Positives and Warmth. The connection between the Behavioral principle of Give Positives and the discipline domain of Warmth flows from the fact that a setting in which caregivers give lots of praise and positive reinforcement, and in which the ratio of praise to punishment is very high (three to five praises for every punishing comment or act), is nothing if not warm. Although behaviorists conceptualize reinforcement in terms of its role in modifying child behavior, there is no question that caregivers who follow the behaviorist prescription for discipline are likely to come across as very warm and loving.

Encourage Participation and Warmth. The connection between the Cognitive principle of Encourage Participation and the discipline domain of Warmth is a little less obvious, but it does exist. When a caregiver allows a child to participate as an equal in discussing, devising, and implementing the rules that govern a family or classroom setting, that caregiver is telling the child, "I respect you and value your views on all matters." Such a stance is a hallmark, I believe, of caregiver Warmth. A second, more obvious, connection to Warmth can be found in the major emphasis in the Cognitive approach on the use of encouragement as a general and frequent form of communication with children.

Encouragement may be seen as a particular (and very careful) type of praise that imparts to a child the notion that he can change, while leaving the motivation to change in the child's own hands. Encouragement is a warm form of caregiver interaction in that it is very empowering and affirmative, in contrast to punishment, which Cognitive theorists see as discouraging and undermining of the child's intrinsic motivation.

Linking Tolerance with Three Principles

The Tolerance domain encompasses caregiver actions that show respect for the autonomy of children and give them room for expression, exploration, and freedom from excessive adult intrusiveness. Each of the three discipline approaches offers a principle that helps a caregiver maintain discipline while exercising Tolerance (see Figure 6.3).

Accept Feelings and Tolerance. The connection between the Affective principle of Accept Feelings and the discipline domain of Tolerance is fairly obvious. When a caregiver accepts an expression of feelings by a child, especially when the feeling is one that the caregiver may not share (or particularly welcome), she is communicating to the child that he is entitled to have an internal life that is his own. It is a way of saying to the child, "I am me, and you are you, and you do not require my permission to have your own thoughts, feelings, and values." This principle may not cover the entire spectrum of Tolerance, but it certainly goes a long way toward establishing a setting (home, classroom, etc.) in which Tolerance is practiced.

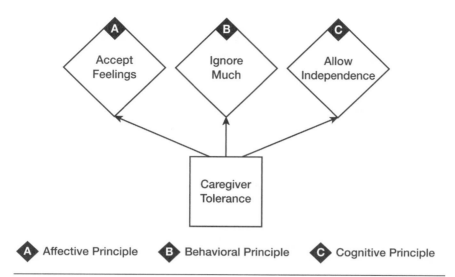

FIGURE 6.3 ABC Principles Associated with the Tolerance Domain

Ignore Much and Tolerance. The connection between the Behavioral principle of Ignore Much and the discipline domain of Tolerance is also obvious. A caregiver who does a great deal of ignoring, and who chooses not to comment on or to punish actions or verbalizations that she may not like but can live with, is a caregiver who comes across as quite tolerant. Although behaviorists do not put a specific emphasis on tolerating expressions of affect, many actions that behaviorists consider ignorable (whining, diversionary tactics, etc.) are behaviors that could be considered symbolic rather than overt expressions of affect. The Ignore Much principle is broader than the Accept Feelings principle, however, in that it also covers many mild forms of overt misbehavior. Although behaviorists do not characterize the Ignore Much principle in terms of promoting caregiver Tolerance (they prefer to characterize it as a tool that contributes to shaping behavior), there is no question that a caregiver who follows the Behavioral discipline approach is one who does a great deal of tolerating.

Allow Independence and Tolerance. The connection between the Cognitive principle of Allow Independence and the discipline domain of Tolerance reflects the fact that the Cognitive approach places a great deal of emphasis on promoting self-reliance, autonomy, and a unique identity within children. It would be difficult to find any other explanation for the Allow Independence principle than as a means to make caregivers more tolerant.

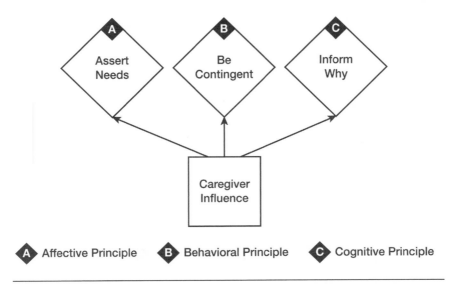

FIGURE 6.4 ABC Principles Associated with the Influence Domain

Linking Influence with Three Principles

The Influence domain encompasses caregiver actions that set limits on unacceptable child behavior and ensure that dangerous, destructive, or otherwise inappropriate acts are not tolerated. Each of the three discipline approaches offers a principle that helps a caregiver exercise Influence in an effective and controlled manner (see Figure 6.4).

Assert Needs and Influence. The connection between the Affective principle of Assert Needs and the discipline domain of Influence stems from the fact that this principle essentially says to caregivers, "You are an adult, so act like one. Don't think that you can let a child do whatever he wants, whenever he wants to do it." It encourages the caregiver to decide what her expectations are regarding behaviors that she will not tolerate and to understand that not communicating those expectations is doing a disservice both to herself and to the child. This principle is a way of motivating caregivers to be more in control, by helping them understand that exerting some degree of Influence is both necessary and good.

Be Contingent and Influence. The connection between the Behavioral principle of Be Contingent and the discipline domain of Influence extends from the purpose of the principle, which is to help caregivers become more skilled and effective in influencing the direction of child conduct. This is accomplished by reinforcing only desired behaviors and by punishing (when they are not ignored) only undesired behaviors. The underlying idea of the principle is that influencing a child requires a significant degree of awareness by a caregiver of how her responses move the child toward or away from a desired end point. Thus, the Be Contingent principle serves as a means for making a caregiver better able to modify child behavior and to perform more effectively in the domain of Influence.

Inform Why and Influence. The connection between the Cognitive principle of Inform Why and the discipline domain of Influence reflects the fact that this principle encourages caregivers to give, or to engineer, responses that let a child know the rationale underlying certain family, classroom, or societal rules and expectations. Particular emphasis is placed on helping a child empathize with others whose rights, property, or feelings are affected by the child's actions. The idea is that mobilizing the child's empathy and judgment will help him become better behaved. Certainly, it is reasonable to view this principle as a vehicle for helping caregivers exercise resolve and good judgment in influencing the behavior of children.

Integrating the Principles around the Desired Outcomes of Discipline

Discipline has two sets of purposes: short-term and long-term. The short-term purposes of discipline are to change a specific behavior of a child from "unacceptable" to "acceptable" and to restore the balance in a caregiver-child system (family, classroom, etc.) from one of conflict to one of harmony. The long-term purposes of discipline are to help children become socially competent and well-adjusted individuals, both when they are young and as they grow into adulthood. Both of these goals are very important, but building social competence is probably more important, especially given that it incorporates the first purpose, because competent children are less likely to behave in ways that are bothersome to adults and that call forth discipline responses.

I discuss using the nine principles to attain the short-term purposes of securing compliance and restoring harmony in the next chapter. Because of the critical place of long-term social competence outcomes in the hierarchy of the ABC model, I devote this space to discussing the links between the nine discipline principles and the long-term outcomes of Happiness, Boldness, and Niceness.

In asserting that discipline influences social competence, it is necessary to say something more about the concept. Social competence (and many other psychological concepts) has proven somewhat difficult to define. One reason is that social competence can be approached either in terms of outcomes or in terms of inputs, and some authors get the two mixed up. A social competence outcome occurs when someone succeeds in a socially valued and age-relevant role, such as earning a high school diploma or landing a job. A social competence input refers to the behaviors or traits, such as cooperativeness, that contribute to those outcomes.

Many kinds of specific behaviors or accomplishments fall under the outcome rubric of social competence; those are not at issue here. It is the input forms of social competence that factor into the ABC model as desired outcomes of discipline, because these are the forms that set the stage for what the child will become in life. Three broad categories of social competence inputs have been identified, and my colleagues and I (e.g., S. Greenspan and Driscoll 1997) have termed these "Temperament," "Character," and "Social Intelligence."

Temperament refers to one's degree of emotional, motivational, and attentional stability, as reflected in the ability to sustain effort, to take things in stride (without flying off the handle), and to maintain a fairly consistent positive mood. Because the attentional component of Temperament is largely affected by innate biological factors (such as genes or the presence or absence of brain damage), the aspect of Temperament featured in the ABC model is mainly focused on positive mood and emotional self-regulation. The common term "Happiness" subsumes many of these qualities, and I use that term to depict the Temperament component of social competence in the ABC model. Clearly, Happiness is a major goal of discipline, as almost any caregiver, when asked what she wishes for a particular child, will offer "to grow up to be a happy person" as her first response.

Character has two subtypes. The first refers to the ability to conform one's behavior to societal expectations and to generally behave in a way that others view positively. In the ABC model, I have reframed this form of Character as "Niceness." A nice child is one whom other children, and adults, want to be around, while a nasty child is one whom others view negatively and wish to avoid, or worse. Clearly, influencing children to be nice is a major goal of discipline. In fact, it is probably the most explicitly emphasized purpose, as evidenced by the fact that dictionary definitions of parent and teacher discipline commonly include phrases such as "maintaining order" and "forming proper conduct."

The other subtype of Character is what I term "Boldness" (the third competence outcome in the ABC model). In this context, Boldness is the ability to assert one's will in situations where to do otherwise would make one vulnerable. It also reflects the development of a unique identity and set of lifestyle preferences. Although excessive Boldness (i.e., when it is not paired with Nice-ness) could make a person insufferable, there is no question that most caregiv-ers want children to grow into adults who are not shrinking violets—that is, who can make their presence known—and, most importantly, who possess the ability to say "no" in situations where others would mislead or coerce them down dangerous or undesired paths. This is an ideal outcome of discipline that is not always articulated by discipline experts (who often portray discipline as solely a matter of imposing one's will on a child). Aside from moral consider-ations (most readers would probably agree that it is wrong to squash a child's identity), caregivers who do not allow a child sufficient room for autonomy are not likely to be successful in the short term (the child is likely to rebel) or in the long term (the child is not likely to be either happy or bold).

A third input form of social competence has been very important in my own research, but I do not emphasize it in the ABC model. This form is Social Intelligence, and it reflects the extent to which a child or adult is "with it" or "out of it" in terms of his awareness and understanding of people and their behavior. Social Intelligence is obviously a significant contributor to success or failure in various social roles and situations. In terms of the ABC model, how-ever, I prefer to view Social Intelligence as a "mediating variable" that operates behind the scenes. Thus, I have not included it in the formal framework of the model.

The notion of social competence used in the model is represented in the three long-term outcomes of Happiness (emotional stability and posi-tive mood), Boldness (autonomous functioning), and Niceness (kindness and appropriateness). In the next three sections, I briefly describe the principles of the ABC model as they contribute to the development of these long-term social competence outcomes.

I want to emphasize that this linking of discipline principles with desired child characteristics is not meant to suggest that children can be programmed to turn out in a specific way. Rather, it is intended to further illuminate the nature and purposes of the various discipline principles and techniques.

Linking Happiness with Three Principles

In the context of the ABC model, Happiness is a long-term social competence outcome that reflects the ability of a child to maintain a generally positive mood, even in the face of occasional setbacks, and to feel good about himself and his life. Each of the three discipline approaches offers a principle that has the effect of helping a child grow into a contented and resilient adult. These principles are shown in Figure 6.5. The Happiness outcome is portrayed at the top of the figure with arrows radiating upward from the three principles (one

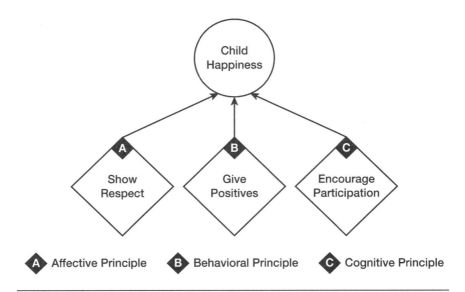

FIGURE 6.5   ABC Principles Contributing to the Outcome of Happiness

from each of the three approaches) below it. The arrows are intended to indicate that the three principles operate in direct support of the social competence outcome of Happiness.

Show Respect and Happiness. The link between the Affective principle of Show Respect and the desired outcome of Happiness is clear. A steady diet of put-downs, sarcasm, and verbal abuse is likely to undermine a child's self-confidence and cause him to become an unhappy person. The intent of the Show Respect principle is to help a caregiver understand that discipline is about changing behavior in a way that does not make a child feel worthless.

Give Positives and Happiness. The link between the Behavioral principle of Give Positives and the desired outcome of Happiness is also clear. A child who gets little or no praise and a steady diet of punishment and criticism is very unlikely to be (or to grow up to be) a happy person. An effect of the Give Positives principle (which calls for a ratio of three to five praises for each punishment over the course of a day) is to create an environment in which children feel good about themselves and about life and are better able to cope with occasional setbacks.

Encourage Participation and Happiness. The link between the Cognitive principle of Encourage Participation and the desired outcome of Happiness

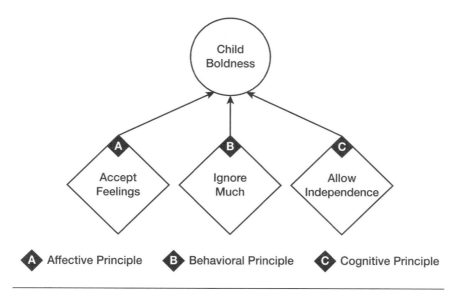

FIGURE 6.6   ABC Principles Contributing to the Outcome of Boldness

may not be self-evident, but I believe it does exist. According to Cognitive discipline theorists, children have a basic need to feel important and in control of their lives. Satisfying this need by giving the child a meaningful role in the governance of the family or classroom unit, for example, is likely to foster happiness, whereas frustrating this need (e.g., through an authoritarian discipline style) is likely to foster unhappiness and resentment.

The intent of the Encourage Participation principle is to help a caregiver understand that discipline must be carried out in a manner that helps a child feel the discipline is not an arbitrary exercise of adult power. By putting so much emphasis on encouragement as a general and very frequent form of caregiver communication, Cognitive theorists aim to help children feel more optimistic and confident in their ability to deal with various life challenges. Optimism, the belief that one can cope with reality however complex and challenging it might be, is an obvious part of the human trait labeled Happiness.

Linking Boldness with Three Principles

In the context of the ABC model, Boldness is a long-term social competence outcome that reflects the ability of a child to assert himself when necessary and to maintain a clear sense of his own preferences and needs. Each of the three discipline approaches offers a principle that has the effect of helping a child grow into a confident and independent adult (see Figure 6.6).

Accept Feelings and Boldness. The link between the Affective principle of Accept Feelings and the desired outcome of Boldness is fairly evident. Few things are as likely to stifle a child's development of self-awareness and self-expression as being denied the opportunity to explore and to communicate how he feels about things. The intent of the Accept Feelings principle is to show caregivers that they can set limits on behaviors without setting limits on the expression of the child's thoughts or feelings.

Ignore Much and Boldness. The link between the Behavioral principle of Ignore Much and the desired outcome of Boldness also does not need much explanation. A setting in which everything is commented on or otherwise responded to is one in which the child does not have much freedom to be himself. An effect of the Ignore Much principle is to give the child a fair amount of room for autonomy.

Allow Independence and Boldness. The link between the Cognitive principle of Allow Independence and the desired outcome of Boldness also is evident. A child who is prevented from having sufficient autonomy in exploring his preferences and values is likely to be inhibited, uncertain, and unable to assert himself when necessary. The intent of this principle (which is probably the one most central to the Cognitive approach) is to help a caregiver understand that promotion of Boldness (i.e., autonomous behavior) is a key aspect of the discipline process.

Linking Niceness with Three Principles

In the context of the ABC model, Niceness is a long-term social competence outcome that reflects the extent to which a child is disposed to abide by reasonable rules, to care about others, and to behave in a way that causes others to like him. Each of the three discipline approaches offers a principle that has the effect of helping a child grow into an adult who is respectful of others and is a pleasure to be around (see Figure 6.7).

Assert Needs and Niceness. There is a clear connection between the Affective principle of Assert Needs and the desired outcome of Niceness. Children raised in an environment of extreme permissiveness (such as those who experience a total absence of limit-setting by their caregivers) have a great deal of difficulty coming to understand that they live in a world where the needs and feelings of other people count as much as their own. The intent of the Assert Needs principle is to convey to caregivers that being a good caregiver is not

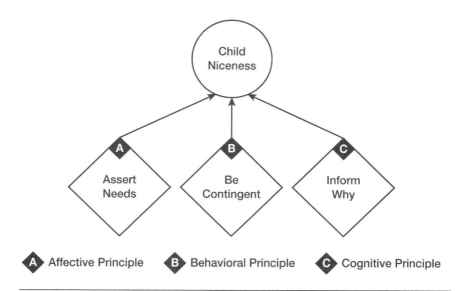

FIGURE 6.7 ABC Principles Contributing to the Outcome of Niceness

just a matter of making a child happy but also involves educating him about the importance of being a kind, considerate, and well-behaved person.

Be Contingent and Niceness. The link between the Behavioral principle of Be Contingent and the desired outcome of Niceness may not be as evident but nonetheless is very strong. When a caregiver does not clearly differentiate between desired and undesired actions (e.g., when she praises bad behavior and punishes good behavior), the child becomes confused as to what is expected and may go down the path of misbehavior under the mistaken impression that it is preferred. An effect of the Be Contingent principle is to help a caregiver become more skilled in shaping nice behavior and guiding a child to social acceptability.

Inform Why and Niceness. The link between the Cognitive principle of Inform Why and the desired outcome of Niceness is obvious, but it must be pointed out that in the Cognitive discipline literature, informing is to be done more through subtle manipulation of consequences than through direct verbal exhortation, which often can turn into a put-down or a power struggle. Disciplining a child through physical intimidation or by statements such as "Because I said so" is not likely to contribute to the development of internalized societal values and sensitivity toward the needs and feelings of others.

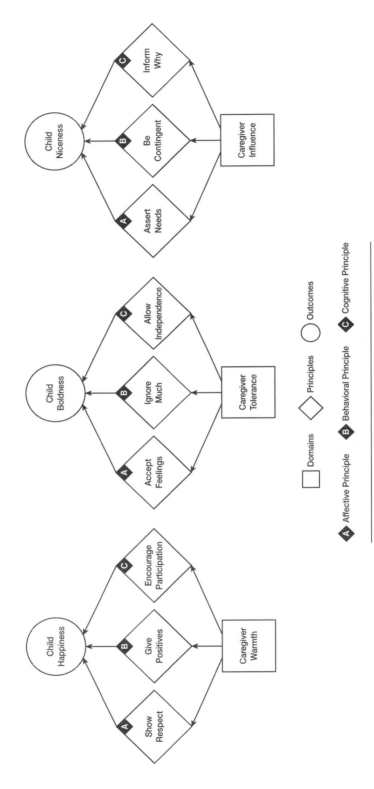

FIGURE 6.8 The ABC Model of Discipline

The intent of the Inform Why principle is to help a caregiver understand that the best way to influence a child to be a responsible person is to help him learn and display empathy for and understanding of others.

The Power of ABC:
Integrating Domains, Principles, and Outcomes

At last, the essence of the ABC model emerges as a framework that empowers the caregiver to take full advantage of the complementarity of the Affective, Behavioral, and Cognitive approaches. The foregoing discussions demonstrate how the nine principles (three from each approach) are integrated hierarchically. Each approach has been shown to have one principle that helps a caregiver perform competently in each of the three domains of discipline: Warmth, Tolerance, and Influence. In addition, these principles have been shown to support three long-term social competence outcomes for children: Happiness, Boldness, and Niceness. Assembling these building blocks (as depicted in Figures 6.2 through 6.7) produces the structure shown in Figure 6.8, which represents the fully integrated network that is the ABC Model of Discipline.

Discussion of the model to this point has focused on the long-term goals of discipline in supporting children in becoming socially competent and well-adjusted individuals, both in their youth and in adulthood. In the next chapter, the emphasis shifts to short-term goals of shaping child behavior to meet standards of acceptability and promoting harmony in family and classroom settings. There I reformulate the nine principles to create an integrated and comprehensive system of specific techniques—a tool kit—that can address virtually any child-rearing challenge while pursuing the long-term goals of Happiness, Boldness, and Niceness.

7

The ABC Tool Kit

Using the Nine Principles
to Deal with Discipline Problems

After criticizing an assortment of writings on the subject of discipline for failing to offer a tool kit to help caregivers implement the ideas expressed, the time has come to present my own tool kit. In this chapter, I describe a set of specific techniques for applying the ABC Model of Discipline. In building the ABC framework around domains of discipline—Warmth, Tolerance, and Influence—I have identified a coherent set of nine principles (three each for the Affective, Behavioral, and Cognitive approaches) that support short-term solutions to behavioral challenges and long-term social competence outcomes of Happiness, Boldness, and Niceness. Based on these nine principles, I offer eighteen concrete techniques that can be applied in a mix and match fashion to create a rich and flexible discipline environment that is not restricted to any one particular school of psychological thought.

The Situation-Specific Nature of Discipline

The principles of the ABC model work only if the caregiver who applies them has both (1) a reasonably good understanding of the principles and how to use them and (2) an ability to read child behaviors reasonably well and to know when to apply which principle. This does not require an advanced diploma, or even a course in discipline, but it does require some degree of common sense and at least an average amount of sensitivity toward people and social situations. One of the problems I have with tough-guy authors on child-rearing, such as John Rosemond (whose approach I profile briefly in Chapter 1), is that they give caregivers very general advice, such as "Show the child who is boss," that ignores the real situations that individual caregivers face. To suggest that a single stance—toughness—is appropriate for every situation implies that every child behavior is the same and that every caregiver needs to be tougher. A caregiver who approaches every situation as an opportunity to be coercive is, of course, unlikely to be effective, either in the short term (getting a child to do what she wants) or in the long term (helping the child become socially competent).

Authors writing within all three of the major discipline approaches encourage caregivers to think about what type of situation they are facing before deciding how to respond. Affectively oriented authors encourage caregivers to determine whether they have a problem and/or the child has a problem and to respond with an acknowledgment of the child's problem, even when asserting a limit to relieve their own problem. Behaviorally oriented authors encourage caregivers to determine whether a child's behavior is praiseable, ignorable, or punishable and then to respond appropriately. Cognitively oriented authors encourage caregivers to determine whether a child's behavior is indicative of a brewing power struggle and to avoid the fight by selecting consequences that flow logically from the behavior rather than assertively from the caregiver's size or status.

Various formulas and teaching devices have been developed to help caregivers become better at making these kinds of discriminations and more proficient in applying the various discipline principles. Thomas Gordon's decision window is such a device, as are the discrimination training and bug-in-the-ear methods behaviorists employ. A major purpose of all of these methods is to break the caregiver's tendency to rely on habitual responses and to help her become more sensitive to the meaning underlying the child's behavior and, thus, better able to respond appropriately.

Turning Theory into Practice: Applying ABC Principles to Challenging Situations

In pages that follow, I explore specific application of the nine ABC principles in pursuit of the short-term objective of dealing with challenging behaviors. An advantage of working with the entire ABC model over adhering strictly to any one of its three constituent approaches is that the caregiver has more principles to draw upon. Figure 7.1 lists two techniques for each of the nine principles that make up the ABC model—in essence, this is the model's tool kit. In the figure, and throughout this chapter, the techniques are presented in the form of succinct and concrete operational statements directed to the caregiver. The foregoing chapters have focused on development and application of the ABC model in an approach-centric fashion. Figure 7.1 represents a reshuffling of the principles out of their approach groupings (Affective, Behavioral, Cognitive) and into new groupings by discipline domain (Warmth, Tolerance,

Warmth-Related Principles

A. **Show Respect** principle (Affective approach)

   1. Do not comment on the child's character, motives, or overall patterns of behavior

   2. Use I-messages ("I feel x when you do y because z") when setting limits

B. **Give Positives** principle (Behavioral approach)

   1. During any day, do much more praising than punishing

   2. Praise behaviors that you like and would like to see more of

C. **Encourage Participation** principle (Cognitive approach)

   1. Use problem-solving (compromise) communications and meetings

   2. Use discipline methods that are encouraging, not discouraging

Tolerance-Related Principles

A. **Accept Feelings** principle (Affective approach)

   1. Set limits on actions but not on underlying feelings

   2. Use active listening ("You feel x about y") when the child is upset

B. **Ignore Much** principle (Behavioral approach)

   1. During any day, do a lot more ignoring than punishing

   2. Ignore behaviors that you do not like but can live with

C. **Allow Independence** principle (Cognitive approach)

   1. Treat the child as an individual and do not make comparisons

   2. Do not blur adult-child boundaries (e.g., through guilt or love withdrawal)

Influence-Related Principles

A. **Assert Needs** principle (Affective approach)

   1. Set limits on acts that are dangerous, destructive, or otherwise unacceptable

   2. Be aware of when an act is problem for the child as well as for you

B. **Be Contingent** principle (Behavioral approach)

   1. Do not punish desirable behaviors or praise undesirable behaviors

   2. Be aware of which behaviors are praiseable, ignorable, and punishable

C. **Inform Why** principle (Cognitive approach)

   1. Give the child reasons (e.g., explain how his acts affect others) when setting limits

   2. Arrange consequences that have logical (i.e., educational) connection to the child's act

FIGURE 7.1   Tool Kit for the ABC Model of Discipline: Techniques for Applying the Nine Principles

WA1	Warmth domain Affective approach Technique 1 Show Respect principle Do not comment on the child's character, motives, or overall patterns of behavior	WA2	Warmth domain Affective approach Technique 2 Show Respect principle Use I-messages ("I feel x when you do y because z") when setting limits
WB1	Warmth domain Behavioral approach Technique 1 Give Positives principle During any day, do much more praising than punishing	WB2	Warmth domain Behavioral approach Technique 2 Give Positives principle Praise behaviors that you like and would like to see more of
WC1	Warmth domain Cognitive approach Technique 1 Encourage Participation principle Use problem-solving (compromise) communi- cations and meetings	WC2	Warmth domain Cognitive approach Technique 2 Encourage Participation principle Use discipline methods that are encouraging, not discouraging

FIGURE 7.2 ABC Principles for Warmth: Techniques and Notation

Influence). This new organization demonstrates how easy (and beneficial) it can be to mix and match techniques across the "approach divide." Thus, in one situation, a caregiver might choose to pair an Affective technique with a Behavioral technique, while in another situation she might use a different combination.

A simple notational system provides another way of depicting—and remembering—the nine principles and eighteen techniques listed in Figure 7.1. In this system, each discipline technique is identified by combining three symbols: two letters followed by a number. The first letter indicates the domain (W for Warmth, T for Tolerance, I for Influence), the second letter indicates the approach (A for Affective, B for Behavioral, C for Cognitive), and the number indicates the technique (1 or 2). Thus, for example, WA2 specifies the second technique listed under the Affective principle for Warmth. This notation is illustrated in Figures 7.2, 7.3, and 7.4, with one figure addressing

TA1	Tolerance domain Affective approach Technique 1 Accept Feelings principle Set limits on actions but not on underlying feelings	**TA2**	Tolerance domain Affective approach Technique 2 Accept Feelings principle Use active listening ("You feel *x* about *y*") when the child is upset
TB1	Tolerance domain Behavioral approach Technique 1 Ignore Much principle During any day, do a lot more ignoring than punishing	**TB2**	Tolerance domain Behavioral approach Technique 2 Ignore Much principle Ignore behaviors that you do not like but can live with
TC1	Tolerance domain Cognitive approach Technique 1 Allow Independence principle Treat the child as an individual and do not make comparisons	**TC2**	Tolerance domain Cognitive approach Technique 2 Allow Independence principle Do not blur adult-child boundaries (e.g., through guilt or love withdrawal)

FIGURE 7.3 ABC Principles for Tolerance: Techniques and Notation

Warmth techniques, one addressing Tolerance techniques, and one addressing Influence techniques. The complete system is summarized in Figure 7.5.

Figure 7.2 displays the six techniques for attaining competence in the Warmth domain of discipline: two each for the Affective approach, the Behavioral approach, and the Cognitive approach. The first row shows techniques associated with Show Respect, the Affective principle for Warmth: (WA1) "Do not comment on the child's character, motives, or overall patterns of behavior," and (WA2) "Use I-messages ('I feel *x* when you do *y* because *z*') when setting limits." The second row shows techniques associated with Give Positives, the Behavioral principle for Warmth: (WB1) "During any day, do much more praising than punishing," and (WB2) "Praise behaviors that you like and would like to see more of." The third row shows techniques associated with Encourage Participation, the Cognitive principle for Warmth: (WC1) "Use problem-solving (compromise) communications and meetings," and (WC2) "Use discipline methods that are encouraging, not discouraging."

IA1	Influence domain Affective approach Technique 1 Assert Needs principle Set limits on acts that are dangerous, destructive, or otherwise unacceptable	**IA2**	Influence domain Affective approach Technique 2 Assert Needs principle Be aware of when an act is a problem for the child as well as for you
IB1	Influence domain Behavioral approach Technique 1 Be Contingent principle Do not punish desirable behaviors or praise undesirable behaviors	**IB2**	Influence domain Behavioral approach Technique 2 Be Contingent principle Be aware of which behaviors are praiseable, ignorable, and punishable
IC1	Influence domain Cognitive approach Technique 1 Inform Why principle Give the child reasons (e.g., explain how his acts affect others) when setting limits	**IC2**	Influence domain Cognitive approach Technique 2 Inform Why principle Arrange consequences that have logical (i.e., educational) connections to the child's act

FIGURE 7.4 ABC Principles for Influence: Techniques and Notation

Figure 7.3 displays the six techniques for the domain of caregiver Tolerance. The first row shows techniques associated with Accept Feelings, the Affective principle for Tolerance: (TA1) "Set limits on actions but not on underlying feelings," and (TA2) "Use active listening ('You feel *x* about *y*') when the child is upset." The second row shows techniques associated with Ignore Much, the Behavioral principle for Tolerance: (TB1) "During any day, do a lot more ignoring than punishing," and (TB2) "Ignore behaviors that you do not like but can live with." The third row shows techniques associated with Allow Independence, the Cognitive principle for Tolerance: (TC1) "Treat the child as an individual and do not make comparisons," and (TC2) "Do not blur adult-child boundaries (e.g., through guilt or love withdrawal)."

Figure 7.4 displays the six techniques for the Influence domain of caregiver discipline. The first row shows techniques associated with Assert Needs, the Affective principle for Influence: (IA1) "Set limits on acts that are dangerous,

Dom	Appr	Tech	Operational Statement of the Technique (Principle)
W	A	1	Do not comment on the child's character, motives, or overall patterns of behavior (Show Respect)
W	A	2	Use I-messages ("I feel x when you do y because z") when setting limits (Show Respect)
W	B	1	During any day, do much more praising than punishing (Give Positives)
W	B	2	Praise behaviors that you like and would like to see more of (Give Positives)
W	C	1	Use problem-solving (compromise) communications and meetings (Encourage Participation)
W	C	2	Use discipline methods that are encouraging, not discouraging (Encourage Participation)
T	A	1	Set limits on actions but not on underlying feelings (Accept Feelings)
T	A	2	Use active listening ("You feel x about y") when the child is upset (Accept Feelings)
T	B	1	During any day, do a lot more ignoring than punishing (Ignore Much)
T	B	2	Ignore behaviors that you do not like but can live with (Ignore Much)
T	C	1	Treat the child as an individual and do not make comparisons (Allow Independence)
T	C	2	Do not blur adult-child boundaries (e.g., through guilt or love withdrawal) (Allow Independence)
I	A	1	Set limits on acts that are dangerous, destructive, or otherwise unacceptable (Assert Needs)
I	A	2	Be aware of when an act is a problem for the child as well as for you (Assert Needs)
I	B	1	Do not punish desirable behaviors or praise undesirable behaviors (Be Contingent)
I	B	2	Be aware of which behaviors are praiseable, ignorable, and punishable (Be Contingent)
I	C	1	Give the child reasons (e.g., explain how his acts affect others) when setting limits (Inform Why)
I	C	2	Arrange consequences that have logical (i.e., educational) connections to the child's act (Inform Why)

W = Warmth Domain   A = Affective Approach   1 = Technique 1
T = Tolerance Domain   B = Behavioral Approach   2 = Technique 2
I = Influence Domain   C = Cognitive Approach

FIGURE 7.5 The Complete Notational System for the ABC Model of Discipline

destructive, or otherwise unacceptable," and (IA2) "Be aware of when an act is a problem for the child as well as for you." The second row shows techniques associated with Be Contingent, the Behavioral principle for Influence: (IB1) "Do not punish desirable behaviors or praise undesirable behaviors," and (IB2) "Be aware of which behaviors are praiseable, ignorable, and punishable." The third row shows techniques associated with Say Why, the Cognitive principle for Influence: (IC1) "Give the child reasons (e.g., explain how his acts affect others) when setting limits," and (IC2) "Arrange consequences that have logical (i.e., educational) connection to the child's act."

Figure 7.5 brings together the information from Figures 7.2, 7.3, and 7.4 into a single chart that illustrates the complete notational system for the ABC model. The balance of this chapter is devoted to illustrating use of the model and the notational system in guiding caregiver responses to various child-rearing challenges and situations. To stimulate the learning process, the discussion is framed as a series of quizzes in which I pose a caregiving problem and invite the reader (before reading my own take on the matter) to come up with an analysis or solution, based if possible on the notational system.

Using the ABC Notational System to Analyze Effective and Ineffective Discipline

I illustrate application of the ABC techniques and use of the notational system by portraying effective and ineffective caregiver responses to challenging child-rearing situations and then describing each response in terms of which of the eighteen techniques listed in Figure 7.5 was used or should have been used. Although a caregiver's overall pattern of discipline (say, across the time frame of a day) should attain balance among the three domains of Warmth, Tolerance, and Influence, such balance is not a concern in the short term. Nevertheless, it is typically the case that an effective response will involve the coordinated use of principles from more than one domain. Thus, for example, when dealing with a situation in which a child is upset about something and acts out unacceptably, an effective caregiver will not just set a limit (Influence) but also will address the underlying feeling (Tolerance).

For each of the cases that follow, I begin by presenting a scenario in which a caregiver was faced with a discipline challenge and then describe how she dealt with it. The first four scenarios involve caregivers who responded effectively; in the next four scenarios, caregivers responded ineffectively. In describing the effective responses, I use the ABC notational system to identify the elements of the caregiver's behavior that are relevant to the success of her response style. For the ineffective responses, I focus on the guidelines in Figure 7.5 that were violated. The description of each scenario is followed by a note encouraging the reader to pause before reading on. My purpose in recommending this pause is to give the reader a chance to reflect on the scenario, and perhaps consult Figure 7.5, before reading on to discover whether his or her analysis is similar to the one that I offer.

Effective Response: Case 1

The first case is drawn from my own life experience a number of years ago and involved myself and my sister's oldest child, Jaron. My nephew, who is now a medical resident, was at that time about five or six years old. Several people, including Jaron, were attending a family event. When we were leaving, my sister offered to give a ride to an elderly aunt. We were short one set of seat belts and someone (not Jaron, who was safely in his car seat) was going to have to sit on another person's lap for the short ride home. Jaron got out of his car seat and announced loudly that everyone in the car was going to have to wear a seat belt. When someone tried to reason with him, he started screaming and would not back down. At that point, the elderly aunt said, "That's all right. I will wait by the side of the road, and you can come back and pick me up after you drop Jaron off at the house." Everyone was prepared to go along with this solution, but I decided to intervene.

I went over to Jaron and asked a series of questions, giving him a brief time to respond to each: "You really want everyone to wear a seat belt, don't you?" "It is important to you that we all follow the law and ride in a safe manner, isn't it?" "It really bothers you when someone rides in the car without wearing a seat belt, doesn't it?" Then I said, "I really admire you for wanting all of us to do the right thing. It's really wonderful that you know what is safe and what is not safe. But it is not fair to Aunt _____ to have to leave her by the side of the road. And the rule is that adults, and not children, get to decide who rides in the car." Then I picked Jaron up and buckled him into his car seat. He made no further objection, and I said, "Thank you, Jaron, for listening to what I had to say."

▷ *Note to the Reader:* Please pause briefly to formulate your own analysis before reading on.

Analysis of Effective Response: Case 1. The first thing to do in analyzing this case is to put aside any moral qualms one might have about modeling non-wearing of seat belts and keep in mind that the main issue here has to do with the inappropriateness of letting a five-year-old child use emotional blackmail to impose his will on a carload of adults. The point of my intervention was to show Jaron that he did not have that power and to model for the other adults a third choice that lies between caving in and using physical force.

This was a fairly standard Affective intervention, employing all three Affective principles. My initial action involved two Tolerance-related techniques. The first, TA2, used active listening, with what some have called "machine-gun reflection" (a string of rapid-fire reflective questions). This had the effect of almost immediately stopping Jaron's crying and carrying on. I also used TA1, setting a limit, but still allowing an outlet for feelings. Influence was exerted through IA1, as I set a limit when Jaron's behavior violated my standards of acceptable conduct. Warmth entered into the mix through WA2, in my use of I-messages, and through WA1, my neutral and nonattacking tone. WB2 was also involved in that I praised Jaron's stated beliefs about the importance of wearing seat belts.

This case nicely illustrates the power of the active listening technique in defusing a conflict that could have escalated into a major scene. By shifting back and forth between (mainly Affective) principles involving all three domains, I was easily able to bring about a satisfactory resolution to this standoff.

Effective Response: Case 2

This case is taken from *Backtalk: Four Steps to Ending Rude Behavior in Your Kids,* by Audrey Ricker and Carolyn Crowder (1998). The case involves Cary (who appears to be a teen) and her mom. When Mom came home from work, Cary informed her in an accusing tone that there was no Crystal Light (a sugar-free soft drink) in the house and demanded to know why her mom had not bought more when she had asked her to. Cary then demanded to know how she could be expected to stick to her diet when her mother could not remember to buy the drink. All this was said in a very snide tone of voice accompanied by much eye rolling and such.

Mom felt irritated but managed to control her temper. She told Cary that she would not be taking her to the mall after dinner to meet her friend as she had earlier agreed to do. She said, "When I feel disrespected, I feel all of my energy getting used up. Because you have used up my energy, I won't be driving you to the mall." Cary started screaming, and Mom ignored it, saying she would go work in the garden if Cary kept screaming. Cary sulked during dinner, and Mom ignored it. After dinner, Cary asked her mother nicely if she would reconsider, but Mom said nothing and went to watch TV. Cary accepted the decision and called her friend to say she would not be coming to the mall.

> *Note to the Reader:* Please pause briefly to formulate your own analysis before reading on.

Analysis of Effective Response: Case 2. A number of principles appear to be applicable to this case, with the mother's intervention appearing to be mostly in the Cognitive mode. First off, Mom had a clear conception that disrespectful back talk was not something she was willing to accept. Two techniques are applicable here: IA1 ("Set limits on acts that are . . . unacceptable") and IB2 ("Be aware of which behaviors are praiseable, ignorable, and punishable").

Mom's punishment was logical and thus educational (IC2, "Arrange consequences with logical . . . connections to the child's act"). In saying "if you make me tired by attacking me, don't expect me to have the energy to drive you," she was conveying a lesson about social reciprocity: "If you expect someone to do you a favor, it is not a good idea to attack the person beforehand."

The thing that was most admirable about Mom's behavior, and most characteristic of the Cognitive approach, is that she refused to get caught up in a power struggle with her daughter. She ignored Cary's screaming (TB2, "Ignore behaviors that you do not like but can live with") and resisted the temptation to throw disparaging insults back at Cary (WA1, "Do not comment on the child's character, motives, or overall patterns of behavior"). Mom admits to one mistake, which was to warn Cary she would leave the room if Cary did not calm down. Such "if" threats are generally ineffective, so caregivers are encouraged to let their contingent acts (IB1 and IC2) and not their threats do their teaching whenever possible. Thus, Mom felt she should have left the room (or not) rather than threaten to do so.

Effective Response: Case 3

This case is taken from *Liberated Parents/Liberated Children*, by Adele Faber and Elaine Mazlish (1975). The book tells the story of a parent support group led by Haim Ginott. The case involved Nell, a single-parent member of the group, and Ken, her son. Nell viewed Ken as an irresponsible kid who was always forgetting things and always managing to mess up in school and elsewhere. Ken shared this assessment and lacked self-confidence. Nell's habitual response to Ken's failures was to berate him in an effort to change his behavior. One day, Ginott was talking to the group about the importance of realistic praise (using I-messages), and Nell said she could not think of anything to praise in Ken. Ginott told her to treat her son not as he currently was but as the person she hoped he could become. A lightbulb went on in Nell's head, and she resolved to change.

A few days later, Ken came home from school at midday to retrieve the lunch bag he had forgotten in the morning. Instead of berating him for forgetting, Nell said she was pleased that he had remembered, even if it was at the last minute. Later, when Ken was making hot chocolate (before, Nell had never allowed him near the stove), he let the milk boil over. Nell calmly handed him a towel and said, "Sometimes we can learn from a mistake," to which Ken replied, "Yes, I learned to turn the heat down when boiling milk." Finally, Nell handed Ken some money and a shopping list and asked him to go to the store. Ken came home a little later and apologetically said he had lost the money. Nell stifled her anger and gave him some more money and sent him back to the store. Ken returned with the items and left a note that read, "Dear Mom and a half, I got everything except the tomatoes. They were too soft."

➤ *Note to the Reader:* Please pause briefly to formulate your own analysis before reading on.

Analysis of Effective Response: Case 3. To me, this is a heartwarming story that shows that caregivers can change the nature of their relationship with children when they achieve insight into the true nature of their own behavior. This mother, Nell, obviously loved her son, but her communications with him had always been disparaging and negative. By suddenly recognizing what she was doing, she was able to translate the love she felt into loving rather than rejecting actions. The wonderful result is that once she began to treat Ken as a capable young man, he began to act like one.

The path Nell traveled in this story started at a point where she was very low on Tolerance and very low on Warmth and ended at a point where she was very high on both. In increasing her Tolerance level, Nell followed TB2 ("Ignore behaviors that you do not like but can live with") to overlook Ken's returning home to retrieve his lunch, his mishap with the spilled milk, and his losing the money. This change automatically brought about increased Warmth, as Nell achieved better ratios of ignoring to punishment (TB1) and praise to punishment (WB1). Warmth was also increased through WA2, when Nell used an I-message to praise Ken for remembering his lunch, even though he was late in doing so. She also increased Warmth through WC2 ("Use discipline methods that are encouraging, not discouraging").

Tolerance was also increased through TC1 ("Treat the child as an individual"), in that Nell began to accept Ken as a person in his own right without comparing him to other children. The Allow Independence principle was also pursued by letting Ken do things on his own for the first time (such as cooking and shopping) without being overly restrictive because of fear of failure. As this story illustrates, acquiring the courage to fail is often a prerequisite for success.

Effective Response: Case 4

This case is taken from *SOS Help for Parents*, by Lynn Clark (2005), and involves three-year-old Gloria and her parents. Gloria had a bad habit of grabbing toys from her younger sister. Her parents recognized that letting Gloria keep the toys would be reinforcing grabbing behavior, so they always took the toys away from her. However, this response did not work, and Gloria persisted in grabbing her sister's toys.

The parents implemented a three-part intervention, which worked nicely in moving Gloria from grabbing toys to sharing them and engaging in cooperative play behavior. The first part was to place Gloria in time-out or to give her a verbal reprimand whenever she grabbed one of her sister's toys. The second part of the intervention was to teach Gloria toy-sharing skills. Her parents did this by first modeling toy trading with Gloria's sister. Gloria's father would do this several times and then get Gloria to practice trading toys. Sometimes Gloria offered her sister several toys before she took one.

The third part of the intervention was to reinforce Gloria's newly acquired skill by praising her for sharing toys with her sister. Gloria became quite adept at toy trading, and the quality of her play with her sister improved dramatically. Occasionally, Gloria would revert to grabbing one of her sister's toys. When that would happen, her parents would punish her with a reprimand or a time-out. But, for the most part, the combination of mild punishment paired with reinforcement worked nicely in maintaining Gloria's newly learned behavior.

➤ *Note to the Reader:* Please pause briefly to formulate your own analysis before reading on.

Analysis of Effective Response: Case 4. This case illustrates the power of the Behavioral approach in ending a negative behavior and building a positive alternative behavior in a young child. It also illustrates one of the central points I have been making throughout this book: For discipline to be effective—that is, not only to alter a child's behavior but also to build social competence—it is not enough to be punitive. Sole reliance on punishment would have "worked" only by turning Gloria's parents into ever-vigilant toy grabbers themselves. It would not have moved Gloria to a new level of social skill, and it would not have achieved anything close to harmony in the family.

The first step in eliminating Gloria's toy snatching involved IB2 ("Be aware of which behaviors are praiseable, ignorable, and punishable"). Gloria's parents had a clear idea of what their goal was, and they responded in a differential manner to toy-grabbing versus toy-sharing behavior. Their method also embodied IA1, in that they determined that toy grabbing was unacceptable to them, and they set a limit whenever it occurred.

What made this intervention successful, however, was that Gloria's parents used a behavioral "microteaching" technique to help her learn the alternative behavior they wanted her to acquire. They did this through a combination of modeling, supervised practice, and a great deal of praise and reinforcement (WB2, "Praise behaviors that you like and would like to see more of"). In this way, they solved a bothersome problem while maintaining a positive relationship (WB1) with their daughter.

Ineffective Response: Case 1

The first example of an ineffective caregiver response is drawn from *Setting Limits in the Classroom*, by Robert J. MacKenzie (1996). The case involves Jerry, an eighth-grade schoolteacher. Mackenzie observed Jerry engage in what he calls a "mixed dance" scenario, where Jerry started off too permissive and ended up too punitive and hostile. Another form of mixed dance could involve the opposite shift: starting off punitive and then caving in. Following is a typical scene from Jerry's classroom.

While Jerry was teaching, two girls started talking and passing a note back and forth. Jerry ignored them altogether. Their talking and giggling got louder, but still no response came from Jerry. They passed the note to a boy, and his reaction caused the girls to giggle louder. Jerry glanced at them but kept on teaching. On the other side of the room, two boys were flicking objects at each other. Finally, one of the boys went too far, and Jerry responded in a pleading tone, "Come on, guys." They stopped. The girls started up again, and Jerry made a pleading comment to them. Then the boys started up again. Again, Jerry made no response. Then the girls started wrestling over the note.

At this point, Jerry exploded, "I've had it!" He handed both girls passes and sent them to the office (Jerry held the school record for sending students to the office). He threatened to send one of the boys to the office too if he did not settle down. The class remained quiet for a while.

➤ *Note to the Reader:* Please pause briefly to formulate your own analysis before reading on.

Analysis of Ineffective Response: Case 1. Jerry presents an interesting paradox: a permissive teacher who repeatedly engages in power struggles and frequently uses the most extreme form of punishment. Jerry's biggest problem is a violation of IB2 ("Be aware of which behaviors are praiseable, ignorable, and punishable"). He clearly does not have a problem with TB2 ("Ignore behaviors that you do not like but can live with"), but he is not being fair to the students who are there to learn when he allows the class to be disrupted so frequently by troublemaking students. In going overboard on TB2, Jerry is violating IA1 ("Set limits on acts that are . . . unacceptable"). To treat all of his students fairly, Jerry needs to establish more firmly in his own mind the dividing line between the kinds of behaviors he is willing to tolerate and the kinds that are unacceptable.

Jerry's discipline is also very inconsistent, because for most of the hour he conveys the message that the disruptive behaviors are tolerable, or even desirable (by paying occasional attention to them), only to suddenly use extreme measures when he has had enough. With his glances and pleading, Jerry is violating IB1 ("Do not . . . praise undesirable behaviors").

Jerry also needs to be more creative in his choice of punishments, because sending a child to the office may be reinforcing (another violation of IB1). IC2 ("Arrange consequences that have logical [i.e., educational] connections to the child's act") might be applicable. There is also an implicit praise deficit here, because so much of Jerry's time is taken up with punishing; thus, Jerry is probably violating WB1 ("Do much more praising than punishing"). WC2 ("Use discipline methods that are encouraging, not discouraging") is another technique that Jerry needs to consider in switching to more effective and creative discipline responses.

Ineffective Response: Case 2

This case is taken from *Confident Parenting*, by Mel Silberman (1988). It involves a divorced mother, Adele, and her adolescent daughter, Julie. The two have a relationship that is more like that of sisters than mother and daughter. According to Silberman, they "looked, talked, and thought alike." Ever since the divorce, Adele had hovered over Julie and had become overly involved in her life (e.g., by reading her diary). Upon reaching adolescence, Julie began to rebel (e.g., by being very rude to Adele's friends). Adele overreacted to Julie's behavior, and mother and daughter engaged in constant conflict.

▷ *Note to the Reader:* Please pause briefly to formulate your own analysis before reading on.

Analysis of Ineffective Response: Case 2. The basic problem with this family is Adele's trying to be Julie's friend rather than her mother. This behavior likely was well intentioned: a desire to make up for the loss of Julie's father. But children need their parents to act like parents, not like friends, and a parent who tries to act like her child's peer is asking for trouble. One reason for this is because the parent loses all authority, and it becomes difficult to impose limits when they are called for.

The ABC principles most violated by Adele involved aspects of Tolerance, and she performed especially poorly on the two Cognitive techniques for Tolerance. In trying to be her daughter's peer, Adele violated TC2 ("Do not blur adult-child boundaries"). This technique was also violated when Adele took it upon herself to read Julie's diary. Such an intrusion into a child's privacy and autonomy is always likely to be resented and reflects a lack of understanding that one's child is not an extension of oneself. Adele also violated TC1 ("Treat the child as an individual") by not giving Julie the freedom to have a life that did not involve her. Adele also violated all of the Behavioral and Affective techniques for Tolerance by being unable to ignore any of her daughter's behaviors, including her verbal comebacks and complaints.

Although Adele's main problem was in the area of Tolerance, it is likely that she lost the ability to set limits when they were called for, such as when Julie acted rudely toward her mother's friends. By reacting to everything Julie did (i.e., by having such low Tolerance), Adele put herself in a position where the things that bothered her a lot did not stand out from the things that bothered her less. Adele needs to adopt a more coherent strategy of focusing on the things that really matter (IB2).

Ineffective Response: Case 3

This case comes from another book by Robert J. MacKenzie (2001), *Setting Limits with Your Strong-Willed Child*. It involves Rick and Linda and their thirteen-year-old daughter, Lisa. Weeks before the family's session with MacKenzie, Lisa came home with a failing report card. When she saw it, Linda said, "Ds are not acceptable in this household." Lisa replied, "I've got six weeks until the semester [ends]. . . . That's plenty of time to get [my grades] up." Mom replied, "You have more time than you think . . . because you're not going anywhere after school until those grades come up." Lisa protested being grounded, and Linda then took away Lisa's phone privileges for six weeks. Linda said, "Keep it up if you want to lose even more privileges."

When Rick came home from work, mother and daughter got into a shouting match, with Linda accusing Lisa of being lazy and disrespectful and Lisa accusing her mom of being mean and unfair. Dad tried to intervene, and Lisa called her mom a "bitch." Her dad ended up removing one of the last privileges available to Lisa. In the weeks leading up to the session, Lisa sulked when she was not engaging in mutually insulting verbal sparring with her parents.

➤ *Note to the Reader:* Please pause briefly to formulate your own analysis before reading on.

Analysis of Ineffective Response: Case 3. In this analysis, I focus mainly on Linda, because her response to the report card started this war, and her relationship with Lisa is particularly problematic. As the basic problem in this family is a tendency to get into power struggles, the key to restoring harmony is for Linda to learn how to avoid such power struggles without giving up her influencing role as a parent.

The precipitating problem was Lisa's poor report card, and the thing that turned it into a war was Linda's decision to take ownership of the problem. That was a big mistake, because the solution to this problem will only come if Lisa owns the problem, and a punitive approach will only motivate her to keep on failing. Thus, the first of Linda's violations was of TC2 ("Do not blur adult-child boundaries"), because as much as any parent wants her child to get good grades, it is necessary to always keep in mind that it is the child's responsibility, and not the parent's, to put in the work needed to get those grades. A better way to deal with Lisa's report card would be to make an empathic comment (TA2) about Lisa's disappointment and then use a problem-solving approach (WC1) to see if Lisa could come up with a remediation plan.

The excessive use of punishment, especially overly harsh punishment, such as taking away all privileges (violation of WB1), needs to be reversed through WB2 (finding things to praise) and WC2 (using encouragement rather than discouragement). Finally, the best way to avoid power struggles is for Linda to learn to ignore Lisa's screaming (TB1) and to understand (TA1) that Lisa's anger toward her is not something that she has to respond to or punish.

Ineffective Response: Case 4

This case is drawn from *Discipline without Shouting or Spanking*, by Jerry Wykoff and Barbara C. Udell (1984). It involves two-and-a-half-year-old Audrey and her mother. Audrey's main problem was compulsive overeating. She was known at her preschool as a "walking bottomless pit." When food was present, it seemed Audrey could never get enough. This was becoming a health problem, but it was also a behavior problem, because preschools only have so many cookies and other treats to go around.

Audrey's mom tried to deal with the problem by angrily screaming things such as "You've had enough cookies to last your lifetime" whenever she saw her daughter reaching for a cookie. She also threatened to take away her tricycle if she did not stop eating. None of these things seemed to help.

➤ *Note to the Reader:* Please pause briefly to formulate your own analysis before reading on.

Analysis of Ineffective Response: Case 4. This is one more bit of evidence (as if more were needed) that punishment alone, especially when it takes the form of verbal reprimand or threats, is not likely to be effective in changing an undesired behavior pattern. Eating (or not eating, which was my modus operandi when I was a child) is a volitional act that cannot be changed through force alone. It is essential to win the child's cooperation if the behavior is to be changed.

With a medically related disorder such as this, it is essential to start off with a consultation with the child's physician to establish whether the problem stems from some biological condition and to receive guidance regarding the basics of a healthy diet for the child. Assuming that Audrey does not have a medical condition that drives her overeating, the task here is to come up with a reinforcement-based, rather than a punishment-based, intervention plan. First of all, it would be useful to determine whether Audrey's parents had inadvertently established her eating pattern by using food as a reward for all sorts of behaviors (violation of IB1) and thus were reinforcing her overeating. If that is the case, they need to come up with other pleasurable rewards.

Secondly, it is essential to reduce the negative nature of the relationship (violation of WB1) and to eliminate the use of pejorative terms, such as "bottomless pit" (violation of WA1). The parents should seek to make greater use of encouragement rather than discouragement (WC2), including encouragement for behaviors other than eating (so that does not become the focus of their relationship). If Audrey were a little older, it would also be advisable to work with her in a collaborative problem-solving manner (WC1) to come up with an agreed-upon plan.

8

Developing an Effective Discipline Style

Using the ABC Model to Refine the Caregiver's Approach to Discipline

My contributions to the literature on discipline began with an articulation of the three principles of the Affective approach (S. Greenspan 1978), continued with publication of a model integrating the Behavioral and Affective approaches (S. Greenspan 1983), and took another step forward when I brought the Cognitive approach into my model (S. Greenspan 1985). Initially, I felt most comfortable with the Affective approach, but when I became a parent, I found myself operating much of the time in the Behavioral approach. Now that my kids are approaching adulthood, I find that the Cognitive approach feels very comfortable. But I switch back and forth all the time (e.g., using active listening when feelings are involved), and I no longer feel the need to restrict myself to a single approach. The main thing I try to do is to strike a balance among the domains of Warmth, Tolerance, and Influence, and all three approaches help me do that, both in the short term (dealing with discipline situations) and in the long term (fostering healthy social development).

The power of the ABC Model of Discipline is that it emphasizes all three domains of discipline and articulates concrete principles for operating within those domains. The structured nature of the model highlights how any adequate theory of discipline must also address the three domains. Unlike the proponents of get-tough discipline, such as James Rosemond, who emphasize Influence almost exclusively, I maintain that a competent caregiver (one operating within the ABC model, for example) is someone who also displays great Warmth and Tolerance. The key to success is knowing when and how to use the principles associated with each domain. Those who profess expertise in the field of discipline, yet claim that being assertive and punitive are enough, are preaching a misleading message. For readers who have considered and assimilated the information in this book, I trust that I do not have to explain why the get-tough message is so far off the mark.

Why Are Caregivers Attracted to Bad Advice?

The big question to ask with regard to dispensers of dubious discipline advice is not "Why is their advice so flawed?" but rather "Why, in light of their flawed advice, are they so popular?" There are several likely reasons, starting with the fact that these individuals have an authoritative and convincing style, helped in some cases by the fact that they write well and display an engaging persona on the lecture circuit. Certainly, both of these are true of Rosemond, who is profiled in Chapter 1. A friend of mine who attended one of Rosemond's workshops twenty years ago reported that he was very entertaining. Rosemond bills himself on his website as "America's Funniest Psychologist," which presumably refers more to his speaking style than to his message.

My friend also told me that Rosemond disclosed that he and his son had gone through significant conflict when his son was a teenager. I must admit this does not surprise me, not for what it says about adolescence (research, and my own experience, shows that living with teenagers can be very peaceful and harmonious), but because this is exactly what one might expect in any family following Rosemond's advice to say "no" at least three times a day. I find it interesting that Rosemond refers in especially negative terms to the teenage years (personally, I find his frequent use of labels such as "brat" to characterize the average American child to be rather shocking). Rosemond's very dim view of adolescents probably reflects the fact that his drill-sergeant approach is particularly unlikely to work with this age-group, which is better equipped than younger children to recognize and to resist bullying.

A second reason why Rosemond and other peddlers of bad advice are so popular is that consumers of the discipline literature lack an independent theoretical framework that can help them tell good advice from bad advice, or recognize the difference between superficially adequate and truly adequate theorizing. In fact, it is partly to remedy this deficiency in theoretical information for caregivers that I finally undertook to formalize the ABC model and write this book.

The third, and likely most important, reason for the popularity of those who offer bad advice, particularly when that advice takes the form of "You're not being tough enough," is that such advice plays into the beliefs already held by many caregivers, especially those who are having problems with child noncompliance.

The irony of so-called experts telling caregivers that the solution to their discipline problems is to be tougher is that most of the caregivers who turn in desperation to child-rearing experts are already too much inclined, rather than too little inclined, to be tough. For proof of that, one only has to look at most of the "before" segments in the TV series *Supernanny* (whose star, Jo Frost, lacks even a college degree and whose message, although packaged more sweetly than Rosemond's, also consists mainly of advising caregivers to "be tougher"). What these segments show are ineffective parents who almost never praise and are constantly threatening or applying punishment, most typically time-out. But discipline based only on Influence is no more likely to succeed than is a dance performed by a dancer who knows only how to move forward and has no idea how and when to move backward or to the side.

The Dance of Discipline

The ABC Model of Discipline is my attempt to show how the three approaches—Affective, Behavioral, and Cognitive—are congruent in many ways and how principles within and across the approaches can be used in a coordinated and flexible manner. It is a mistake to think that, even in a simple situation, any one principle can stand alone. When a skilled caregiver deals with most discipline situations, she usually calls upon two or more principles (and domains) simultaneously. For example, she may decide to ignore one behavior (Tolerance) while setting a limit on another (Influence), but doing so in a way that acknowledges the child's underlying feeling (Tolerance) and does not attack the child's self-esteem (Warmth). She may then acknowledge the child's feelings about the limit being set (Tolerance) and a short while later praise the child (Warmth) when he is engaging in acceptable behavior incompatible with the behavior that triggered her initial discipline response (Influence). Thus, while the discipline principles can be viewed and discussed as separate elements, their effective use almost always involves putting them together, as a caregiver effortlessly moves back and forth among them. Effective discipline, to achieve both short-term (behavior change and restoration of system harmony) and long-term (growth in social competence) goals, always involves attaining a balance between, and coordinated use of, principles from across the three domains.

Several authors have used the analogy of a dance to describe the intuitive, effortless, and flexible way in which a skilled caregiver interacts with a child and responds to his cues and moves. In the context of parenting, Evelyn Thoman and Sue Ellin Browder (1987) refer to this as "dance parenting," and John Gall (2003) likens it to "dancing with elves." The dance metaphor can be used negatively, however, as Robert J. MacKenzie (1996) does when he refers to "the classroom dance of ineffective discipline." Mackenzie uses the analogy to refer not so much to the skilled moves of a confident caregiver but rather to the tendency of unskilled caregivers to take the verbal bait offered by challenging and resistant children. Such a dance (which resembles the coercion cycle described in Chapter 3) takes the form of a child doing something disruptive, a caregiver making a weak plea for compliance, the child ignoring the plea, and the situation escalating through a mutual exchange of insults and culminating in the adult doing something coercive enough to stop the cycle temporarily.

Here, however, I prefer to use the dance metaphor to refer to the discipline style of a highly effective parent or teacher. Herbert L. Foster (1974) uses a game metaphor in his classic book *Ribbin', Jivin' and Playin' the Dozens,* but a dance metaphor would work just as well. Foster's book addresses a critical problem in education, especially in urban settings where large numbers of children are failing and thus are motivated to deflect attention away from learning. The problem stems from the fact that many of the teachers who take jobs in urban settings are young and inexperienced and have received very inadequate training in the theory and practice of discipline.

Rather than respond intuitively and assertively to the challenging probes thrown out by bored and alienated students, inexperienced teachers respond woodenly and fail to understand the game the students are playing. As a result, things do not go well in their classes. These teachers quickly become demoralized by their inability to maintain order, and they feel burned out (another term for inadequate). Severely frustrated, they are likely to leave the teaching profession prematurely. Foster's book shows how teachers and administrators who thrive in such an environment do so because they are able to engage in a kind of playful, but often quite firm, dance. In this dance, effective caregivers show an intuitive sense of when to be assertive, when to back off, and when to praise, and they do so in a confident, effortless, and even joy-filled manner.

Although Foster did not know about the (not-yet-articulated) ABC model or its nine principles, his numerous examples of effective caregiver responses, many of which involve sidestepping a potential power struggle by making a humorous response, all fit nicely within the model. This illustrates an important point—namely, that the ABC model, and the three domains of discipline effectiveness, did not emerge off the top of my head but were revealed in studies that examined caregivers in the real world. Effective caregivers are effective because they already demonstrate an intuitive use of the principles that constitute the ABC model. Caregivers who wish to become more effective at discipline can do so by applying principles that were developed by studying skilled caregivers and analyzing the reasons why they are effective.

The trick for any caregiver in adopting the ABC model, or one of the three approaches that make up the model, is to become proficient enough at applying it that it becomes second nature. When a caregiver understands the principles well enough, she can respond to situations intuitively and in a way that is natural and comfortable. In this way, caregiver-child interaction becomes a form of dance, and the kind of good feeling that is experienced by everyone in the system brings the caregiver a sense of confidence and joy. Obviously, one cannot get to this point of "flow" (automatic excellence) overnight, but it is important for any caregiver to understand that with practice, effort, and perseverance, she can become as proficient at the dance of discipline as she is at real dancing or at performing any other activity she has mastered to the point where she can do it automatically, without having to think too much about the precise details of what she is doing.

In addition to invoking dance and game metaphors, some have also described skilled discipline as involving a degree of playfulness. The play metaphor is relevant in two ways. The first has to do with the exhilaration that a caregiver feels when she becomes more competent in influencing and relating to children. As with the acquisition of any important skill, a newly effective caregiver will for a while go out of her way to look for opportunities to practice, refine, and play with her new discipline schemas until they have been fully mastered. A second, and more long-lasting, aspect of the play metaphor is that as caregiver-child relationships become less negative, mutual laughter and playfulness are more likely to prevail. Some authors (e.g., Sherman 1995) have even made humor a centerpiece of their discipline advice, using such descriptors as "The Laughing Classroom" (Loomans 1993) and "Playful Parenting" (Weston and Weston 1993, 1996). I see this as a valid line of advice, although my preference is that humor emerge naturally as a feature of healthy classroom or family settings rather than as a result of caregivers' trying too hard to be funny or popular.

Attitude Adjustment for Caregivers

For a caregiver to change her discipline practices, it may be necessary for her to first change her attitudes toward discipline and toward children. Few things are more difficult for people to change than their habitual behavior patterns, especially when those patterns are well entrenched and are called forth by certain "button-pushing" actions of others. Here are some of the attitude adjustments that caregivers may need to make when attempting to bring their discipline practices more in line with the ABC model.

Adopting a More Positive Attitude

All three discipline approaches encourage caregivers to maintain a relationship with children that can be characterized as positive. In the Affective approach, this begins by resolutely avoiding put-downs or general comments about a child's motives, intentions, or personhood. In the Behavioral approach, positivity takes the form of a great deal of praising and reinforcing. In the Cognitive approach, a positive relationship is built on encouragement and making a child feel he is a valued member of the family or class unit.

For caregivers who have a habit of being negative and critical, switching over to a more positive mode of interacting with children can be difficult. However, asking a child a question when one's initial impulse is to criticize can be a source of revelation (and liberation) for a caregiver. Hearing how hurtful and undermining one's comments have been (perhaps in the context of a family or classroom council meeting) can be a source of transforming insight. Most people do not want to think of themselves as mean or hurtful, and becoming more aware of how they are perceived can be a catalyst for meaningful behavior change on the part of the caregiver.

Adopting a More Tolerant Attitude

All three discipline approaches have as a core tenet that ineffective caregivers need to do a better job of recognizing when they do not have a problem. In the Affective approach, caregivers are encouraged to understand that a child's expression of affect may reflect a problem the child is having, but the expression itself is not necessarily problematic for the caregiver. In the Behavioral approach, caregivers are encouraged to understand that to effectively stop child behaviors they do not like and cannot live with, it is necessary for them to ignore child behaviors that they do not like but can live with. In the Cognitive approach, caregivers are encouraged to understand that effective discipline requires them to avoid getting into power struggles with children and that the best way to avoid a power struggle is to step back and not respond to all provocations. Switching over from treating many child behaviors as problems to treating all but a few of them as nonproblems is a shift that can be difficult, because it often calls for something in the nature of a personality transformation.

Adopting a More Assertive Attitude

The flip side of a caregiver's knowing when she does not have a problem is knowing when she does. Then it behooves her, according to all three discipline approaches, to do something about it. In the Affective approach, that involves setting a limit—often beginning with a communication about how the child's act made the caregiver feel—and communicating some general rule (e.g., "Chairs are not for kicking"). In the Behavioral approach, an unacceptable behavior calls forth some form of punishment, which can range from verbal disapproval to something involving a "response cost" (e.g., loss of privilege) to the child. In the Cognitive approach, caregivers are encouraged to think up an undesired consequence that has some teaching value—namely, one that is tied logically to the offense ("If you don't get ready, then you'll miss the party")—and that can be implemented without a power struggle.

Although the majority of ineffective caregivers have the problem of being over- rather than underassertive, many caregivers do have great difficulty asserting themselves with children. This can be a reflection of an overprotective attitude (e.g., fear of psychologically harming the child) or of certain naive beliefs (e.g., "Love should be enough"). In some cases, caregiver underassertiveness may reflect a more general personality style or certain cultural practices, such as a tendency in some cultures to communicate displeasure very subtly and indirectly.

As with the other forms of attitude change discussed here, a caregiver can become more assertive when she comes to understand how important it is both for her own effectiveness (and happiness) and for the well-being of the child. Assertion Training programs can help caregivers become more assertive, in part by teaching them that being assertive does not require them to be aggressive or violent; many nonassertive people do not understand the difference. Part of Assertion Training (see the discussion of the Assertive Discipline approach in Appendix B) involves role-playing the use of a more emphatic tone of voice. This can be very important, as in the case of a mother who learned to utter more assertive words but did so in such a weak and imploring tone of voice that her overly aggressive young child did not get the message.

Does the Model Apply to Special Populations?

A caregiver might say, "This model is well and good for disciplining normally developing children, but will it work with children who have brain-based behavior disorders or who are so far gone in their pattern of oppositional behavior that something else must be tried?" My response to this question is, yes, the model still applies, even when it must be supplemented with other methods (such as medication), although it may be necessary to define more precisely what one means by "work."

A child with autism (a behavior disorder now understood to reflect abnormalities in brain development), for example, will not be cured by use of the nine principles of the ABC model or, most likely, through any other intervention. (As the brother of an adult with an autistic spectrum disorder who has been treated by outstanding clinicians, including Leo Kanner—who gave the disorder its name—I feel I have earned the right to say that.) But even if he is not cured by use of the ABC model, a child with autism is more likely to become better adjusted if his caregivers are competent than if they are incompetent. Furthermore, a child with autism has just as much right to, and need for, clear limits as well as freedom from unreasonable limits as any other child, and the ABC model's emphasis on increasing the caregiver's insight into the expression of affect (an area where autistic individuals are particularly deficient) could be of great benefit. So, although the ABC model is not a cure-all for conditions that may be incurable, there is every reason to think that it "works" with all children, even those who have biologically based disorders, in optimizing their adjustment and in maximizing the degree of harmony in their living environment.

The notion that certain populations are so impaired, or so disadvantaged, that they should be granted an exemption from normal expectations or treatment can itself actually add to, rather than diminish, their handicaps. For example, I know of one family where the parents felt so sorry for their intellectually challenged teenage son that they set very few limits on his actions, in the mistaken belief that "at least this way, he will get some enjoyment out of life." As a result, his routine became so disordered (e.g., staying up all night, raiding the refrigerator, trashing the house, etc.), and the family's, and his own, quality of life became so bad that an out-of-home placement became more likely than might otherwise have been the case.

William Glasser (1965) gives a similar example of a university-based summer program for disadvantaged teenagers that was intended to spur their interest in going to college. Although the young people had signed a contract stating that they were expected to show up for classes, the program administrators did not enforce this rule, feeling it was too much to expect from individuals from such chaotic backgrounds and who had already experienced so much school failure. As a result, the attendance rate plummeted to the point where very few participants were taking advantage of the program. Instead, they were learning the lesson that rules are not to be taken seriously, which would only serve them poorly in future school or work settings. Furthermore, the failure to make reasonable, or any, behavior demands on these young people was based on a mistaken view of them as being more fragile and incompetent than they actually were.

With respect to the application of the ABC model to children with well-entrenched patterns of oppositional or noncompliant behavior, it should be noted that many of the leading figures in the caregiver discipline literature (e.g., Ginott, Glasser, Patterson, and Forehand) earned their spurs working with such populations. In fact, one could argue that they were extending to the general population methods that had already been used successfully with the most difficult children, rather than the other way around. This is not to downplay the challenge in getting disturbing children to behave "normally," nor is it to deny the difficulty in transforming highly dysfunctional family or classroom patterns into something healthier. But with skilled and perseverant application of the nine principles of the ABC model, there is no doubt that the great majority of children and caregivers can be helped substantially.

Does the Model Apply across Cultures?

Two related criticisms of the ABC model—pertaining to culture and race—are that (1) certain underlying assumptions about the nature of social competence (e.g., the desirability of a child becoming bold) do not apply equally across all cultures and (2) cultural and racial subgroups differ according to the extent to which certain discipline practices (e.g., shaming or spanking) are valued and considered normative. Without denying the obvious fact that culture plays an important role in discipline, I feel these criticisms are overstated.

In every culture, there are children and adults who are considered socially competent and others who are considered socially incompetent. The long-term purpose of discipline is the same in every culture—namely, to help children develop into individuals who are socially competent (i.e., who can survive and thrive socially in the culture in which they grew up or choose to live). I believe that caregivers who are skilled at attaining a balance between Warmth, Tolerance, and Influence will be successful in helping children adapt socially to the particular demands of the community and culture in which they live, even if the weight given to some of the domains may vary. The ABC model offers considerable flexibility regarding the kinds of behaviors that are deemed acceptable or unacceptable to caregivers, and this flexibility is intended in part to accommodate cultural differences. As for use of extreme caregiver punishments—such as hitting with a belt (which is a crime in many places)—I think it is an exaggeration to assert that these techniques produce socially competent children. They certainly do not, in my opinion, produce happy children, regardless of how some of the adult victims of abusive family or educational practices might later try to nostalgically justify their experiences.

Developmental Factors in Applying Discipline

Discipline authorities generally understand that the age of the child is an important consideration in deciding how to respond to various behaviors. Age is certainly a factor in deciding when and how to apply discipline, but the decision also involves such things as personal preference and the specific nature of the challenge being presented. I prefer to combine principles from the Affective, Behavioral, and Cognitive approaches, mixing and matching as the occasion arises and as the age of the child dictates. Thomas W. Phelan's (2010) book *1-2-3 Magic: Effective Discipline for Children 2–12* illustrates what I see as the downside of becoming too tightly wedded to a particular technique or age-group in offering a system of discipline.

Phelan's curriculum is somewhat eclectic in that he borrows from all three approaches. From the Affective approach he mentions (essentially as an add-on at the end of the book) the technique of active listening. Cognitive techniques he advocates include family councils and natural consequences. Among the Behavioral techniques Phelan emphasizes are positive reinforcement, charting, and, especially, time-out. In fact, time-out is really the central technique of *1-2-3 Magic*, which is probably why Phelan explicitly (in his subtitle) gives his book an applicability ceiling of age twelve, as many people consider time-out to be too coercive and demeaning to use with adolescents (who are also big enough to put up quite a struggle if they decide to resist time-out).

One difference between time-out as used by behaviorists and time-out (called something else) as used by Phelan is that Phelan suggests sending a child to his room (unless he has too much fun there) instead of to a designated time-out area. In fact, the main reason why behaviorists do not advocate sending a child to his room is because he is likely to find that reinforcing—hence the original full name for time-out: "time-out from reinforcement." The *1-2-3* in Phelan's title is derived from the method he advocates for cluing a child that time-out is imminent: giving a "1" and a "2" warning and then following through with a time-out if "3" is reached before a child stops the offending behavior. Although *1-2-3 Magic* contains some good ideas, I am bothered by the fact that Phelan puts so much emphasis on punishment (the "1-2-3 time-out" method takes up the first half of the book) and so little on avoiding power struggles.

Phelan does not, from what I can tell, indicate why the *1-2-3 Magic* framework is unsuitable for children younger than two or older than twelve. Presumably, age twelve is the ceiling because time-out is not really appropriate for adolescents (as noted earlier). I assume age two is the floor for several reasons: (1) infants cannot be expected to stay in a time-out area; (2) they are not really able to participate in a discussion setting, such as a family council; and (3) they cannot readily grasp verbal concepts (and, thus, a punitive orientation is both ineffective and cruel with infants).

Personally, I feel that all approaches—Affective, Behavioral, and Cognitive—are applicable to children and youths of all ages, as long as two points are kept in mind: (1) punishment is really a very small part of any valid approach (his emphasis on punishment makes me reluctant to recommend Phelan's books) and (2) an approach is defined not by any single method (such as time-out) but rather by certain underlying principles.

One problem with emphasizing a specific technique, as Phelan does, is that many caregivers think they understand a discipline system if they can use that technique, even if they use it excessively and inappropriately. For many caregivers, their understanding of discipline begins and ends with the use of timeout, and this belief is, unfortunately, reinforced by Phelan. Time-out is simply one of many forms of punishment a caregiver could use, and even if used, it should be used infrequently and in conjunction with much praising and much ignoring. Once again, I can refer to the *Supernanny* TV series for an example of "how-not-to": most of the ineffective caregivers featured on the program were already using or threatening time-out much of the time, and it was all too clear how little good that did.

One factor in determining the developmental appropriateness of a particular discipline technique is the amount of verbal comprehension that is required. There are those who feel that family or class council meetings are inappropriate for very young children, precisely because of the amount of talking and listening that goes on. The same argument can be made against using some Affective techniques, such as active listening and I-messages, with very young children. Most Cognitive and Affective experts, however, feel that it is important to use techniques such as family councils and active listening with children of all ages, even infants. Exposing young children to such techniques may benefit them by modeling certain ways of responding. Besides, it is better to overestimate than to underestimate a child's comprehension ability.

At one time, I felt that the Behavioral approach is perhaps best suited for use with very young children, because caregivers following this approach have little need to say anything. As I began to realize the broad flexibility of that and the other approaches, however, I came to understand that all three discipline approaches are suitable for use across the age spectrum, again with the proviso that certain specific techniques (such as time-out) may need to be shelved for children of certain ages. If one thinks of the Behavioral approach in terms of broad guiding principles (do a lot of praising, do a lot of ignoring, and be contingent when praising and punishing), then it is hard to think of any age where such an approach is not applicable. The same can be said for the principles associated with the Cognitive and Affective approaches. Thus, I have structured the ABC Model of Discipline as a system that integrates the three approaches to operate within common domains of discipline in pursuit of common goals. The framework is sufficiently interwoven that it remains robust even in the face of the necessary age-related adjustments in application of certain techniques.

Do Caregivers Really Make a Difference?

In asserting a connection between caregiver (especially parent) discipline and child social-competence outcomes, I am putting myself in opposition to a stance taken by Judith Rich Harris (1998) in her book *The Nurture Assumption*. Harris's argument, influenced a great deal by her own experience as a parent, is that the importance of parents has been greatly exaggerated by Freudians and behaviorists, both of whom see the role of parents as of critical importance for the healthy development of children. According to Harris, a major determinant of whether a child becomes socially competent or incompetent has to do with the peer group he is lucky or unlucky enough to fall in with.

Harris notes that her position was influenced greatly by her experience in raising two daughters. The older daughter (for whom Harris was the biological mother) became an honors student on the fast track to life success, while the younger daughter (whom Harris adopted) was a poor student with an oppositional attitude who experienced lots of life difficulties. Harris argues that the major difference, as both daughters were exposed to the same upbringing, was that the girls hung out with very different friends, and the younger daughter fell under the sway of a deviant set of peers. Harris also reviews an extensive body of research literature and argues that it shows much less support for the importance of parents than has been claimed.

Harris's book, as might be expected, generated considerable controversy among parenting scholars (Borkowski, Ramey, and Bristol-Power 2000; Collins et al. 2000), some of whom have argued that the research literature provides much more support for the importance of parents than Harris asserts. Here I just want to briefly put in my two cents, as the controversy does have implications for what I am writing about in this book.

First of all, it is wrong to assume that the parenting environment is the same for a happy and cooperative child as it is for a sibling who is unhappy and uncooperative. Ideally, one would like to think that parents treat all of their children the same, but it is well known (Bell and Harper 1977) that caregivers respond differently to children who challenge them, as illustrated in the coercion cycle that has come up several times in this book. A child who defies his parent is more likely to trigger a negative response from the parent, which in a kind of feedback loop only exacerbates the child's disobedient tendencies. Harris is correct in asserting that the initial difference in temperament may have little to do with parenting, but it may also have little to do with peers or other aspects of the social environment. Many biological factors—such as genetics, birth stressors (prenatal and perinatal), allergies, infections, brain injuries, and so forth—contribute to individual differences in temperament, a term that encompasses a range of traits, many of which have a biological component (as I discuss below).

Regarding peers, Harris fails to consider the alternative explanation: that children seek out peer groups that fit with their own lifestyles and self-images. Undoubtedly, peers can and do influence the development of children, and any child has the potential to be led astray by peers. But I suspect that Harris's younger daughter may have had problems in development that made her particularly vulnerable to negative peer influences long before she became involved with the friends whom Harris considers to be the main cause of the girl's difficulties.

The fact that Harris's younger daughter was adopted is, to me, of great significance. It is a well-established fact that adopted children have a much higher (three or more times) incidence of adjustment problems than do children who are not adopted. One possible explanation relates to the fact that mothers who give their babies up for adoption tend to be younger and poorer, and thus are often less likely to get adequate medical care and more likely to ingest drugs and alcohol during pregnancy. We are only beginning to understand the pervasiveness, destructiveness, and invisibility of fetal alcohol spectrum disorder (Edwards and S. Greenspan 2011). Furthermore, children who are adopted sometimes spend weeks or months (sometimes even years) in chaotic and non-nurturing child-rearing environments, including multiple foster homes (or orphanages, still used in Eastern Europe) before being adopted. It is likely, however, that the greater mental-health difficulties of many adolescents and adults who are adopted are in part attributable to the extra challenges they face in devising satisfactory identities (Brodzinsky, Schecter, and Henig 1993; McRoy, Grotevant, and Zurcher 1988).

Harris is undoubtedly justified in arguing that it is a mistake to attribute a good or bad outcome solely to a child's parents. But a better approach would have been to explore how parenting combines with other factors, including the child's temperament, rather than to pose the issue as simply one of parents versus peers. There is a considerable literature on innate child temperament (and related biological factors), and the general finding is that the competence of caregivers does make a huge difference, especially for children with difficult temperaments or who are otherwise at risk.

The notion of temperament refers to aspects of a child's personality that appear almost from birth, which including such traits as emotional reactivity, approachability, soothability, self-regulation, rhythmicity of sleep and eating, fearfulness, openness to new experiences, response to people, sensitivity to change, and persistence. Parents who have more than one child know that siblings (even twins) come out of the womb with different temperaments, although to an outsider these differences sometimes seem smaller than they do to family members. One likely explanation for these temperament differences is that the process of being born is inherently stressful, and—except for those born via cesarean section (and who do not suffer too much before the expedited delivery)—all of us come into the world having experienced some degree of birth-induced brain damage. (This could explain why even identical twins, in spite of having the same genetic makeup and the same caregiving environment, sometimes have very different temperaments and academic and adjustment histories, because it is known that the second-appearing twin is more likely to experience prenatal and perinatal complications.) Difficulties related to temperament and birth trauma are typically subtle and usually can be transcended, but sometimes they pose significant challenges for caregivers.

In a study in New York, Alexander Thomas, Stella Chess, and Herbert G. Birch (1968) rated babies according to their temperaments as "easy," "difficult," and "slow-to-warm-up." They found that by middle childhood, easy babies tended to develop into socially competent and mentally healthy children, regardless of how competent their parents were. For the difficult babies, however, having a skilled parent could make all the difference between a good and a bad outcome.

In a long-term longitudinal study on the Hawaiian island of Kauai, Emmy E. Werner and her colleagues (Werner, Bierman, and French 1971) found somewhat the same thing, except that their starting point was whether or not a child had been born with perinatal anoxia (oxygen deprivation at birth, typically caused by a difficult birth or a cord wrapped around the neck). As with the New York study, Werner found that a skilled parent can help a child overcome initial risk factors but that combining an unskilled parent with an at-risk child is a formula likely to lead to problems down the road.

How does all this discussion of biological factors relate to the ABC model? The point I have been making is that in discipline (as in so many areas of life) one size cannot fit all. Sensitivity to inherent differences among children is one of the hallmarks of a competent caregiver. Although caregivers should always avoid any appearance of playing favorites (e.g., having different sets of rules or rewards for different children), caregiver awareness of differences among children is an important factor both in the effectiveness of discipline and in its impact on the child. For example, my wife and I were a little more emphatic when setting a limit with our younger son Eli than with our older son Alex, because Alex was more sensitive (i.e., his feelings were more easily hurt) but also because Eli was less likely to listen to us when we were too quiet. However, we treated both children equally in terms of having the same expectations and in being careful to communicate in a manner that was respectful (but I did come a little closer to the line with Eli, in part because I knew that he enjoyed the insult game and experienced it as playful rather than hurtful).

Of the three discipline approaches, the Cognitive approach has the most to say about the need to respect children's innate differences. This reflects the emphasis of the founder of this approach, Alfred Adler, on the idea that adult mental-health problems often reflect an unresolved need to win the approval of one's parents by competing with and besting one's siblings. Although this emphasis can be found in the writings of all of the Cognitive experts, it is most explicitly developed in a book for parents appropriately titled *Your Child Is a Person,* by Chess, Thomas, and Birch (1965), whose longitudinal temperament study was cited above. Another book that addresses the need for caregivers to be sensitive to innate temperamental differences of children is *The Challenging Child,* by the late child psychiatrist Stanley I. Greenspan (1995), whose work is mentioned in Chapter 2.

Ultimately, yes, caregivers *do* make a difference. Implicit throughout my discussion is the notion that caregivers who are skilled in the three major discipline domains (Warmth, Tolerance, and Influence) are more likely to facilitate the development of social competence (i.e., outcomes of Happiness, Boldness, and Niceness) in children. The principles of the Affective, Behavioral, and Cognitive approaches provide many avenues to reach these important goals.

Can one guarantee that a caregiver who adheres to the ABC Model of Discipline will produce perfect children? Of course not. Many factors contribute to a healthy child outcome, including the child's own choices and, yes, peer influences.

I am fairly confident, however, that a caregiver who is incompetent in her application and balancing of the three domains of discipline is much more likely to end up with children who are incompetent and unhappy than is a caregiver who competently uses those domains. Furthermore, the purpose of the outcomes component of the ABC model is to highlight that a major goal of discipline (in addition to the short-term goal of managing conflict and attaining harmony) is to facilitate healthy long-term development in children. Despite my reservations about Judith Rich Harris's views regarding the relative roles of peers and parents in the outcome for a child, she makes one point with which I wholeheartedly concur: Having a kind and loving relationship with a child should be pursued not because it produces a particular outcome but because it is the best and only kind of relationship one can imagine any adult wanting to have with a child.

APPENDIX A

Glossary

ABC Model of Discipline   A framework I have developed for integrating the three major approaches to discipline, which I term "Affective," "Behavioral," and "Cognitive." For each approach, the model delineates three principles, one linking each of the three domains of discipline ("Warmth," "Tolerance," and "Influence") with a desired long-term social competence outcome ("Happiness," "Boldness," and "Niceness," respectively). The three-tiered framework of the model is depicted in Figure 6.8. The purpose of the model is to (1) help caregivers understand the psychological theory underlying various discipline curricula, (2) provide caregivers with a broader set of concepts and skills than might be found in curricula operating within only a single approach, and (3) empower caregivers with information that will allow them to detect discipline advice that is invalid (e.g., an overly narrow prescription that emphasizes only one or two of the three discipline domains).

Accept Feelings   One of the nine principles in the ABC Model of Discipline. The principle is stated as "Caregivers should provide symbolic outlets for the expression of feelings." Accept Feelings is the Affective principle for Tolerance, the discipline domain that helps facilitate development of the desired child social competence outcome of Boldness. This principle is derived from the psychoanalytic notion that maladaptive behaviors are motivated by strong feelings and that getting in touch with those feelings helps in the child's development of self-regulatory controls over his behavior. The principle is also based on the ethical belief that everyone—children as well as adults—has a right to have and to express feelings, and such expressions are healthy and acceptable, even when they are accompanied by overt behaviors that may need to be curtailed. The basic technique by which this principle is implemented (other than by not doing anything) is through active listening, which is a caregiver communication technique that takes the form "You feel x about y."

Active Listening   A technique in which a feeling is reflected back to an individual through a comment that takes the form "You feel *x* about *y*." This technique is applied frequently in the Affective approach to discipline (Tolerance domain) as a means for the caregiver to accept and to facilitate affective expressions by a child. See **Reflection.**

Affective Approach   One of the three major approaches to discipline education. This "neopsychoanalytic" approach is loosely derived from the ideas of Sigmund Freud and Carl Rogers. The basic idea underlying this approach, which was expressed in a widely read book by Dorothy Baruch and later in books by Haim Ginott and Thomas Gordon, is that child misbehavior stems from strong feelings and that the best way to deal with such behavior and to promote healthy socioemotional development in the child is to allow an acceptable outlet for those feelings while setting limits on unacceptable expressions of those feelings. The three elements, or principles, of the Affective approach are (1) Show Respect (Warmth domain, Happiness outcome), (2) Accept Feelings (Tolerance domain, Boldness outcome), and (3) Assert Needs (Influence domain, Niceness outcome). See individual glossary entries or Figure 5.1 for formal statements of the principles.

Allow Independence   One of the nine principles in the ABC Model of Discipline. The principle is stated as "Caregivers should not interfere with the efforts of a child to solve his own problems and to develop his own lifestyle preferences." Allow Independence is the Cognitive principle for Tolerance, the discipline domain that helps facilitate development of the desired child social competence outcome of Boldness. This principle reflects the Adlerian notion that a key task of child development is the development of a unique identity that one can feel good about. In implementing this principle, caregivers are encouraged to treat children as individuals by never comparing them to other children, by maintaining clear adult-child boundaries (e.g., by avoiding guilt-tripping), and by allowing children to take as much ownership as possible of their own problems and to find solutions to those problems.

Applied Behavioral Analysis   The basic science from which the Behavioral approach to discipline is derived; also known as "ABA." Applied behavioral analysis uses learning theory, particularly as developed by B. F. Skinner and other operant behaviorists, to understand the relationship between environmental factors and changes in targeted behaviors. A fundamental characteristic of ABA is a rejection of hypothetical (i.e., internal and indirectly observable) psychological constructs in favor of a focus on overt observable behaviors. The basic concepts in the Behavioral approach to discipline—such as reinforcement, extinction, and punishment—are derived from the applied behavioral analysis framework.

Assert Needs   One of the nine principles in the ABC Model of Discipline. The principle is stated as "Caregivers should let a child know when he has done something unacceptable." Assert Needs is the Affective principle for Influence, the discipline domain that helps facilitate development of the desired child social competence outcome of Niceness. This principle is derived from two ideas: (1) an ethical notion that it is unfair for only a child's feelings to be considered and that a caregiver's feelings should be acknowledged as well and (2) a developmental notion that a child needs limits and that a caregiver who fails to set limits is doing a child a disservice. There is some disagreement between the two main groups of proponents of the Affective model regarding how forcefully this principle should be implemented, with those (such as Thomas Gordon) who espouse Carl Rogers's nondirective approach recommending a negotiation stance, while those (such as Haim Ginott) who are Freudians recommending a more insistent stance. All Affective discipline experts, however, stress the importance for the child's healthy development, as well as for the caregiver's sanity, of letting a child know when his behavior is bothersome or problematic.

Be Contingent   One of the nine principles in the ABC Model of Discipline. The principle is stated as "Caregivers should not punish behaviors they like and should not praise behaviors they dislike." Be Contingent is the Behavioral principle for Influence, the discipline domain that helps facilitate development of the desired child social competence outcome of Niceness. This principle reflects the behaviorist notion that social learning occurs in children as a function of the skill with which caregivers respond to child behaviors. Although caregivers are generally encouraged to respond with much praise for desirable behaviors and by either punishing or (more typically) ignoring undesirable behaviors, the Be Contingent principle is worded negatively: "not punish behaviors they like and . . . not praise behaviors they dislike." This phrasing emphasizes that caregivers have a range of acceptable options within the categories of liked or disliked child behavior as long as they avoid encouraging misbehavior or discouraging good behavior. See **Consistency.**

Behavioral Approach   One of the three major approaches to discipline education. This approach is derived from the ideas of B. F. Skinner and his colleagues and adherents. A core belief of the operant conditioning literature is that behavior in an organism (pigeon, rat, child, etc.) is shaped by the environmental contingencies that *follow* the behavior rather than by the contingencies that precede it (a feature of the older classical conditioning literature). The key contingency in this approach is "positive reinforcement" (i.e., something desired by the organism that therefore serves as a motivator). Applied to discipline, this means that caregivers should be careful to respond contingently to child behaviors in a manner that increases adaptive (desired) behaviors and reduces maladaptive (undesired) behaviors. Three types of contingencies are featured in the Behavioral approach: "praise" (positive reinforcement), "ignoring" (lack of response, including adult attention [which serves as a powerful reinforcer]), and "punishment" (an adult response intended to terminate a child misbehavior). In operant theory, undesired behavior is "extinguished" more effectively by ignoring it (paired with differentially praising the next-appearing desired behavior) than by punishing it. The three elements, or principles, of the Behavioral approach are (1) Give Positives (Warmth domain, Happiness outcome), (2) Ignore Much (Tolerance domain, Boldness outcome), and (3) Be Contingent (Influence domain, Niceness outcome). See individual glossary entries or Figure 5.5 for formal statements of the principles.

Boldness   One of the three desired social competence outcomes in the ABC Model of Discipline. (The other two are Happiness and Niceness.) Boldness (and the linked discipline domain of Tolerance) is an aspect of social competence that is sometimes ignored by discipline experts, particularly those with an authoritarian bent, who act as if unquestioning obedience is the best and only purpose of discipline. However, Boldness should be considered an important aspect of social competence because it enables a child to develop a sense of his own preferences and needs and makes it possible for him to say "no" to unwanted or harmful demands. Each of the three major discipline approaches in the ABC model has a principle in the Tolerance domain that has the hoped-for effect of promoting the outcome of Boldness in children: (1) Accept Feelings (Affective approach), (2) Ignore Much (Behavioral approach), and (3) Allow Independence (Cognitive approach).

Boundary Issues   Factors relating to maintenance of clear, if necessarily flexible, lines of demarcation between the needs, roles, and perspectives of adults and the needs, roles, and perspectives of children. Discipline problems often result from overly fuzzy, rigid, or confused setting of boundaries, as when a caregiver imposes her needs or perspectives on a child, views her role as that of a peer or playmate rather than an adult, or views the child as more of an adult than is legally or morally acceptable (as in sexual abuse). All three discipline approaches emphasize the importance of boundary issues, but these are especially emphasized in the Affective and Cognitive approaches. In the Affective approach, boundary issues are addressed in the recognition that a child's feelings do not have to be the same as the caregiver's and in the assertion that a caregiver has a responsibility to have her needs and values respected. In the Cognitive approach, boundary issues are addressed in the recognition that development of individual lifestyle choice is one of the central tasks of healthy socioemotional development, and, consequently, children (such as siblings) should be treated as individuals and enabled to develop their own identities. In the Behavioral approach, even though there is less explicit discussion of boundary issues, the advice to caregivers to ignore minor annoyances and to concentrate on major ones has the effect of respecting the child's right to have a sphere of activity free from adult intrusion and control. The term "enmeshment" is sometimes used to describe a dysfunctional family style that has amorphous boundaries, with excessive intrusiveness by members into each other's lives.

Bug-in-the Ear   A technique for improving discipline competence by equipping a trainer with an FM transmitter and a caregiver with an earpiece that has an FM receiver in it. This technique is sometimes used by Behavioral discipline trainers as a means of providing *in vivo* (real-world) as opposed to *in vitro* (simulated, through discussion of scenarios) feedback. Typically, the trainer observes the caregiver and one or more children from behind a one-way mirror and prompts the caregiver whenever an opportunity to praise, to punish, or to ignore presents itself or is missed; the trainer praises the caregiver when she responds appropriately to such opportunities.

Burst of Extinction   A term used by behaviorists to refer to the common tendency of children and youth to escalate an offensive behavior during the initial period when a caregiver is attempting to extinguish it through differential reinforcement (a combination of ignoring behavior one does not like but can live with and reinforcing incompatible behavior one likes and wants to see more of). This behavior is kind of a limit-testing by the child to see if and when the caregiver will cave in; therefore, it is important for the caregiver to stand firm during this period, because the ignored behavior will eventually decrease in frequency but will continue if the caregiver starts attending to it again.

Chaotic Discipline   One of the four types of caregiver discipline identified by Diana Baumrind. Within Baumrind's two-factor model, which includes elements she called "Control" (equivalent to the ABC domain of Influence) and "Warmth" (equivalent to the ABC domain of Warmth), Chaotic discipline results when caregivers exercise low levels of Control/Influence and low levels of Warmth. These are caregivers who basically ignore children and set few limits but erupt occasionally with very aversive communications, often characterized by violence. Children exposed to Chaotic discipline are, not surprisingly, at the highest risk of developing delinquent, antisocial, and maladaptive patterns of behavior. For more detail on Baumrind's model, see **Harmonious Parenting.**

Child Abuse   A term used in legal as well as human-services circles to refer to a pattern of caregiving that is so dangerous or destructive as to be considered grounds for civil or criminal proceedings intended to protect affected children and to punish or restrict offending caregivers. Abuse can take one or a combination of three forms: (1) "physical abuse" refers to infliction of tissue damage through use of harsh physical punishment, such as whipping, burning, pinching, or hitting; (2) "sexual abuse" refers to inappropriate genital contact with a child; and (3) "emotional abuse" (not surprisingly, the hardest to define or to document) refers to excessive use of psychologically damaging punishment, such as shaming, ridicule, and isolation. Abuse is often found in combination with child neglect.

Child Neglect   A term used in legal as well as human-services circles to refer to a habitual inability of caregivers to provide a sufficiently safe, stimulating, or nurturing environment for children under their care. Child neglect is often seen in chronically disorganized caregivers, for whom mental illness, substance abuse, or intellectual limitations can contribute to poor judgment around such issues as medical care, hygiene, nutrition, and physical protection from harm. Although child neglect is the most common reason for termination of parental rights (sometimes merging into abuse when children are harmed as a result of lax supervision), it is also a highly nebulous classification, given the general absence of clear standards for adequate caregiving. This lack of clear standards, as well as a lack of meaningful measures of caregiver adequacy, sometimes results in discriminatory action by child protective workers who may be tempted to impose their own cultural values concerning what constitutes adequate child care.

Choice Theory   An approach to relating to children, also known as "Control Theory," that was developed by William Glasser and that grew out of a counseling framework he termed "Reality Therapy." The purpose of Choice Theory is to help a child understand that his actions, such as those that habitually get him in trouble, are not automatic reactions to external events (or the actions of others) but are conscious choices that are influenced by his own thoughts and the things he tells himself about those events. The idea is to help a child develop self-regulatory skills by getting him to understand the connection between his responses and the (often unintended) negative social consequences that sometimes flow from those responses.

Coercion Cycle   A term coined by Gerald Patterson and colleagues to refer to a short-term cyclical interaction that starts when a child engages in some minor misbehavior, which coerces the caregiver into making a nattering response (e.g., "Stop it"), which coerces the child into stopping briefly. This cycle typically starts over again a few minutes later, when the child engages in the same or a somewhat different minor misbehavior. The reason why such a cycle (characterized by mutual infliction of pain between child and caregiver) tends to repeat itself *ad infinitum* is because the child's brief stopping is negatively reinforcing the caregiver (who deludes herself into thinking that the nattering worked), while the adult's nattering is positively reinforcing the child's misbehavior by paying attention to it. The way to break such a cycle is for a caregiver to begin to ignore minor misbehaviors (saving punishment for a smaller class of major misbehaviors) and look for opportunities to more frequently praise the occurrence of desirable behaviors.

Cognitive Approach   One of the three major approaches to discipline education. This approach is based on the ideas of Alfred Adler, the pioneering psychiatrist who introduced such concepts as self-esteem, birth order, and sibling rivalry. The basic idea underlying this approach is that child misbehavior stems from a combination of a desire for power, a need to stake out one's own identity, and a failure to understand why good behavior is in the child's own best interest. The three elements, or principles, of the Cognitive approach are (1) Encourage Participation (Warmth domain, Happiness outcome), (2) Allow Independence (Tolerance domain, Boldness outcome), and (3) Inform Why (Influence domain, Niceness outcome). See individual glossary entries or Figure 5.9 for formal statements of the principles.

Consistency   A term that refers to a caregiver's making similar responses over time to various classes of child behaviors, such that a child has some idea of what is desired or undesired by a caregiver and has some idea of what he can or cannot get away with. Many assume wrongly that the Behavioral approach advocates absolute consistency, but that is true only up to a point (see **Be Contingent**). In fact, the important thing for behaviorists is not always reinforcing a praiseworthy behavior but rather never punishing a praiseworthy behavior. Some inconsistency (in not always praising a desired behavior) is actually beneficial, because it makes for a more natural and comfortable situation for caregivers, and it is more likely to create intermittent reinforcement, which is more powerful than continuous reinforcement at maintaining a desired child behavior.

Control   Another term for what I call "Influence," which is one of the three discipline domains in the ABC Model of Discipline. As used in research by Diana Baumrind and others, Control/Influence is one of the dimensions (along with Warmth) by which caregivers can be ranked when measuring their discipline competence. Baumrind described the ideal caregiver as one who is "Authoritative," scoring high on both Warmth and Control/Influence. The weakness in Baumrind's model is that it does not take into account the critical domain of Tolerance. For more detail on Baumrind's model, see **Harmonious Parenting.**

Council Meetings   A central method (termed either "class councils" or "family councils") in the Cognitive approach to discipline, intended to mediate disputes, solve problems, and create a spirit of cooperation and compromise within classroom and family settings. The method, involving regular (usually weekly) meetings attended by caregivers and children, was developed by Rudolf Dreikurs, a disciple of Alfred Adler, and was based on the idea that child misbehavior is in part motivated by a need for attention, power, and an enhanced sense of adequacy. By creating a cooperative framework, it was believed that children would learn that these needs could be met empathically and constructively. The council method is embedded within Encourage Participation, the Cognitive principle for the domain of Warmth.

Decision Window   A technique invented by Thomas Gordon and used within the Affective approach to help a caregiver decide upon the types of child behaviors that reflect a problem the child is having (and thus call for a reflective comment or no action) and the types of child behaviors that are problematic for the caregiver (and thus call for an I-message, and perhaps a reflective comment if the behavior also indicates a problem for the child). The technique also has utility in helping caregivers develop a better understanding of their own values, expectations, and response styles regarding discipline.

Differential Reinforcement   A key concept of the Behavioral approach, defined as the pairing of ignoring (extinction) a child behavior the caregiver does not like but can live with and praising an incompatible behavior the caregiver likes and wants to see more of. Differential reinforcement is a very powerful technique for building child social competence (i.e., increasing the child's ratio of desirable to bothersome behaviors). An example of differential reinforcement would be a caregiver's ignoring a child when he whines about having fish for dinner and then praising him when he eats most of it.

Discipline   The caregiving process by which adults attempt to influence the short-term behavior (cessation or initiation of activities) and long-term (socio-emotional) development of children. Although the term is often assumed to be synonymous with "punishment," punishment is only one of the techniques used to discipline children, and caregivers who are highly effective at discipline typically use punishment very sparingly. The term "behavior management" is used synonymously with discipline, particularly in school or institutional settings, and especially by experts who have a Behavioral orientation.

Discrimination Training   A set of training techniques used by adherents of the Behavioral approach, whereby caregivers are made more aware of when to praise, when to punish, and when to ignore child behaviors. Typically, the training involves initial simulations using videotaped or written scenarios, followed by monitored interaction with actual children using bug-in-the-ear feedback from a trainer.

Diversionary Tactic   A common technique used by children to sidetrack caregivers from following through on the imposition of a limit. An example would be a young boy picking up a jar of something in a store and, upon being told to put it back, then asking his mother to read the contents of the label on the jar. The intent of the boy's diversionary tactic (asking his mom to read the label) is to divert his mother from following through on the limit (making him put the jar back). Caregivers often fall for these tactics because they have trouble coordinating the competing goals that are involved (in this case, following through on the limit versus supporting the child's interest in reading). Diversionary tactics should never be responded to, as they weaken the ability of a caregiver to set limits in an effective manner.

Domains of Discipline   Foundational elements in the conduct of discipline that contribute to favorable outcomes in both the short term and the long term. The three domains in the ABC Model of Discipline are Warmth, Tolerance, and Influence. These domains emerged from factor analytic research studies of the characteristics of effective caregivers and are applicable to all three approaches that make up the ABC model (Affective, Behavioral, and Cognitive approaches). Each domain supports a specific long-term social competence outcome. The domain of Warmth supports the outcome of Happiness, Tolerance supports Boldness, and Influence supports Niceness.

Effectiveness Training   A curriculum—often with a prefix applied, such as "Parent Effectiveness Training" (PET) or "Teacher Effectiveness Training" (TET)—for training caregivers in the Affective approach to discipline. Devised by psychologist Thomas Gordon and derived from the ideas of Carl Rogers (the inventor of nondirective, or client-centered, psychotherapy), PET/TET teaches three core discipline techniques: (1) active listening (e.g., "You feel x about y"), (2) use of I-messages (e.g., "I feel x when you do y because z") as opposed to you-messages (e.g., "You are an ungrateful little fool who never listens"), and (3) use of the decision window (a graphic device intended to help a caregiver know when she and/or a child does or does not have a problem and to guide her discipline response or nonresponse accordingly). A difference between Gordon and Haim Ginott (the other major developer of the Affective approach) is that Gordon (who had many Cognitive/humanistic leanings) felt that caregiver-child differences should be resolved through negotiation, while Ginott was more comfortable with the idea of an adult's imposing her will on a child (albeit carefully, in line with the Accept Feelings and Show Respect principles).

Encourage Participation   One of the nine principles in the ABC Model of Discipline. The principle is stated as "Caregivers should allow a child to participate in making and applying rules." Encourage Participation is the Cognitive principle for Warmth, the discipline domain that helps facilitate development of the desired child social competence outcome of Happiness. This principle is derived from ideas in the personality theory of Alfred Adler relating to his belief that a basic human motivation is the need to feel important and effective. Child misbehavior, thus, can be considered to be in part motivated by a sense of powerlessness and unimportance. Application of the Encourage Participation principle can take many forms, one of the main ones being family or class councils, a collaborative problem-solving method developed by an Adler disciple, Rudolf Dreikurs.

Floortime   A technique involving a caregiver's getting down on the floor and talking with a young child about his feelings. Developed by the late psychiatrist Stanley I. Greenspan (no relation), floortime is intended to help young children develop greater empathy and to help caregivers become more skilled in talking the language of emotion with children. Although floortime is a general tool for use with all young children, it has become widely used with autistic children, given that an inability to take the perspective of others is one of the defining features of autistic spectrum disorders.

Give Positives   One of the nine principles in the ABC Model of Discipline. The principle is stated as "Caregivers should do a lot more praising than punishing." Give Positives is the Behavioral principle for Warmth, the discipline domain that helps facilitate development of the desired child social competence outcome of Happiness. This principle is derived from the behaviorist notion of positive reinforcement, whereby contingently praising a child behavior that one likes and wants to see more of (i.e., right after it occurs) serves to increase the frequency of such behaviors. Thus, reinforcement is important not only in increasing Happiness but also as a very powerful tool (especially when used in conjunction with contingent ignoring and, infrequently, punishing) for increasing the frequency of adaptive behaviors and reducing the frequency of maladaptive behaviors. Although behaviorists generally do not talk about hypothetical personality constructs, such as Happiness, and prefer to discuss reinforcement mainly in terms of its central role in building skills in the child, I think it is reasonable to point out that a much-praised (and little-punished) child is more likely than not to be a happy child.

Happiness   One of the three desired social competence outcomes in the ABC Model of Discipline. (The other two are Boldness and Niceness.) Clearly, Happiness is a major goal of discipline, as almost any caregiver, when asked what she wishes for a particular child, will give as her first answer "to grow up to be a happy person." The term, as used here, refers to a quality of child temperament describing someone who has a generally positive and stable mood and an ability to deal effectively with frustration and adversity. Each of the three major discipline approaches in the ABC model has a principle in the Warmth domain that has the hoped-for effect of promoting the outcome of Happiness in children: (1) Show Respect (Affective approach), (2) Give Positives (Behavioral approach), and (3) Encourage Participation (Cognitive approach).

Harmonious Parenting   A pattern of caregiver discipline identified by Diana Baumrind wherein parents do very little controlling yet children are well behaved, well adjusted, and socially competent. Baumrind first developed a two-factor system for describing caregivers, involving elements she called "Control" (equivalent to the ABC domain of Influence) and "Warmth" (equivalent to the ABC domain of Warmth). In Baumrind's scheme, caregivers fell into one of four categories: "Authoritarian" (high on Control, low on Warmth), "Permissive" (low on Control, high on Warmth), "Authoritative" (high on Control, high on Warmth), and "Chaotic" (low on Control, low on Warmth). She regarded the ideal form of discipline as Authoritative. In follow-up studies, she detected a fifth pattern, which she named "Harmonious," in which only moderate application of Control/Influence produced highly socially competent children. Baumrind attributed this result to the children's having become so well behaved (as a result of earlier more assertive discipline) that caregivers no longer had to set many limits, or else did so by the merest of glances. However, others (myself included) believe that Harmonious caregivers are high on a third domain—Tolerance—and are able to differentiate between situations where a controlling response is or is not called for. Thus, Harmonious discipline, rather than being a special case within Baumrind's typology, likely highlights a weakness in her model. A two-factor (Control/Influence plus Warmth) discipline model is inadequate, and a third factor (Tolerance) is needed. Harmonious discipline is superior to Authoritative discipline in that it enables caregivers to respond differentially to situations without feeling the need to respond to all child misbehaviors, even of a minor nature, with toughness.

Ignore Much   One of the nine principles in the ABC Model of Discipline. The principle is stated as "Caregivers should do a lot more ignoring than punishing." Ignore Much is the Behavioral principle for Tolerance, the discipline domain that helps facilitate development of the desired child social competence outcome of Boldness. This principle is derived from the behaviorist notion of extinction, whereby not giving either reinforcement or punishment to a child behavior that one does not like but can live with enables the behavior to die out on its own. Ignoring is most effective, however, if it is paired (through differential reinforcement) with praise (reinforcement) immediately after the next-occurring behavior that one likes and would like to see more of. This is especially powerful if the praised behavior is something that is incompatible with the ignored behavior. An example would be praising a child for eating his vegetables after ignoring him when he complained about having to do so.

I-message   A term coined by Thomas Gordon to describe a method used in the Affective approach for setting a limit in a manner that conforms to the Show Respect principle (i.e., refraining from commenting on a child's character, motives, or overall patterns of behavior, even when setting limits on a specific objectionable action). I-messages take the form "I feel x when you do y because z." By thus briefly focusing on an objectionable act in relation to her feelings, the caregiver is less likely to make the child feel attacked.

Influence   One of the three discipline domains in the ABC Model of Discipline. (The other two are Warmth and Tolerance.) In the ABC model, Influence is linked logically to the desired child social competence outcome of Niceness. The basic idea behind Influence is that caregivers should provide guidance and direction to the behavior of children. Each of the three major discipline education approaches has a principle for helping caregivers act competently in the domain of Influence. The three discipline principles associated with Influence are (1) Assert Needs (Affective approach), (2) Be Contingent (Behavioral approach), and (3) Inform Why (Cognitive approach).

Inform Why   One of the nine principles in the ABC Model of Discipline. The principle is stated as "Caregivers should help a child understand the reasons underlying rules and expectations." Inform Why is the Cognitive principle for Influence, the discipline domain that helps facilitate development of the desired child social competence outcome of Niceness. This principle is derived from the Adlerian notion that altruism (i.e., being "nice") is the key to developing positive mental health, and the key to becoming altruistic is becoming empathic (i.e., moved by the plight of others). By framing discipline consequences for a child's misbehavior as an opportunity to help him understand the impact of his behavior on others, the hope is that the child will acquire a better understanding of why good behavior is in everyone's interest.

Lecturing   An extended verbal explanation that often accompanies the setting of a limit by a caregiver. This is something generally to be avoided, as it is experienced by a child as a put-down and is often tuned out. For this reason, the Affective I-message formula ("I feel x when you do y because z") uses very few words instead of a long-winded lecture. Similarly, Behavioral and Cognitive experts emphasize that caregiver consequences, rather than extended verbalizations, are more power-ful (and less strife-filled) methods for bringing about improved child behavior.

Limit-Setting   Communication from a caregiver to a child that he needs to stop some offensive behavior; also known as "negative injunction." The term is espe-cially used in the Affective approach, where one formulation of Assert Needs (the principle for Influence), developed by Haim Ginott, follows this formula: "One should set a limit whenever a child does something dangerous or destructive or that violates one's standards of acceptability." The Assert Needs principle is based on the notion that children need limits and that caregivers have a right to have their feelings communicated, but that there should be a clear understanding of the kinds of situations in which limit-setting should or should not be done. The last phrase in Ginott's formulation—"standards of acceptability"—is intended to allow for individual and cultural variability across caregivers regarding what kinds of behaviors are problematic for them. Although symbolic expressions (e.g., words, whining) are generally exempted from limits under the Affective principle of Accept Feelings, there are occasions (such as when the verbalization takes the form of an obscenity or is overly rude) when a caregiver may choose to set a limit, depending on whether a child's use of particular words qualifies under her defini-tion of unacceptable conduct.

Logical or Natural Consequences   A basic technique advocated by Cognitive experts, in which a punishment for a misbehavior is designed to be educational while avoiding arbitrary use of power. Punishment for a child who leaves a bike outside in a rainstorm would provide an example of the two types of conse-quences. A natural consequence for that behavior would be letting the bike rust and become unusable, while a logical consequence would be locking it up and not letting the child use it for a period of time. In both cases, the objective is to help the child come to understand that putting a bike away is for his own benefit rather than something that must be done simply because an adult said so. Cognitive experts tend to prefer natural over logical consequences (more educational, less coercive) but prefer both over punishments that have no connection to the offending action.

Moral Judgment The quality of one's understanding of ethical situations, as reflected in the ability to identify the fairest, and most empathic, course of action. Becoming a kind person (i.e., an outcome of Niceness) is one of the major tasks of child development, and each of the three major discipline approaches has a principle intended to facilitate the development of this quality. Moral development is most explicitly emphasized in the Cognitive approach, however, because having a prosocial orientation is one of the defining features of good mental health according to the writings of Alfred Adler, whose personality theory undergirds the Cognitive approach.

Nattering A recurrent pattern of an adult's responding to minor child misbehaviors (such as grabbing items off supermarket shelves) with weak limit-setting comments along the lines of "Stop it" or "How many times have I told you not to do that?" Though intended as a form of mild punishment, nattering can still become reinforcing to the child because it also represents adult attention, especially when a caregiver has a profound praise deficit (i.e., she rarely pays attention to desirable child behaviors, and her nattering is so constant that it becomes a kind of background noise). Nattering is a key element in what has been termed a "coercion cycle" and is commonly found in families or classrooms marked by caregiver ineffectiveness and unhappiness.

Natural Consequences See **Logical or Natural Consequences.**

Niceness One of the three desired social competence outcomes in the ABC Model of Discipline. (The other two are Happiness and Boldness.) Niceness refers to those prosocial behaviors, such as kindness and friendliness, that cause other people (children as well as adults) to like someone. Clearly, Niceness is a major goal of discipline, as almost any caregiver, when asked what she wishes for a particular child, will give as her second answer (after "to grow up to be a happy person") "to grow up to be a decent person." Each of the three major discipline approaches in the ABC model has a principle in the Influence domain that has the hoped-for effect of promoting the outcome of Niceness in children: (1) Assert Needs (Affective approach), (2) Be Contingent (Behavioral approach), and (3) Inform Why (Cognitive approach).

Nondirective Therapy An influential theory of counseling, also known as "client-centered therapy," that was invented in the mid-twentieth century by an

American psychologist, Carl Rogers. The theory can be considered neopsycho-analytic in that although it lacks some of the trappings of classical Freudian analysis (such as dream interpretation), it shares an emphasis on helping an individual get in better touch with his feelings. This is done by use of a core technique known as reflection or active listening, in which a feeling is reflected back to a client through a comment along the lines of "You feel x about y." This approach is considered humanistic because it is grounded in the notion that all human beings, and their feelings, are deserving of "unconditional positive regard" without judgment or condemnation. Both of these notions are central to the Affective approach to discipline, in that caregivers are encouraged to accept and to facilitate affective expressions by a child, through the use of active listening responses, and to set limits in a way that avoids attacking a child's feelings of self-worth.

Outcomes   In the context of the ABC Model of Discipline, behavioral or personality traits that allow an individual to function successfully in interpersonal relations and socially valued and age-relevant pursuits in life. In the model, social competence outcomes are not specific accomplishments (such as earning a high school diploma or landing a job), but rather are the traits that support such accomplishments. All three approaches that make up the ABC model (Affective, Behavioral, and Cognitive approaches) recognize three desired long-term social competence outcomes: Happiness, Boldness, and Niceness. Each outcome is considered a logical outgrowth of effective caregiving in a particular domain of discipline. Happiness is linked with the domain of Warmth, Boldness is linked with Tolerance, and Niceness is linked with Influence.

Permissive Parenting   One of the four types of caregiver discipline identified by Diana Baumrind. Within Baumrind's two-factor model, which includes elements she called "Control" (equivalent to the ABC domain of Influence) and "Warmth" (equivalent to the ABC domain of Warmth), Permissive parents operate at a low level of Control/Influence and a high level of Warmth. These individuals were found by Baumrind to have children who were less socially competent than were children whose parents exercised more Control/Influence. More recent scholarship has suggested that a pattern of discipline Baumrind designated "Harmonious" (medium on Control, high on Warmth) is the most effective. For more detail on Baumrind's model, see **Harmonious Parenting.**

Power Struggles   A key concept in the Cognitive approach to discipline that relates to a nonproductive standoff in which a caregiver tries to forcefully impose her will on a child while the child resists, sometimes violently. Cognitively oriented authors stress the importance of avoiding power struggles when dealing with undesirable child behaviors. Power struggles are counterproductive for several reasons: (1) they foster resentment and cause a child to focus more on justifying his own position (and plotting revenge) than on taking the caregiver's perspective, (2) they typically lack an educational component and thus are unlikely to help the child develop an understanding of the need for certain kinds of conduct, and (3) they encourage the child to develop a habit of blaming or using others rather than taking responsibility for his own behavior. For these reasons, a caregiver is encouraged not only to avoid engaging in her own power struggles with a child but also to resist efforts by the child (such as through tattling) to ensnare her in his power struggles with peers or siblings. The use of logical or natural consequences is a recommended means of exercising Influence precisely because it enables the caregiver to educate the child about the importance of good behavior while at the same time avoiding any element of struggle or power assertion.

Praise An expression of verbal approval directed to a child by a caregiver for some act of which the caregiver approves. In the Behavioral approach, the term "praise" is sometimes used as if it were synonymous with positive reinforcement, regardless of whether verbalization is involved. In the ABC model, the Behavioral principle for the domain of Warmth, Give Positives, is stated as "Caregivers should do a lot more praising than punishing." Interpreting praise broadly, this means that one should do a lot more reinforcing than punishing.

Praise Deficit A ratio of praise (positive reinforcement) over punishment that is very low, approaching or lower than one to one. Praise deficits are commonly found in families or classrooms where kids are poorly behaved, owing to the fact that when punishment is constant, children tend to tune it out. Caregivers with praise deficits tend to operate on the twin mistaken assumptions that good behavior is to be taken for granted and that only through corrective feedback can a child's behavior improve. Ironically, such caregivers want to be in control but fail to recognize that they are allowing the child to set the agenda. A goal of most Behavioral interventions with ineffective caregivers is to bring their praise-over-punishment ratio up to some multiple (optimal would be a ratio of at least four or more to one). This is done by encouraging caregivers to ignore many child behaviors that they previously would have punished and to praise many behaviors that they previously would have ignored (in the process becoming less perfectionistic in terms of what child behaviors they see as deserving of praise).

Principles of the ABC Model of Discipline Nine statements (three each for the Affective, Behavioral, and Cognitive approaches) that define the essentials of competent caregiving. Each principle links a discipline domain (Warmth, Tolerance, or Influence) with a desired long-term social competence outcome (Happiness, Boldness, or Niceness). The nine principles and their linkages within the framework of the complete model are depicted in Figure 6.8. Figures 5.1, 5.5, and 5.9 provide formal statements of the principles and show linkages for the Affective, Behavioral, and Cognitive approaches, respectively.

Psychoanalysis   An important intellectual framework invented by Viennese psychiatrist Sigmund Freud at the end of the nineteenth century and periodically modified by him and his followers through the first half of the twentieth century. Both as a theory of personality and as a theory of psychotherapy, psychoanalysis has influenced practice in many areas, including caregiver discipline. The essence of psychoanalysis is that people who are unhappy or ineffective possess strong feelings (anger, sexuality, etc.) that have gone underground into their "unconscious." The key to making these people happier and more effective is to assist them in consciously understanding who they really are and how they came to be alienated from themselves. The Affective approach to discipline grew out of psychoanalytic theory, as reflected in the core notion that a key to effective caregiver discipline is helping children better understand and articulate the feelings underlying various forms of bothersome conduct.

Punishment   One of the three types of caregiver responses in the Behavioral discipline approach. (The other two are praise and ignoring.) Punishment is defined technically as "A caregiver response that has the effect of stopping or reducing the frequency of some offending child behavior." In lay parlance, punishment is often equated with a harsh caregiver response, such as spanking, but within the Behavioral approach, punishment takes in a much broader range of responses, including a simple verbal command, such as "Stop doing that." A common form of mild punishment advocated by behaviorists, primarily for young children, is time-out. Within the Behavioral approach, punishment is something to be used infrequently (i.e., a caregiver should punish only behaviors that she does not like and cannot live with). The Give Positives principle of the Behavioral approach states "Caregivers should do a lot more praising than punishing." In quantitative terms, in a relatively large unit of time (such as a day), "a lot" means a ratio of three to five praises (positive utterances or gestures) for each punishment (negative utterances or gestures).

Ratio of Response   A concept important in the Behavioral discipline approach, involving the relative frequency, within any day, of a caregiver's praising, punishing, and ignoring. The basic rule of thumb is that there should be considerably more praising than punishing and considerably more ignoring than punishing. This ensures that the caregiver will display Warmth (by doing much praising) and Tolerance (by doing much ignoring) while also exerting Influence (by providing direction, through contingent pairing and coordinated use of praise and punishment) when called for.

Reflection   The basic technique used by nondirective and neo-Freudian psychotherapists and a core means for implementing Tolerance within the Affective discipline system; also known as "active listening." Reflection takes the form "You feel *x* about *y*" and may be followed up by one or more additional reflective statements. Within a discipline context, for example, when Paul punches Johnny while yelling, "Don't kick my book bag," the caregiver would say, "You are really mad at Johnny." After Paul says, "Yes, he is always kicking my things," the caregiver would follow up with "You hate it when Johnny messes with your stuff." After Paul replies "Yes," the caregiver would respond with a limit-setting I-message along the lines of "But the rule in this classroom [house etc.] is that people are not to be hit." The caregiver could then continue with a discussion of alternative, acceptable ways Paul could let Johnny know how he feels.

Reinforcement   The central process for the Behavioral approach that explains how a caregiver increases the frequency of a target behavior in a child. Its most common form is positive reinforcement, which serves to increase the frequency of a target behavior by praising or rewarding it. An example of this would be smiling or saying "Thanks" after a child takes out the garbage. A less common form is negative reinforcement, which increases the frequency of a target behavior by removing some aversive stimulus. An example would be telling a child he is no longer restricted from going out with friends after he has brought his grades up to an acceptable level.

Sarcasm   A disrespectful way of communicating that involves a combination of irony and a disparaging tone of voice, as when one says "You really are smart" in a tone that says "You really are dumb." Sarcasm is used frequently by teachers, and by parents, who fail to understand that its main effect is to make a child resent the caregiver or, worse, develop feelings of worthlessness.

Shaping   The process of teaching a child a new skill or behavior sequence primarily through the use of positive reinforcement of "successive approximations" of the desired behavior; used mainly within the Behavioral approach. This reinforcement is relatively continuous until the behavior becomes well established. After the desired behavior sequence has been established, a caregiver is encouraged to shift to a more natural intermittent pattern of reinforcement, wherein the behavior is still reinforced frequently, but not every time it occurs.

Show Respect   One of the nine principles in the ABC Model of Discipline. The principle is stated as "Caregivers should refrain from commenting on a child's character, motives, or overall patterns of behavior, or from otherwise assaulting a child's sense of worth." Show Respect is the Affective principle for Warmth, the discipline domain that helps facilitate development of the desired child social competence outcome of Happiness. This principle is derived from the notion of "unconditional positive regard" developed by Carl Rogers, which asserts that one's intrinsic worth as a human being remains constant, no matter how morally deplorable the nature of one's thoughts or acts. In terms of caregiver discipline, this translates into the advice to avoid commenting on a child's character, motives, or overall patterns of behavior, even when one is setting limits on a specific objectionable action. The principle is also reflected in the use of I-messages (which take the form "I feel x when you do y because z") rather than you-messages (which take the form "You [never think, are naughty, etc.]").

Sibling Rivalry   Competition or rivalry among children in the same social system, typically involving attempts to hurt each other by vying for the attention and approval of adults. A fairly universal phenomenon that typically diminishes in adolescence and adulthood, sibling rivalry can persist and take pathological forms (as in the Biblical story of how Cain killed his younger brother, Abel, because of jealousy over Abel's getting preferential treatment). Alfred Adler, whose ideas provide the theoretical foundation for the Cognitive approach, was one of the first to have written about this phenomenon (although he did not coin the term) within the context of a personality theory based on the notion of a child's being motivated to attain a sense of his own significance. In terms of the Cognitive approach, child behaviors reflecting sibling rivalry should never be encouraged or rewarded, and children should always be treated as individuals and never compared to one another.

Social Competence   The desired long-term outcome of discipline. This term refers to the extent to which an individual is able to interact with other human beings in a manner that is effective and valued by others. Social competence can be viewed either in terms of roles successfully played (e.g., friend, student, worker) or (more commonly) in terms of particular traits that contribute to the successful playing of those roles. Three interrelated social competence traits have been emphasized in the literature: "Character" (the extent to which one is cooperative and prosocial, while at the same time assertive when necessary), "Temperament" (the extent to which one is emotionally stable and can focus attention on demanding tasks), and "Social Intelligence" (the extent to which one can understand social situations and people, including others and oneself). A modified version of this scheme (splitting Character into Niceness and Boldness, emphasizing the Happiness aspects of Temperament, and treating Social Intelligence as an indirect "intervening variable") is used as one of the integrative devices in the ABC Model of Discipline.

Social Intelligence   An aspect of social competence that has to do with the ability to understand people and social situations. It is enhanced in children when caregivers set limits while providing explanations that help the child appreciate the impact his behavior has on other people and the possible consequences this may have for his own interests being met. The Cognitive approach to discipline is to a large extent based on the idea that a key aspect of helping children become morally admirable individuals is enhancing their social intelligence.

Social Skills Conventional social behaviors that contribute to people's being valued, such as saying hello, maintaining eye contact, observing reciprocity norms, and so forth. Because these are concrete and observable actions, they are often targets for Behavioral interventions aimed at improving social competence in at-risk populations by increasing the frequency of valued social skills. In the absence of also improving social intelligence, however, social skills often fail to generalize to novel social situations.

Symbolic Expression The basic Affective discipline notion that caregivers should always allow (and ideally facilitate, through active listening) symbolic expressions of feelings, even when setting limits on overt (dangerous, destructive, or unacceptable) expressions of those feelings. A symbolic expression is one that uses words (such as "You're a mean mommy"), while an overt expression uses physical force (such as hitting a caregiver or kicking a chair). An appropriate response to a purely symbolic expression is either to ignore it or to make a comment, such as "You are really mad at me for not letting you stay up late."

Temperament A child's degree of emotional, motivational, and attentional stability, as reflected in his ability to sustain effort, to take things in stride (without flying off the handle), and to maintain a fairly consistent positive mood. For purposes of the ABC model, I reframe Temperament as Happiness. Clearly, Happiness is a major goal of discipline, as almost any caregiver, when asked what she wishes for a particular child, will give as her first answer "to grow up to be a happy person."

Time-out A mild form of punishment promoted in Behavioral discipline manuals for use especially with young children. Shorthand for "time-out from reinforcement," this term refers to a technique in which a caregiver removes a misbehaving child from the setting in which the misbehavior occurred and orders him to sit without moving or speaking in a spot where he has no interaction or eye contact with peers or adults for a specified period of time (one commonly used rule of thumb is a minute for each year of age). The power of the technique stems from the facts that (1) interaction with, and attention from, others is important to children, and removing it can be an effective motivator of better behavior and (2) the technique takes the element of argument and protracted struggle out of the equation. As with any form of punishment, time-out is effective when used sparingly and in combination with a shift toward greater caregiver use of praising and ignoring. Unfortunately, many caregivers mistakenly think that time-out is all that is needed to be effective at discipline; such overuse of the technique (as advocated in Thomas Phelan's books, where it is the core technique) is a perversion rather than an implementation of the Behavioral approach. The Behavioral approach, like the other two approaches, is grounded in positive relationships, and one can become effective at discipline without ever having to use time-out or any other form of punishment very much, if at all.

Token Economy A Behavioral method by which a caregiver rewards a child for good behavior by awarding points that can be traded for items or treats of the child's choosing. Because a token economy is a reinforcement rather than a punishment device, points should typically not be taken away for bad behaviors. The method is most often used to build competence in children who are severely lacking in it, and for that reason token economies are often found in institutional settings, such as residential treatment centers. Token systems typically have levels of progression built into them, such that when a child or youth reaches certain adjustment milestones, he will graduate to a more natural (i.e., less micromanaged) method for receiving periodic bonuses.

Tolerance One of the three discipline domains in the ABC Model of Discipline. (The other two are Warmth and Influence.) In the ABC model, Tolerance is linked logically to the desired child social competence outcome of Boldness. The basic idea behind Tolerance is that caregivers should maintain clear boundaries between themselves and the children in their care and allow the children some degree of autonomy. Each of the three major discipline education approaches has a principle for helping caregivers be competent in the domain of Tolerance. The three discipline principles associated with Tolerance are (1) Accept Feelings (Affective approach), (2) Ignore Much (Behavioral approach), and (3) Allow Independence (Cognitive approach).

Tough Love An approach to discipline that owes its name to a 1968 book with that title by Bill Milliken. Developed mainly to encourage parents of drug-using youths to become less enabling, the approach is based on the proposition that caregivers should not continue indefinitely to forgive intolerable and illegal behavior. However, when used as a general discipline framework, Tough Love has been taken to extreme lengths and appears to be encouraging parents to think that toughness, including threat of ultimate "parent-child divorce," is the best stance to take when dealing with all challenging child behaviors. This authoritarian approach seems to characterize application of the framework in the United States (through such abusive practices as youth boot camps), while in Great Britain a more balanced application, grounded in notions of character development, seems to have taken root.

Toxic Caregiving An unusually cruel, disparaging, manipulative, and unfair pattern of discipline that is often found in mentally ill caregivers and that makes it extremely difficult for children exposed to such a pattern to themselves develop good mental health. One of the hallmarks of toxic caregiving is extreme inconsistency, both across occasions (continually shifting demands and responses) and toward different children in the same setting (blatant playing of favorites).

Traditional Parenting An approach to caregiver discipline developed by John Rosemond that is based on a hierarchical view of the proper nature of the relationship between adults and children. This approach can be considered highly authoritarian, as there is much emphasis on Influence and punishment, with no emphasis on (and, in fact, a disputation of the importance of) Tolerance and Warmth. This lack of balance among the three discipline domains is also reflected in a thin range of technical options, as virtually every proposed response involves some form of punishment, regardless of the nature of the depicted situation or child.

Triangulation A term borrowed from the family therapy literature, which in the context of caregiver discipline refers to a phenomenon where one child tries to recruit a caregiver as an ally in his campaign (to become more powerful) against another child. A common example of triangulation is tattling, as when a child tells his mother that a sibling broke a family rule, and the mother responds by punishing the sibling. The best caregiver response to a triangulation game, stressed especially by Cognitive discipline experts, is to ignore it, thus communicating to the child that (1) he does not rank any higher in the family (or classroom) hierarchy than any other child and (2) underhanded scheming against others is not the key to success or happiness.

Warmth One of the three discipline domains in the ABC Model of Discipline. (The other two are Tolerance and Influence.) In the ABC model, Warmth is linked logically to the desired child social competence outcome of Happiness. The basic idea behind Warmth is that caregivers should maintain relationships with children that are kind and loving. Each of the three major discipline education approaches has a principle for helping caregivers be competent in the domain of Warmth. The three discipline principles associated with Warmth are (1) Show Respect (Affective approach), (2) Give Positives (Behavioral approach), and (3) Encourage Participation (Cognitive approach).

APPENDIX B

Using the ABC Model
to Evaluate Discipline Advice

W riters in the field of discipline often do not make clear which theoretical framework they are using or which other authors they may have borrowed ideas from. Readers are expected to accept discipline advice unquestioningly, as if the author had some direct pipeline to the Almighty. Lack of such theoretical openness makes it difficult for a reader to get beneath technical advice and understand an author's deeper message. It also makes it difficult for a reader to know whether an author is making sense or nonsense. In this appendix, I illustrate a technique for helping readers understand more fully the theoretical framework from which an author is operating. The technique also enables a reader to know whether an author's ideas have validity or whether he or she is so "full of it" that the ideas should be rejected.

The technique involves focusing on an author's major points, either those stated overtly or those revealed in portrayed examples. The reader can do this by writing down all (or a representative sample) of an author's pronouncements and checking off the ABC principles that are touched on, either affirmatively or contradictorily. In this way, one can determine if an author (1) fits into one of the three major approaches, (2) has an eclectic message that cuts across two or more approaches, or (3) has an idiosyncratic approach that falls outside any of the three major approaches. In the last case, the reader will also be alerted to the need to decide whether an author's message runs sufficiently against the ABC model that there is a possibility he or she might be leading people down a wrong path.

Here I use this technique to profile three discipline methods. These are the "Love and Logic" method of Foster Cline and Jim Fay, the "Assertive Discipline" method of Lee and Marlene Canter, and the method espoused in *From Chaos to Calm* by Janet Heininger and Sharon Weiss. These methods are ones that I had not read about before undertaking this exercise. However, I was sufficiently certain after looking them over that all would turn out to be relatively adequate (that turned out to be true for two of the three). I also chose methods that seemed to differ substantially from each other. Because I deliberately chose to analyze methods that I knew relatively little about, my background descriptions are fairly brief.

Using the ABC Model to Analyze the Love and Logic Method

Background

Parenting with Love and Logic: Teaching Children Responsibility (Cline and Fay 1990) was written by Foster Cline, a child and adult psychiatrist, and Jim Fay, a former teacher and school principal. Together, they founded the Colorado-based Cline-Fay Institute, now known as the Love and Logic Institute. Information about the institute and its publications and workshops can be obtained at www.loveandlogic.com. The company's products, including a companion book, *Teaching with Love and Logic*, are aimed at both parents and teachers. In fact, Fay notes on the institute's website that the method first grew out of his efforts as an educator to build classroom structures that "would teach children responsibility and self-discipline, while still giving kids the message that adults cared about them."

Fay notes that the method makes frequent use of the word "love" and acknowledges that "some people are uncomfortable when I bring up love in education. . . . 'This shouldn't be a popularity contest,' they say. But I started out as a parent and a teacher with lots of lecturing, threats, rewards, and punishments—and they didn't work." According to the website, "the love and logic philosophy teaches character" in three phases: "A child making a mistake, an adult feeling empathy and compassion for the child, and the kid learning from the consequences of his or her actions."

This philosophy is expanded in the introduction to the book under consideration, where Cline and Fay write

> Effective parenting centers around love: love that is not permissive, love that doesn't tolerate disrespect, but also love that is powerful enough to allow kids to make mistakes and permit them to live with the consequences of those mistakes. The logic is centered in the consequences themselves. Most mistakes do have logical consequences. And those consequences, when accompanied by empathy—our compassionate understanding of the child's disappointment, frustration, and pain—hit home with mind-changing power. It's never too late to begin parenting with love and logic. (1990, 12)

Conceptual Analysis

Based on the descriptive statements quoted above, with use of such terms as "logical consequences" and an emphasis on allowing the child to learn from his mistakes, it would seem that this book, and the whole Love and Logic curriculum, is rooted squarely in the Cognitive approach. However, in reading through the 1990 edition of the book (which has since been revised and expanded), I did not find a single citation of Dreikurs or any other discipline author, or any acknowledgment that the book was inspired by, or is part of, a larger movement. The authors create the impression, perhaps unintentionally, that their curriculum emerged totally out of their own experience and thinking. That may be true to some extent, but they did not invent the term "logical consequences," and I would be surprised if they were not influenced to some degree by Dreikurs and other like-minded authors.

The Love and Logic framework is imparted mainly through numerous brief "tips" and "pearls." No single statement summarizes the Love and Logic conceptual framework, although one can find many conceptual statements among the twenty-three tips that precede the presentation of the pearls. Some of these tips might be considered procedural, such as Tip 1, which cautions caregivers to use their "head" (i.e., the Cline-Fay framework) rather than their "gut" (i.e., old power-oriented habits) when disciplining children. An analysis of twenty-eight points from the Love and Logic framework (drawn primarily from the tips, not counting the purely procedural advice) is contained in Table B.1.

As suspected, the Love and Logic method falls squarely in the Cognitive camp. Twenty-two (78 percent) of the twenty-eight points involve Cognitive principles, while 18 percent involve Affective principles, and only 4 percent involve Behavioral principles. Although Cline and Fay describe their curriculum as emerging from their own experience, the resemblance to the standard Cognitive approach is striking. The major way in which Cline and Fay diverge from other Cognitively oriented experts is that the term "family council" is not mentioned even once. Apparently, council meetings involve a little too much democracy for the slightly power-oriented tastes of Cline and Fay.

There is a nice balance among the three domains. Thirty-nine percent of the points involve Influence principles, 36 percent involve Tolerance principles, and 25 percent involve Warmth principles. Given that the word "love" is in the title of the curriculum, I would have expected a little higher Warmth score, but 25 percent is still fairly high. In most of the examples used by Cline and Fay, Warmth is conveyed more in an absence of anger than in a surfeit of hugs, kisses, or endearments. Thus, a better name for this curriculum might be "Detachment and Logic." Warmth is encapsulated more in offering encouragement that a child can avoid a negative consequence in the future than in what one might consider a warm and fuzzy relationship.

If I have a problem with the Love and Logic method, it is in the authors' willingness to allow consequences that (to me) fall somewhere between neglectful and dangerous. Sending a child away hungry (as opposed to, say, denying him a treat) when he acts out at the dinner table is a violation of his basic right to adequate nutrition. Dropping a child off at the side of the road and letting him walk home could be grounds for judicial intervention, depending on the child's age, the distance, and what happens to him during the journey. Love and Logic is a fine exemplar of the Cognitive approach, but on occasion the authors take logic to an unrealistic extreme.

TABLE B.1 Content Analysis of the Points Made by Cline and Fay

Points made in *Parenting with Love and Logic*	Domain	Approach
Letting a child fail is important for him to later succeed	Tolerance	Cognitive
Building self-concept gives a child the courage to try hard things	Warmth	Cognitive
It is important to let a child decide things for himself	Tolerance	Cognitive
Give lots of hugs and loving messages	Warmth	Behavioral
Letting a child freeze is best way for him to learn to wear a coat	Influence	Cognitive
If there is any chance a child can fix a problem himself, let him	Tolerance	Cognitive
Giving a neglected dog away is the best way to teach a child to feed it	Influence	Cognitive
The best solution occurs when a child makes it himself	Tolerance	Cognitive
In almost all cases, let a child learn from consequences	Influence	Cognitive
Use thinking words, not fighting words	Influence	Cognitive
The consequence for misbehaving at the table is that a child goes hungry	Influence	Cognitive
Instead of saying "no," say, "yes, when you do _____"	Influence	Cognitive
When a child complains about a consequence, sympathize but do not relent	Warmth	Affective
Do not make a child's success your own, or he will sabotage it	Tolerance	Cognitive
Allow more freedom to a child as he gets older	Tolerance	Cognitive
Avoid control battles	Tolerance	Cognitive
Always offer a child choices	Tolerance	Cognitive
If a child will not get ready before the car leaves, let him walk	Influence	Cognitive
Save words for happy times; keep anger inside when a child misbehaves	Warmth	Affective
Do not respond to a child's anger, just keep repeating the consequence	Tolerance	Cognitive
Offer choices in a calm, nonhysterical manner	Warmth	Cognitive
The best consequence of bedtime hassles is letting a child be tired the next day	Influence	Cognitive
Consequences should help a child think about his behavior	Influence	Cognitive
The best consequence is one that occurs naturally	Influence	Cognitive
Empathize with a child when he suffers a bad consequence	Tolerance	Affective
If a child acts out on the way to the mall, hire a babysitter and make him pay for it	Influence	Cognitive
Be warm and sympathetic when a child is disappointed	Warmth	Affective
Do not reprimand a child when he fails at something	Warmth	Affective

Using the ABC Model to Analyze
the Assertive Discipline Method

Background

Assertive Discipline is a method developed in the mid-1970s by a husband and wife team, Lee and Marlene Canter. They established a California-based firm, Canter and Associates, to promote their ideas about discipline, particularly to educators. Information about Canter and Associates can be obtained at the website www.canter.net. Nothing much about the founders of this method can be gleaned from the website or from their books. On the back of *Assertive Discipline for Parents* (Canter and Canter 2001), it is noted that "Lee Canter's professional background is in child psychology and family counseling. Marlene Canter's background is in special education." No information about academic degrees is given, so it is probably safe to assume that neither of the Canters holds a doctorate (in my experience, educators and human-services professionals rarely pass up an opportunity to advertise a doctorate, even of the matchbook kind).

Unlike some experts, such as Thomas Gordon, who first developed their ideas in work with parents and then extended them to teachers, the Canters first developed their ideas in work with teachers and then extended those ideas to parents. However, the overwhelming emphasis of Canter and Associates remains products and training aimed at helping educators become more effective in dealing with students.

Conceptual Analysis

The book I analyze here is *Assertive Discipline: A Take Charge Approach for Today's Educator* (Canter and Canter 1988). Unlike most books on discipline aimed at teachers or parents, this book includes some preliminary discussion of theoretical matters. This is reflected not in the provision of a list or elaborated statement of core principles (in that sense, the book is no different from others) but in a discussion of the body of theory from which the book sprang. Unfortunately, that body of theory has nothing to do with discipline or child development.

The Canters indicate that the inspiration for their book, and for the Assertive Discipline method, came out of the literature on "Assertion Training." Assertion Training is a quasi-therapeutic self-help movement that was very popular in the late 1960s and early 1970s, around the time the Canters developed their discipline method. In the introduction to the book, the authors note that "'*Assertive Discipline*' is based primarily upon the principles of Assertion Training, which has evolved from social learning theory research. Assertion Training skills, therefore, have been developed by professionals who have conducted extensive research in the area of interpersonal communication" (1980, 10).

Assertion Training, according to the Canters, has the purpose of teaching individuals to "identify wants and feelings in interpersonal situations," to verbalize those wants and feelings, to persist in verbalizing those wants and feelings, and to use eye-gaze and nonverbal gestures that support the assertive verbalizations. Skills taught in Assertion Training sessions include being able to say "no" without feeling guilty; accepting and giving compliments; communicating thoughts that a listener might not want to hear; standing up for one's rights, even when being pressured; and being able to make requests of others.

In terms of applying the principles and methods of Assertion Training to classroom teachers, the Canters aim to help teachers (1) recognize situations where they need to be more assertive, (2) develop better verbal communication skills around limit-setting and praise, (3) become less aggressive (in the case of overly hostile teachers prone to yelling), (4) become more positive (in the case of overly negative teachers), (5) become more confident (in the case of "overwhelmed" teachers), and (6) acquire the skills to deal effectively with whatever behavior challenges they might encounter. The basic presentation technique used in the book is to set up scenarios and then provide three prototypical responses: (1) a "non-assertive" response style, in which the teacher is overly passive in getting her own needs and wants across; (2) a "hostile" response style, in which the teacher expresses her needs and wants in a manner that "abuses the rights and feelings of the children" (17); and (3) an "assertive" response style, in which the teacher is able to communicate her own wants and needs (i.e., set limits) in a manner that is likely to "maximize the teacher's potential to get her needs met without violating the best interests of the students" (18).

My initial guess, after reading the introductory material and before reading any of the case material, was that the Assertive Discipline method would most likely be categorized as a variant of the Affective approach. The emphasis on wants and needs (synonyms for "feelings"), the empowering of caregivers to get their needs met, and the admonition to do so in a manner that allows the child to get his needs (feelings) acknowledged and his self-worth respected all sound very similar to ideas expounded by Haim Ginott and Thomas Gordon. Determining whether this guess was correct requires taking a closer look at the specific situations and proposed solutions discussed by the Canters.

Content Analysis

Assertive Discipline presents many scenarios, and for each scenario provides a series of responses representative of a teacher's "assertive," "hostile," or "non-assertive" response style. I have analyzed a number of these scenarios, listing the major points made by the Canters about what they consider important in dealing with each one. Nine scenarios are presented in Table B.2, with a total of twenty-five points.

My original guess that Assertive Discipline would fall in the Affective camp was supported to an extent, with one major qualification. Seventeen (68 percent) of the points do involve Affective principles, with the balance divided between Behavioral (20 percent) and Cognitive (12 percent) principles. However, Tolerance

TABLE B.2 Content Analysis of the Points Made by Canter and Canter

Points made in *Assertive Discipline*	Domain	Approach
SCENARIO 1: Children are pushing and shoving.		
Use "assertive limit-setting" to communicate the need to stop	Influence	Affective
Follow this up with action ("Go to the end of the line")	Influence	Cognitive
Do not use sarcasm or degrading comments	Warmth	Affective
Positively recognize and support compliant behavior	Warmth	Behavioral
SCENARIO 2: A boy is stealing supplies and lying about it.		
State what you will not tolerate	Influence	Affective
Take the boy to the principal's office and call his parents	Influence	Cognitive
Do not label the child (e.g., "You little thief")	Warmth	Affective
SCENARIO 3: A young child who does not share is observed sharing.		
Give a hug and praise the child	Warmth	Behavioral
Comment on feelings about the act, not the child	Warmth	Affective
SCENARIO 4: The child who is often a "class clown" is doing work nicely.		
State how pleased you are	Warmth	Affective
Describe the behavior, not the child	Warmth	Affective
SCENARIO 5: The child is not starting work after being prompted to do so.		
Assert to the child the need to comply	Influence	Affective
State a consequence (stay after school) when he resists	Influence	Cognitive
Use assertive eye-gaze and body posture when stating the consequence	Influence	Affective
SCENARIO 6: A child is fighting. He uses sidetracking tactics when confronted.		
Assert the limit	Influence	Affective
Do not respond to diversionary tactics	Tolerance	Behavioral
SCENARIO 7: One child is poking another child. When the teacher tells him to stop, he starts to cry.		
Repeat telling the child to stop poking	Influence	Affective
Do not respond to his crying	Tolerance	Behavioral
SCENARIO 8: A child will not do his work and gets belligerent with the teacher.		
Make an assertive statement ("You will do your work")	Influence	Affective
Ignore anger	Tolerance	Behavioral
Perform a "broken record" repeating of the assertion	Influence	Affective
Threaten a consequence (principal's office) if the child persists	Influence	Affective
SCENARIO 9: A child was very disruptive. Putting him in time-out in the classroom and calling his parents did not work.		
The teacher warned the child he would be sent to another classroom	Influence	Affective
When the child persisted, the teacher sent him away	Influence	Affective
The teacher responded calmly when the child complained about the other classroom	Tolerance	Affective

is given very short shrift, with only 16 percent of the points being coded in the Tolerance domain. Furthermore, although the Canters do suggest that the child's affective expressions should be ignored, they do not once suggest using active listening. As that is the hallmark of the Affective approach, it is difficult for me to believe that the Canters were much influenced by Affectively oriented authors, although I did see one noncredited use of Gordon's "I-message" term.

As one might infer from the title *Assertive Discipline,* the predominant recommended response involves use of Influence principles. There is some emphasis on Warmth, as in the suggestion to praise, to avoid disrespectful labeling, and to create a positive classroom milieu. However, Warmth is not emphasized enough, in my opinion, and Tolerance, as I noted, is given way too little emphasis. Although there is an effort to rein in the negative behaviors of overly hostile teachers, the main concern of the Canters seems to be to prop up the resolve of overly meek teachers. The effort is to make teachers assertive without crossing over into aggression.

The Canters' focus on guilt-ridden passive teachers is very much in line with the emphasis of Assertion Training in general. However, although Assertive Discipline cannot be considered "Influence only" (unlike the methods of John Rosemond, whom I discuss briefly in Chapter 1), it comes awfully close. There are just too many threats to call the principal or the child's parents, and these "nuclear" options come in much too early, in my opinion. Although Assertive Discipline likely will make a weak teacher stronger, it will not necessarily make her more skilled. That is because skill at discipline involves the coordinated use of Influence, Tolerance, and Warmth in a kind of "dance of discipline" (discussed in Chapter 8), and I see very little evidence in their book that the Canters know how to dance that dance, let alone teach it effectively.

Using the ABC Model to Analyze the Method of *From Chaos to Calm*

Background

I ran across *From Chaos to Calm: Effective Parenting of Challenging Children with ADHD and Other Behavioral Problems* (Heininger and Weiss 2001) while browsing the child-rearing section of my local bookstore. I was not familiar with the book or its two authors, Janet E. Heininger and Sharon K. Weiss. After briefly looking through it, I thought it would be an interesting book to analyze using the ABC model, in part because of its focus on dealing with children with difficult temperaments.

Unlike the other two books profiled in this appendix, this book is not part of a series and has not resulted in the creation of a discipline training institute or even a website. Another unusual aspect of the book is that the first author, Heininger, does not have training in an educational or mental-health discipline. Instead, she has a doctorate in history, has served as a foreign-policy expert for the U.S. State Department and Congress, and has published one other book, *Peacekeeping in Transition*, which focuses on the role of the United Nations in Cambodia. According to the biographical sketch on the back of *From Chaos to Calm*, Heininger's main interest and qualification for writing the book is that the younger of her two children is described as "a son with ADHD."

The second author, Weiss, who holds a Master's degree in Education, with emphasis on Special Education and Counseling, does have relevant professional credentials and experience (not that being a parent of a child with ADHD should be dismissed as irrelevant experience). She has a website, www.sharonkweiss.com, that describes her as follows: "Sharon Weiss is a nationally known behavioral consultant in private practice in Northern Virginia. Her areas of expertise include parent and staff training in behavior management and crisis intervention. She has worked as a teacher of special needs children, program coordinator and supervisor of behavioral intervention programs for behavior disordered children." In addition to being second author of *From Chaos to Calm*, Weiss is a coauthor of another discipline book, *Angry Children, Worried Parents: Seven Steps to Help Families Manage Anger* (Goldstein, Brooks, and Weiss 2004).

The introductory chapter of *From Chaos to Calm* explains that the book tells the story of a one-year intervention that Weiss conducted with Heininger; her husband, Jamie Reuter; and their family. The purpose of the intervention was to help the parents and their son, Theodore Reuter, devise strategies for coping more effectively with Theodore's ADHD.

Conceptual Analysis

Weiss describes herself as a "behavioral consultant," and that title is typically applied to professionals who operate within a Skinnerian, or behaviorist, framework. Therefore, I assumed that the book would reflect the Behavioral perspective on discipline. This assumption was strengthened by the number of charts in the book (charting problem and good behaviors, as well as progress, is a staple of the Behavioral approach) and by Heininger's mention in the acknowledgments that she and Theodore had participated in a Social Skills training program known as "Stepping Stones." Social Skills training is an intervention commonly used and recommended by behaviorists, which is another indication that the book likely describes a discipline intervention with many Behavioral components. However, Social Skills training also involves teaching and rehearsing of self-regulatory and interpersonal strategies, so it seemed possible that the book would describe an intervention with Cognitive and Affective dimensions as well.

As with most discipline books aimed at parents or teachers, I searched in vain for a clear or concise statement of the book's theoretical orientation. There is an extensive bibliography, listing books representing all three discipline approaches, in addition to books dealing with medical aspects of ADHD and related conditions,

TABLE B.3   Content Analysis of the Points Made by Heininger and Weiss

Points made in *From Chaos to Calm*	Domain	Approach
Keep a record of difficult situations, with details	Influence	Behavioral
To establish or change routines, ask yourself what you really want	Influence	Affective
Put routines in visual form, so the child does not have to be reminded	Influence	Behavioral
Ask how one can make routines desired by the child	Influence	Cognitive
Decide what is really essential, and ignore the unessential	Tolerance	Behavioral
Give incentives to reinforce compliance with routines	Warmth	Behavioral
Get the child's input in developing routines	Warmth	Cognitive
Insist that items not in the child's backpack the night before do not go to school	Influence	Cognitive
Do not bring an item to school if the child fails to pack it	Influence	Cognitive
Give the child rewards for adhering to his morning routine checklist	Warmth	Behavioral
Develop documentation for compliance with routines	Influence	Behavioral
Use a timer, and give rewards for tasks completed before it rings	Warmth	Behavioral
Do not take misbehavior personally, and do not attribute bad motives	Tolerance	Affective
Make exceptions clear	Influence	Affective
Focus on positive child behaviors, not negative ones	Warmth	Behavioral
Ignore moaning and venting	Tolerance	Affective
Enlist the child's help in figuring out solutions	Warmth	Cognitive
Keep rules few and short	Influence	Behavioral

such as Asperger's Disorder. The authors create the impression that they put the intervention together over the course of a year and that it is unique, particularly because of its emphasis on ADHD. That is probably true to a large extent, but I think the intervention's distinctness is mainly a product of its eclectic nature, with techniques and methods drawn from a variety of sources and combined in a manner that is not typical.

One problem I have in conducting a conceptual analysis of the book is that I find it to be overwritten, with pages and pages of distracting and unnecessary tangents, personal asides, and descriptions. To simplify my task here, I discuss only material appearing in the occasional boxes labeled "rules," "tips," or "pointers." As many of these pointers deal with issues specific to ADHD (e.g., concentration aids, support groups, seeking professional help, techniques for making prescription renewals easier), I include only items that specifically touch on discipline. Because there is much repetition of points from one box to the next, I have cut out some items that I consider redundant. In addition, I stopped my analysis about two-thirds of the way through the book, when the discussion switched to specific problems, and the proposed solutions became especially repetitious.

The data in Table B.3 confirm my initial impression that the discipline intervention described in *From Chaos to Calm* is primarily in the Behavioral mode. Of the eighteen tips or pointers listed, 50 percent involve Behavioral principles. At the same time, the intervention is somewhat eclectic, as 28 percent of the tips involve Cognitive principles and 22 percent of them involve Affective principles.

The breakdown among the discipline domains shows a nice balance between Influence and Warmth principles, with 50 percent of the tips involving Influence principles and 33 percent of them involving Warmth principles. The Tolerance domain was a little low, with only 17 percent of the tips involving Tolerance principles. This figure may be somewhat misleading, however, because several of the Behavioral items coded as Influence or Warmth tend to have Tolerance embedded in them and could just as easily have been coded as Tolerance. Two examples of such items are "Focus on positive child behaviors, not negative ones" (coded as Warmth but a combination of Warmth and Tolerance) and "Keep rules few and short" (coded as Influence but a combination of Influence and Tolerance).

The results of this analysis show that, in spite of all of the novel material dealing with ADHD and related disabilities, the discipline intervention in *From Chaos to Calm* is a fairly standard Behavioral discipline curriculum, with a few Cognitive and Affective principles thrown in. There is a fairly adequate balance of emphasis across the three domains, although I would have liked a little more discussion of the crucial, but often underemphasized, domain of Tolerance.

Conclusion

My purpose in providing this brief appendix is to model for readers a way they can evaluate discipline books and decide whether a book fits into a particular psychological approach and whether or not it is any good. In assembling these examples, I did not attempt comprehensive coverage of the discipline literature (I am saving that for a subsequent book); I simply picked three books more or less at random. Two of those books are (like mine) applicable to both classrooms and family settings, while the third is aimed only at parents.

Purely by accident (I had not read any of these books beforehand, although I had heard a little about *Parenting with Love and Logic*), it turns out that the method espoused in one book (*Assertive Discipline* by Lee and Marlene Canter) falls more or less in the Affective discipline camp, the method of another (*From Chaos to Calm* by Heininger and Weiss) falls more or less in the Behavioral camp, and the method of the third (*Parenting with Love and Logic* by Cline and Fay) falls more or less in the Cognitive camp. I say "more or less" in each case because the methods all borrow some principles from other approaches, and none of them is a full-fledged exemplar of the camp I assigned it to (e.g., Cline and Fay omit one important feature of the Cognitive approach [council meetings], while the Canters omit a crucial aspect of the Affective approach [active listening]). Furthermore, none of the authors explicitly ground their advice in the broader discipline literature, thus implying that the methods originated with them, even though little of the advice offered is novel. Only one of the books, the one by the Canters, even mentions a theoretical foundation, but that theoretical foundation—Assertion Training—has nothing to do with child development.

Only one of the books, *Parenting with Love and Logic*, has an equal balance among Warmth, Influence, and Tolerance, while the other two give short shrift to Tolerance (although, as mentioned, that conclusion may be a little overstated for *From Chaos to Calm*). For that reason, I consider Cline and Fay's book to be the most adequate of the three and the Canters' book to be the least satisfactory. However, none of the these books is horrendous, as the books of one of the authors profiled early in Chapter 1 truly are. In my analyses, I used a somewhat labor-intensive content analytic technique that I applied systematically to sequentially sampled bits of advice. I do not expect readers to go to that much trouble but I do want to show caregivers how they can become more critical consumers of the discipline literature and determine for themselves whether or not a discipline "expert" really deserves that descriptor. Of course, one additional lesson that can be drawn from this exercise—if I may be a little vain—is that the only discipline manual you will ever need may be the one you have just finished reading.

References

Baruch, D. W. 1949. *New ways in discipline: You and your child.* New York: McGraw-Hill.

Baumrind, D. 1967. Child care practices antedating three patterns of preschool behavior. *Genetic Psychology Monographs* 75:43–88.

———. 1971. Harmonious parents and their preschool children. *Developmental Psychology* 4:99–102.

Becker, W. C. 1964. Consequences of different kinds of parental discipline. In M. L. Hoffman and L. W. Hoffman (eds.), *Review of child development research,* Vol. 1, 169–208. New York: Russell Sage Foundation.

———. 1971. *Parents are teachers: A child management program.* Champaign, IL: Research Press.

Bell, R. Q., and L. V. Harper. 1977. *Child effects on adults.* Hillsdale, NJ: LEA Associates.

Borkowski, J. G., S. L. Ramey, and M. Bristol-Power (eds.). 2000. *Parenting and the child's world: Influences on academic, intellectual and socio-emotional development.* Mahwah, NJ: Erlbaum.

Brodzinsky, D., M. D. Schecter, and R. M. Henig. 1993. *Being adopted: The lifelong search for self.* New York: Anchor.

Canter, L. C., and M. C. Canter. 1988. *Assertive discipline: A take charge approach for today's educator.* Santa Monica, CA: Lee Canter Associates.

———. 2001. *Assertive discipline for parents.* Rev. ed. New York: Harper and Row.

Chess, S., A. Thomas, and H. G. Birch. 1965. *Your child is a person: A psychological approach to parenthood without guilt.* New York: Viking.

Clark, L. 1995. *SOS help for parents: A practical guide for handling common everyday behavior problems.* 3rd ed. Bowling Green, Kentucky: SOS Programs and Parents Press.

Cline, F. W., and J. Fay. 1990. *Parenting with love and logic: Teaching children responsibility.* Colorado Springs, CO: Pinon Press.

Cohen, L. J. 2002. *Playful parenting.* New York: Ballantine Books.

Collins, W. A., E. E. Maccoby, L. Steinberg, E. M. Hetherington, and M. H. Bornstein. 2000. Contemporary research on parenting: The case for nature and nurture. *American Psychologist* 55:218–232.

Deci, E. L., and R. M. Ryan. 1985. *Intrinsic motivation and self-determination in human behavior.* New York: Plenum.

Dinkmeyer, D., and R. Dreikurs. 1963. *Encouraging children to learn: The encouragement process.* New York: Hawthorn Books.

Dinkmeyer, D., and L. Losoncy. 1980. *The encouragement book.* Englewood Cliffs, NJ: Prentice-Hall.

———. 1996. *The skills of encouragement: Bringing out the best in yourself and others.* Delray Beach, FL: St. Lucie Press.

Dinkmeyer, D., and G. D. McKay. 1976. *Systematic training for effective parenting.* Circle Pines, MN: American Guidance Service.

Dinkmeyer, D., Sr., G. D. McKay, and D. Dinkmeyer, Jr. 1998. *The parent's handbook: Systematic training for effective discipline (STEP).* Atascadero, CA: Insight Publishing.

Dobson, J. C. 1977. *Dare to discipline.* New York: Bantam Books.

———. 1996. *The new dare to discipline.* Carol Stream, IL: Tyndale House.

Dreikurs, R., and L. Grey. 1968. *A new approach to discipline: Logical consequences.* New York: Hawthorn Books.

Dreikurs, R., with V. Soltz. 1990. *Children: The challenge.* New York: Plume/Penguin (originally published 1964).

Edwards, W. J., and S. Greenspan. 2011. Adaptive behavior and fetal alcohol spectrum disorders. *Journal of Psychiatry and Law* 38 (4): 419–447.

Erikson, E. H. 1950. *Childhood and society.* New York: Norton.

Faber, A., and E. Mazlish. 1975. *Liberated parents/liberated children.* New York: Avon.

———. 1980. *How to talk so kids will listen and listen so kids will talk.* New York: Avon.

Fay, J., C. Fay, and F. W. Cline. 2000. *The pearls of love and logic for parents and teachers.* Golden, CO: Love and Logic Press.

Fleming, D., with M. Ritts. 2003. *Mom, I hate you! Children's provocative communication: What it means and what to do about it.* New York: Three Rivers Press.

Flicker, E. S., and J. A. Hoffman. 2006. *Guiding children's behavior: Developmental discipline in the classroom.* New York: Teacher College Press.

Forehand, R., and N. Long. 2002. *Parenting the strong-willed child: The clinically proven five-week program for parents of two- to six-year-olds.* Rev. ed. Chicago: Contemporary Books.

Forward, S., with C. Buck. 1989. *Toxic parents: Overcoming their hurtful legacy and reclaiming your life.* New York: Bantam.

Foster, H. L. 1974. *Ribbin', jivin' and playin' the dozens: The unrecognized dilemma of inner-city schools.* New York: HarperInformation.

Frost, J. 2005. *Supernanny.* Los Angeles: Ricochet Productions/ABC.

Furedi, F. 2002. *Paranoid parenting: Why ignoring the experts may be best for your child.* Chicago: Chicago Review Press.

Gall, J. 2003. *Dancing with elves: Parenting as a performance art.* Bloomington, IN: Authorhouse.

Ginott, H. G. 1965. *Between parent and child: New solutions to old problems.* New York: Macmillan.

Ginott, H. G., A. G. Ginott, and H. W. Goddard. 2003. *Between parent and child: The bestselling classic that revolutionized parent-child communication.* New York: Three Rivers Press.

Glasser, W. A. 1965. *Reality therapy.* New York: Harper and Row.

———. 1998. *The quality school teacher: A companion volume to* The Quality School. Rev. ed. New York: HarperCollins.

———. 2003. *For parents and teenagers: Dissolving the barrier between you and your teen.* New York: HarperCollins.

Glasser, W. A., and K. L. Dotson. 1998. *Choice theory in the classroom.* Rev. ed. New York: HarperCollins.

Glenn, H. S., and J. Nelson. 1989. *Raising self-reliant children in a self-indulgent world: Seven building blocks for developing capable young people.* Rocklin, CA: Prima Publishing and Communications.

Goldstein, S., R. B. Brooks, and S. K. Weiss. 2004. *Angry children, worried parents: Seven steps to help families manage anger.* Plantation, FL: Specialty Press/ADD Warehouse.

Goleman, D. 1995. *Emotional intelligence: Why it can matter more than IQ.* New York: Bantam, Doubleday and Dell.

Gordon, T. 1970. *P.E.T.: Parent effectiveness training.* New York: Wyden.

———. 1991. *Discipline that works: Promoting self-discipline in children.* New York: Plume.

Gottman, J., with J. Declaire. 1998. *Raising an emotionally intelligent child.* New York: Simon and Schuster.

Gray, S. W., B. K. Ramsey, and R. A. Klaus. 1982. *From 3 to 20: The early training project.* Baltimore: University Park Press.

Greenspan, S. 1978. Maternal affect-allowance and limit-setting appropriateness as predictors of child adjustment. *Genetic Psychology Monographs* 98:83–111.

———. 1983. A unifying framework for educating caregivers about discipline. *Child Care Quarterly* 12:5–27.

———. 1985. An integrative model of caregiver discipline. *Child Care Quarterly* 14: 30–47.

———. 2006. Rethinking "harmonious parenting" in light of a three-factor model of discipline. *Child Care in Practice* 12 (1): 5–12.

———. 2009. *Annals of gullibility.* Westport, CT: Praeger.

Greenspan, S., and J. Driscoll. 1997. The role of intelligence in a broad model of personal competence. In D. P. Flanagan, J. L. Genshaft, and P. L. Harrison (eds.), *Contemporary intellectual assessment: Theory, tests, and issues,* 131–150. New York: Guilford.

Greenspan, S. I. 1995. *The challenging child: How to understand, raise and enjoy your "difficult child."* Boston: Addison-Wesley.

———. 2003. *The secure child: Helping children feel safe and confident in a changing world.* Cambridge, MA: Da Capo Press.

Greenspan, S. I., with J. Salmon. 1993. *Playground politics: Understanding the emotional life of your school-age child.* Reading, MA: Perseus Books.

Greenspan, S. I., and S. Wieder, with R. Simons. 1998. *The child with special needs: Encouraging intellectual and emotional growth.* Cambridge, MA: Perseus Books.

Harris, J. R. 1998. *The nurture assumption: Why children turn out the way they do.* New York: Free Press.

Heininger, J. E., and S. K. Weiss. 2001. *From chaos to calm: Effective parenting of challenging children with ADHD and other behavioral problems.* New York: Penguin.

Hoffman, M. L. 1975. Altruistic behavior and the parent-child relationship. *Journal of Personality and Social Psychology* 31:937–943.

Hoffman, M. L., and H. D. Salzstein. 1967. Parent discipline and the child's moral development. *Journal of Personality and Social Psychology* 5:45–57.

Hulbert, A. 2003. *Raising America: Experts, parents, and a century of advice about children.* New York: Knopf.

Kennedy, R. W. 2001. *The encouraging parent: How to stop yelling at your kids and start teaching them confidence, self-discipline and joy.* New York: Crown Publishing Group.

Kohn, A. 1993. *Punished by rewards: The trouble with gold stars, incentive plans, A's, praise, and other bribes.* New York: Houghton-Mifflin.

———. 1996. *Beyond discipline: From compliance to community.* Alexandria, VA: ASCD.

Lewis, C. C. 1981. The effects of firm parental control: A reinterpretation of findings. *Psychological Bulletin* 90:547–563.

Loomans, D. 1993. *The laughing classroom: Everyone's guide to teaching with humor and play.* Tiburon, CA: H. J. Kramer.

MacKenzie, R. J. 1996. *Setting limits in the classroom: How to move beyond the classroom dance of discipline.* Roseville, CA: Prima Publishing.

———. 2001. *Setting limits with your strong-willed child.* Roseville, CA: Prima Publishing.

Martin, W. 1999. *The parent's Tao Te Ching: A new interpretation—ancient advice for modern parents.* New York: Marlowe and Company.

McGraw, P. 2004. *Family first: Your step-by-step plan for creating a phenomenal family.* New York: Norton.

McRoy, R. G., H. D. Grotevant, and L. A. Zurcher, Jr. 1988. *Emotional development in adopted adolescents: Origins and development.* Westport, CT: Praeger.

Miller, W. H. 1975. *Systematic parent training: Procedures, cases and issues.* Champaign, IL: Research Press.

Neill, A. S. 1977. *Summerhill: A radical approach to childrearing.* New York: Simon and Schuster.

———. 1978. *Freedom, not license.* New York: Simon and Schuster.

Patterson, G. R. 1982. *Coercive family process.* Eugene, OR: Castalia Press.

Patterson, G. R., and M. E. Gullion. 1968. *Living with children: New methods for parents and teachers.* Rev. ed. Champaign, IL: Research Press.

Phelan, T. 2010. *1-2-3 Magic: Effective Discipline for Children 2–12.* Rev. ed. Glen Ellyn, IL: ParentMagic, Inc.

Ricker, A., and C. Crowder. 1998. *Backtalk: Four steps to ending rude behavior in your kids.* New York: Fireside/Simon and Schuster.

Rosemond, J. 1996. *Because I said so: 366 insightful and thought-provoking reflections on parenting and family life.* Kansas City, MO: Andrews McMeel.

———. 2005. *Family building: The five fundamentals of effective parenting.* Kansas City, MO: Andrews McMeel.

Rousseau, J. 1908 (orig. pub. 1762). *Émile: A treatise on education* (transl. W. H. Payne). New York: D. Appleton and Co.

Ryan, R. M., and E. L. Deci. 2000. Self-determination theory and the facilitation of intrinsic motivation, social development, and well-being. *American Psychologist* 55:68–78.

Seligman, M. E. P., with K. Reivich, L. Jaycox, and J. Gillham. 1995. *The optimistic child.* New York: Harper Collins.

Shapiro, L. E. 1998. *How to raise a child with a high EQ: A parents' guide to emotional intelligence.* New York: Harper Collins.

Sherman, J. R. 1995. *The magic of humor in caregiving.* Golden Valley, MN: Pathway Books.

Silberman, M. 1988. *Confident parenting: Solve your toughest child-rearing problems with a four-step plan that works.* New York: Warner Books.

Skinner, B. F. 1948. *Walden two.* Indianapolis: Hackett.

——. 2002 (orig. pub. 1971). *Beyond freedom and dignity.* Indianapolis: Hackett.

Strunk, W., Jr., and E. B. White. 1959. *The elements of style.* Rev. ed. New York: Macmillan.

Thoman, E. B., and S. E. Browder. 1987. *Born dancing: How intuitive parents understand their baby's unspoken and natural rhythms.* New York: HarperCollins.

Thomas, A., S. Chess, and H. G. Birch. 1968. *Temperament and behavior disorders in children.* New York: New York University Press.

Werner, E. E., J. M. Bierman, and F. E. French. 1971. *The children of Kauai: A longitudinal study from the prenatal period to age ten.* Honolulu: University of Hawaii Press.

Weston, D. C., and M. S. Weston. 1993. *Playful parenting: Turning the dilemma of discipline into fun and games.* New York: Jeremy P. Tarcher.

——. 1996. *Playwise: 365 fun-filled activities for building character, conscience and emotional intelligence in children.* New York: Jeremy P. Tarcher.

Wykoff, J. L., and B. C. Udell. 1984. *Discipline without shouting or spanking: Practical solutions to the most common preschool behavior problems.* Deephaven, MN: Meadowbrook.

York, P., D. York, and T. Wachtel. 1982. *Toughlove.* Garden City, NY: Doubleday.

Zigler, E., and P. K. Trickett. 1978. IQ, social competence, and evaluation of early childhood intervention programs. *American Psychologist* 33:789–798.

Index

Stephen Greenspan is a developmental psychologist who is Clinical Professor of Psychiatry at the University of Colorado and Emeritus Professor of Educational Psychology at the University of Connecticut, where he coordinated the graduate program in Special Education. A widely cited authority on social competence, especially in at-risk children, youth, and adults, he was the 2011 recipient of the John Jacobson Award for Critical Thinking from the American Psychological Association.